CHRISTIAN PHILOSOPHY A–Z

D0898255

Volumes available in the Philosophy A–Z Series

Epistemology A–Z, Martijn Blaauw and Duncan Pritchard
Ethics A–Z, Jonathan A. Jacobs
Indian Philosophy A–Z, Christopher Bartley
Jewish Philosophy A–Z, Aaron W. Hughes
Philosophy of Religion A–Z, Patrick Quinn

Forthcoming volumes

Aesthetics A–Z, Fran Guter
Chinese Philosophy A–Z, Bo Mou
Feminist Philosophy A–Z, Nancy McHugh
Islamic Philosophy A–Z, Peter Groff
Philosophical Logic A–Z, J. C. Beall
Philosophy of Language A–Z, Alessandra Tanesini
Philosophy of Mind A–Z, Marina Rakova
Philosophy of Science A–Z, Stathis Psillos
Political Philosophy A–Z, Jon Pike

Christian Philosophy A–Z

Daniel J. Hill
and
Randal D. Rauser

Edinburgh University Press

© Daniel J. Hill and Randal D. Rauser, 2006

Edinburgh University Press Ltd
22 George Square, Edinburgh

Typeset in 10.5/13 Sabon
by TechBooks India, and printed and
bound in Finland by WS Bookwell

A CIP record for this book is
available from the British Library

ISBN-10 0 7486 2212 8 (hardback)
ISBN-13 978 0 7486 2212 2 (hardback)
ISBN-10 0 7486 2152 0 (paperback)
ISBN-13 978 0 7486 2152 1 (paperback)

Contents

This book is lovingly and gratefully dedicated to our respective parents.

Series Editor's Preface

One of the things that Christian philosophy has going for it is a central text, the New Testament, written in Greek. Greek is a highly appropriate language for philosophy, abstract and capable of fine conceptual distinctions, something the more concrete and basic Hebrew of the Old Testament had difficulty accomplishing. The traditional conflict between Athens and Jerusalem, between philosophy and religion, was often thus muted in Christianity since their religion was from the start pretty firmly established in Athens, at least linguistically speaking. The development of Christian philosophy was rapid since even in the early Christian communities the growth of the religion took place in a cultural environment where philosophy also flourished. Ever since then the ideas and issues of Christianity have been extensively explored using the various philosophical techniques that have arisen within different philosophical traditions. It is often difficult to understand what is going on in Christian philosophy, though, since the blend of philosophy and religion may make the reader unsure precisely what argument is being presented, or how it is supposed to work. It is the aim of Daniel Hill and Randal Rauser's guide to the vocabulary of the debate to throw light on this and other aspects of Christian philosophy, and we hope that readers will find it useful in gaining a pathway through this interesting intellectual territory.

Oliver Leaman

Introduction

Fifty years ago a scan of bookshop shelves would have been as likely to find a dictionary of terms for alchemy as one for Christian philosophy. Indeed, one might well have thought that, though of course there were some Christian philosophers then, they were doomed to the same fate as the dodo. But, in a stunning reversal, today Christian philosophy is among the most vibrant areas of philosophy. While the story of that change is still being written, there are a few key factors. On the negative side, the last fifty years have seen the demise of some historically formidable opponents to Christian philosophy, most perspicuously logical positivism and classical foundationalism, and this demise is due in significant part to the work of Christian philosophers. On the positive side, there has been a revitalisation of Christian philosophy from a number of sources, including the renewal of Catholic philosophy after the broadening of the Second Vatican Council as evident, for instance, in the diversity of the American Catholic Philosophical Association. Another significant factor is the work of several key philosophers coming out of (or sympathetic to important features of) the Dutch Calvinist tradition. Philosophers such as Alvin Plantinga, Nicholas Wolterstorff and William Alston (who, though not a Calvinist, has sympathy with the broad approach of Plantinga and Wolterstorff) have provided a formidable body of original philosophical work, all in accord with, or explicitly building upon, their Christian convictions. This new vibrancy led to the founding of the Society of Christian Philosophers in 1978 and the establishment of its journal *Faith and Philosophy* in 1984. One of the first articles to be published in this journal, Plantinga's seminal address 'Advice to Christian Philosophers' (Plantinga 1984), has served as a clarion call to a new generation to approach philosophy without apology from a distinctively Christian perspective. And Christian philosophers continue to do so.

Although North America has seen the greatest growth in Christian philosophy, there has been a slower revival in other English-speaking countries, particularly in the UK. In England, Oxford University has, and London University's King's College had until recently, a 'named chair' for philosophy of religion held by an eminent Christian philosopher: the chair at Oxford was held recently by Richard Swinburne, who was followed by Brian Leftow; and the chair at London was held most recently by Paul Helm. Each of these has done much to advance the field of Christian philosophy in the UK, not least through the British Society for Philosophy of Religion, which developed out of the UK Society of Christian Philosophers.

All this means that while alchemy remains an obscure footnote in the history of science, Christian philosophy has emerged as one of the liveliest fields in current philosophy. For that reason, the need grows for a manageable reference guide for students and the interested layperson to the specific tasks and concerns of Christian philosophy, and it is to that need that this book is aimed.

Unfortunately, the task of composing a dictionary is a precarious one, as one is bound to leave out certain terms, movements, positions, or individuals that one or more readers will view as an egregious omission. The best way to respond to inevitable disappointment is to be clear on our criteria for including the particular definitions that we have. In short, we have included particular terms, movements, theories and individuals based on two criteria: either they put forward a distinctively Christian philosophy or they suggest a distinctively Christian reply. Of course, not every such theory or individual can be included in a small volume such as this one, but we have tried to include all those that, in our judgement, have had such a significant impact on the field of Christian philosophy that the student or interested layperson is likely to come across them in some context or other. This judgement was not made in a scientifically precise manner, and no doubt some people will still respond that if x is included then so should y be. As long as we have not omitted those that should have been included within the confines of the space permitted we are less concerned about having included those that could (or even should) have been omitted. Nevertheless, the authors would welcome constructive feedback concerning the choice of entries as well as concerning the entries themselves.

Acknowledgements

A dictionary such as this cannot be completed without help from others in the discipline. We therefore gratefully thank all those that came to our aid whether with single suggestions or, as is the case with Paul Helm and Tony Garrood, reading through the entire manuscript. In particular, we'd like to thank the members of the Tyndale-House 2005 Colloquium in Philosophy of Religion, especially Joseph Jedwab, for helpful suggestions. We'd also like to thank Stephen Clark, Lydia Jaeger and Richard Sturch for helpful comments, and two anonymous readers for Edinburgh University Press. We are just as grateful to our wives and families for being so patient during the completion of the task, and particular thanks are extended to James, Marcus and Tim for their patience during the 'holiday'. Thanks are equally due to those that gave prayer support, especially Steve, Phil, Hugh and Chris. Finally, we thank Oliver Leaman, series editor, and the staff of Edinburgh University Press, especially Jackie Jones and Carol Macdonald, for their help and patience.

Christian Philosophy A–Z

A

a posteriori/a priori: A **belief** is *a posteriori* if it is held on the basis of experience, and is *a priori* if it is held on a basis other than experience (or held on no basis at all). Of course, one individual may believe a proposition on the basis of experience and another may believe it on a different basis: for example, you may believe Pythagoras' theorem on the basis of your reasoned proof of it, and I may believe it on the basis that I heard you tell me it was true and that in the past I have found you to be reliable. It follows that this distinction must be drawn at the level of individual token instances of belief, not at the level of propositions believed. Belief in God would be held *a priori* if, for example, it were held on the basis of the **ontological argument**. Belief in God would be held *a posteriori* if, for example, it were held on the basis of the **argument to design**.

See **argument, ontological; belief; argument from/to design; empiricism; rationalism; reason; theology, natural**

Further reading: Geivett and Sweetman 1993; Moser 1987

Abelard/Abailard, Peter (1079–1142): The leading, and most quarrelsome, philosopher and theologian of his time, Abelard was inclined to the nominalistic school of thought concerning **universals**: the view that universals are mere linguistic items that can be predicated of many individuals. Abelard also wrote on the **atonement**, claiming that its value lay in the response it evoked from us, and on the compatibility of divine **foreknowledge and freedom**. He placed high importance on the rational defence of the Christian faith, his high view of **reason** being evident in his *Sic et Non* ('Yes and No'), in which he invites the reader to use reason to reconcile apparently contradictory theological authorities. After his love affair with Héloïse went disastrously wrong, Abelard finished his days as a monk and teacher in a variety of monasteries. The monuments in the cemetery of Père Lachaise to him and Héloïse are a site of pilgrimage for lovers even today.

See **foreknowledge and freedom, problem of; nominalism; philosophy, medieval; universals**

Further reading: Abelard 1849–59, 1855, 1969–87 and 1977; Brower and Guilfoy 2004; Geyer 1919–33; Marenbon 1997

action, divine: Theists, as opposed to deists, believe that God acts *in* the world as well as creating the world. Moreover, most theists believe that God not only conserves the world in being moment by moment, but that he also intervenes in the running of the world from time to time in a miraculous way: so-called 'special divine action'. Philosophical discussion focuses on the one hand on the definition of **divine conservation** and its relation to secondary agency and, on the other, on whether God can do **miracles** and what the difference is between God's miraculous intervention and his ordinary action. Christian philosophers believe that the greatest divine action was the **incarnation**.

See **conservation, divine; deism; incarnation; miracle; theism**

Further reading: Hebblethwaite and Henderson 1990; Morris 1988; Tracy 1994; Wiles 1993

Adams, Marilyn McCord (1943–): A co-founder and past president of the **Society of Christian Philosophers**, Marilyn Adams has done much work in the history of **medieval philosophy**, including a two-volume work on **William of Ockham**. She has also written on the **problem of evil**, asking whether 'horrendous evils' give us reason to doubt the goodness of God. In addition, Adams has written on the question of whether God's **beliefs** about one's future free actions are compatible with their freedom, suggesting that God's fore-belief may not be a '**hard fact**' about the past. She is a priest of the Episcopal Church in the USA, married to **Robert Merrihew Adams**, and is currently Regius Professor of Divinity at Oxford.

See **Adams, Robert Merrihew; foreknowledge and freedom, problem of; hard-fact/soft-fact debate; Ockham, William of; philosophy, medieval; Society of Christian Philosophers**

Further reading: Adams, Marilyn McCord 1987 and 1999

Adams, Robert Merrihew (1937–): A co-founder and past president of the **Society of Christian Philosophers**, Robert Adams has wide-ranging interests: he has written on **ethics**, where his work has included a defence of the **divine-command theory**, has discussed the **problem of evil** and whether there is a best of all possible worlds, and has tackled the question of **middle knowledge**, arguing that God does not have knowledge of what one would have freely done in non-actual circumstances. He has also written an important book on **Leibniz**. He is married to **Marilyn McCord Adams**.

See **Adams, Marilyn McCord; ethics, divine command theory of; knowledge, middle; Leibniz, Gottfried Wilhelm; Society of Christian Philosophers**

Further reading: Adams, Robert Merrihew 1987 and 1994

agnosticism: Agnosticism is variously defined as (1) lack of **belief** in God, (2) lack of belief in God and lack of belief that there is no God, (3) the view that the **existence of God** cannot be proved, and (4) the view that the existence of God cannot be proved and cannot be disproved. Of these, (2) seems best, as (1) and (3) would lump atheists in with agnostics, and (4) would lump many theists in with agnostics too.

See **atheism; theism**

Further reading: Hume 1974; Kenny 2004

Albert the Great (c. 1200–80): Now chiefly remembered as **Thomas Aquinas**' tutor in the Dominican schools at Cologne and Paris, and as the one that introduced him to Aristotle's work, Albert the Great (or Albertus Magnus) did, however, leave a very substantial body of writings of his own, including many expositions of Aristotelian texts and of ancient and Arabic commentaries on Aristotelian texts. His wide-ranging work, which included not just philosophical and theological texts but also, reflecting his empiricist bent, texts on natural history, such as the first Western text on horticulture, merited him the nickname of 'Doctor Universalis'.

See **Aquinas, Thomas; Aristotelianism**

Further reading: Albert the Great 1951–; Meyer and Zimmermann 1980; Weisheipl 1980

Alston, William Payne. (1921–): A leading Christian philosopher, a co-founder and past president of the **Society of Christian Philosophers** and founding editor of the journal *Faith and Philosophy*, William P. Alston also edits the important monograph series Cornell Studies in the Philosophy of Religion, and was President of the Central (then called 'Western') Division of the American Philosophical Association. His philosophy is of a realistic bent, and this shows itself in his work on **truth,** meaning and **metaphysics**, as well as in **philosophy of religion**, in which he has argued, contrary to those that claim it is entirely **equivocal** or analogical, that there is a '**univocal** core' to religious discourse, and that much of our thought about God is literally true. Alston's work in philosophy of religion has also been groundbreaking where it has intersected with his innovative contributions to **epistemology**. Perhaps particularly notable is his defence of the rationality of religious **belief** based on 'mystical perception' – the perception of God associated with **religious experiences**. He has argued that since we treat beliefs based on sense perception as rational we should treat beliefs based on mystical perception as rational too. Alston also taught **Alvin Plantinga** when the latter was a graduate student.

See **analogy; experience, religious; Plantinga, Alvin; Society of Christian Philosophers; univocal**

Further reading: Alston 1989a, 1989b and 1993; Howard-Snyder 2004; Morris 1994.

altruism: Altruism is disinterested benevolence. In other words, an action is altruistic if it is done solely for the benefit of another. Christian philosophers differ on whether it is possible for us to be altruistic. **Hobbes** took the extreme view that altruism was totally impossible. A common Calvinistic line is that altruism is impossible before becoming a Christian, but possible afterwards, though only thanks to the indwelling power of the Holy Spirit. Other Christians claim that altruism is possible, albeit not easy enough to earn one's place in Heaven thereby.

See **Calvinism; Hobbes, Thomas**

Further reading: Gauthier 1970; Hobbes 1839–45; Nagel 1970

analytical philosophy See **philosophy, analytical**

analogy: A word is used univocally in two contexts when it has the same meaning in each. A word is used equivocally in two contexts when it has a totally different meaning in each. A word is used analogically in two contexts when its meaning in one context is similar to, though not identical with, its meaning in the other context. These terms are important in the debate concerning **religious language,** in which **Thomas Aquinas** claimed that most important (non-negative) religious language about God was analogical.

See **equivocal; language, religious; univocal**

Further reading: Ross 1981; Sherry 1976a; Sherry 1976b

annihilationism see **Hell**

Anscombe, Gertrude Elizabeth Margaret (1919–2001): A vigorous, and vigorously Roman-Catholic, English philosopher, Anscombe made contributions to many different philosophical fields: philosophy of mind and action, moral philosophy and the history of philosophy, to name but a few. In each of these fields her admiration for Aristotle was evident: in the philosophy of mind she rejected substance **dualism** in favour of the view that the **soul** was the form of the body, in moral philosophy she defended **virtue ethics,** and she wrote some papers on Aristotle himself. She also did much to translate and promote the writings of her mentor, **Wittgenstein**. Her philosophy was not merely 'pure'; she applied her ethical views, writing pamphlets against the use of the atom bomb and against contraception, and even taking direct action against abortion clinics. She was married to **Peter Thomas Geach**.

See **Aristotelianism; ethics, virtue; Geach, Peter Thomas; Wittgenstein, Ludwig Josef Johann**

Further reading: Anscombe 1981a, 1981b and 1981c; Gormally 1994; Teichmann 2000

Anselm of Canterbury (c. 1033–1109): Sometimes called 'the father of **scholasticism**', Anselm bequeathed to Christian philosophy the method of 'faith seeking understanding' (refined from **Augustine of Hippo**) and an argument, the **ontological argument** for the **existence of God**, to be found in his *Proslogion* ('Address'). Scholarly controversy rages, however, over whether Anselm really meant his meditation, composed, as it was, in a Benedictine abbey, to be understood as an argument to convince the unbeliever, and philosophical argument rages as to whether the ontological argument ought to convince anyone. Many modern Christian philosophers have adopted Anselm's method of thinking through their already held religious commitments. This method may be seen in the *Proslogion* and its companion the *Monologion* ('Soliloquy'), in which Anselm gives a version of the **cosmological argument** for the existence of God and then gives a list of God's attributes with supporting argument, based on his famous definition of God as 'that than which no greater can be conceived'. It may also, however, be seen in some of Anselm's more theological works, such as *Cur Deus Homo* ('Why God Became Human'), which is an investigation into why the **incarnation** and **atonement** were necessary, arguing that God's honour must be satisfied, and that it can be satisfied only by an infinite sacrifice from a member of the offending family, humanity. Anselm's significance can be judged from the fact that the original title of the *Proslogion*, Augustine's phrase '**fides quaerens intellectum**' ('faith seeking understanding'), could well be said to be the slogan of the contemporary revival in Christian philosophy, along with another phrase from Anselm, 'credo ut intellegam' ('I believe in order that I may understand').

See **argument, cosmological; argument, ontological; Augustine of Hippo; fides quaerens intellectum; scholasticism**

Further reading: Anselm of Canterbury 1938–61, 1998 and 2000; Davies and Leftow 2004; Hopkins 1972

antirealism see **realism**

apologetics: Apologetics is the rational defence of the faith. Christian philosophers differ over the importance and methods of apologetics. Some hold that it is a duty on every Christian to be able to give positive arguments in favour of his or her **beliefs**. Others hold that the only duty is to rebut arguments against Christianity. A middling position is held by those that claim that the Christian can and ought to provide negative arguments against non-Christian **worldviews** even if he or she cannot buttress his or her own views with positive arguments. One could also shift the apologetic duty from the individual to the broader Christian community such that individual Christians need not have the resources to defend Christianity so long as there are some individuals within the community that are so able.

See **argument, cosmological; argument, ontological; God, arguments for the existence of**

Further reading: Campbell-Jack, McGrath and Evans 2006; Geisler 1976 and 1998

Aquinas, Thomas (c. 1225–74): Perhaps the most influential Christian philosopher of all time, Thomas Aquinas was born near Aquino, of which his father was Count, in 1225 or 1227. He entered the Dominican Order and studied under **Albert the Great** in Cologne and Paris. Thomas Aquinas himself afterwards taught and wrote there and in many other places, culminating in Naples, where, in 1273, he, so his biographer reports, experienced a heavenly vision that made all that he had written seem as straw. He died on his way to the Council of Lyons and was canonised some fifty years later. His vast written output (the estimates hover around eight million words) contains not one but three systematic theologies (*Summa Theologiae*, which alone runs to nearly two million words, *Summa contra Gentiles* and *Compendium Theologiae*) and writings on many and varied theological and philosophical topics. Perhaps best known philosophically for his 'five ways' to prove the **existence of God** and his brilliant synthesis of **Aristotelianism** and the Bible, Aquinas' theological influence has been rivalled only by that (outside the Bible) of **Augustine of Hippo,** of Luther and of **Calvin.** Aquinas was officially regarded as the philosophical authority for Roman Catholics from Pope Leo XIII's 1879 encyclical until Vatican II. Almost every area discussed in **medieval philosophy** is treated by him: in philosophy of mind he follows Aristotle in claiming that the **soul** is the form of the body; in **ethics** he propounds a natural-law theory; in **epistemology** he argues that knowledge begins with the senses; in **metaphysics** he argues that things are composed of both form and matter – the exceptions being angels, which are pure form, prime matter, which is pure matter, and God, who is being itself. Thomas also made significant contributions to aesthetics, politics and philosophy of law. For Christian philosophers even today the 'angelic doctor' (as he was nicknamed) is still the first port of call when trying to work out a Christian line in some area of philosophy, as is witnessed by the more than 6, 000 commentaries that *The Catholic Encyclopedia* reports as having been written on Thomas Aquinas' work.

See **Albert the Great; Aristotelianism; five ways; philosophy, medieval; soul**

Further reading: Aquinas 1882–, 1920–5, 1955–7, 1963–80, 1993a and 1993b; Clark Mary T. 1972; Davies 1992; Kenny 1969a and 1980; Kretzmann and Stump 1993; Martin 1988; Stump 2003; Velde 2005; Weisheipl 1974

argument, cosmological: The cosmological argument argues for the **existence of God** from the starting point of the existence of the cosmos (or, in **van Inwagen**'s formulation, the possibility of the existence of the cosmos). The argument typically proceeds by way of the **principle of sufficient reason**, which states that everything contingent needs an explanation. Since the universe is contingent, it too needs an explanation. If we find its explanation in something else contingent then we can just ask what the explanation for the contingent whole composed of the universe plus its explanation is. Since, so the argument goes, there cannot be an infinite sequence of explanations, all explanation must find its end and culmination in the existence of a necessary being, God. One particular version of the cosmological argument, known as 'the *kalām* cosmological argument', argues specifically for the proposition that the world must have had a beginning and, therefore, a cause, on the grounds that it is not possible that an infinite amount of **time** should have elapsed. Critics have replied that the assumptions made in the various forms of the cosmological argument are not obviously correct, and, in any case, the argument does not establish any other interesting properties possessed by the necessary being.

See **a posteriori and a priori; God, arguments for the existence of; sufficient reason, principle of**

Further reading: Craig 1979 and 1980; Rowe 1975; van Inwagen 2002

argument, moral: The moral argument (also known as 'the axiological argument') is usually thought of as a type of **argument for the existence of God** based on the existence of moral absolutes. Dostoyevsky captured the core intuition in *The Brothers Karamazov* with Ivan Karamazov's chilling assertion: 'If there is no God, everything is permitted.' The moral argument adds that since it's not true that everything is permissible, there must be a God. That is, the existence of objective moral laws requires an objective moral lawgiver just as laws of a civil society require a lawgiver (the state). A different sort of moral argument is found in **Immanuel Kant**'s *Critique of Practical Reason*. In this version, it is not the putative *existence* of moral norms that requires explanation, but rather the **necessity** that the punitive and exculpatory judgement of human actions according to these moral norms be satisfied. Since it is clearly not satisfied in this life (for example, the wicked prosper while the good suffer), there must be another life where it is satisfied, and a divine authority to ensure as much. Also, if we did not believe in this other life where wrongs are righted we should have no motivation to press on when our good ends are not achieved.

See **dilemma, Euthyphro; God, arguments for the existence of; Kant, Immanuel; Lewis, Clive Staples**

Further reading: Kant 1956; Lewis, C. S. 1952; Owen 1965

argument, ontological: The ontological argument, classically formulated by **Anselm of Canterbury** and later by **Descartes,** has been a bone of philosophical contention for nearly a millennium. One formulation of the argument, derived from Anselm, goes like this:

1. The concept of God is, by definition, the concept of a being than which nothing greater can be conceived.
2. God certainly exists in the mind: even **atheists** have this concept of God.
3. It is greater to exist in reality than in the mind alone.
4. Suppose, for a *reductio ad absurdum*, that God exists in the mind alone.
5. Then there would be a concept of a greater being, namely, a concept of a being just like God but also existent in reality (by (3)).
6. But there cannot be a concept of a greater being than God (by (1)).
7. Therefore, our supposition in (4) was false.
8. Therefore, God exists in reality as well as in the mind.

Doubt has been cast on this argument at almost every turn: many have complained that the concept of God here employed is the concept of the 'God of the philosophers', but certainly not the concept of the 'God of Abraham, of Isaac and of Jacob'; others have complained that, although atheists have a concept of God, there is no sense in which God 'exists in the mind'; **Kant** famously complained that one could not compare objects in respect of existence; and still others have tried to find a logical flaw in the argument's structure. Different versions of the argument have been propounded to try to circumvent these objections. **Plantinga** has devised a modal version of the argument that moves, using the system of modal **logic** S5, from the premise that it is possible that a necessary being exist, to the conclusion that it is necessary that a necessary being exist. Although Plantinga's argument is valid within his system, this has not stopped the debate; many object that we have no good reason to think it possible that a necessary being exist.

See **Anselm of Canterbury; Descartes, René; God, arguments for the existence of; Kant, Immanuel; Plantinga, Alvin**

Further reading: Barnes, Jonathan 1972; Hick and McGill 1967; Oppy 1995; Plantinga 1965 and 1974b

argument from religious experience see **experience, religious**

argument from/to design: The argument to or from design is one of the most popular arguments used by Christian philosophers to justify their **belief** in God or to persuade others of it. Although it dates back to **Plato** (and the pre-Socratics) the first Christian use of it that had lasting impact was **Thomas Aquinas**' deployment of it as the fifth of his **five ways**. Another very well-known form is that given in 1802 by **William Paley**, who drew the famous **analogy** between finding a watch on the heath and inferring a watch-designer on the one hand and finding order in nature and inferring a designer of nature on the other hand. Many sceptical philosophers of the analytical school think, however, that this argument was decisively rebutted by **Hume** in his *Dialogues Concerning Natural Religion*, published twenty-three years earlier. One not so convinced is **Richard Swinburne**, who, in his *The Existence of God*, propounded a rigorous inductive version of the argument, a version that was also compatible with the truth of evolutionary theory.

Swinburne also put forward 'the fine-tuning argument', which claims that the universe is finely tuned for life: had the universe expanded just a tiny bit faster or slower there would have been no life as we know it. Swinburne argued that this cannot plausibly be described as a lucky break and therefore one must postulate a powerful and supernatural designer. The **intelligent-design** movement, associated with Michael Behe and William Dembski, argues that there are instances of irreducible complexity in nature (the knee joint is one oft-cited example) that cannot have evolved by chance and therefore also bespeak a designer. Doubts remain, however, even within the Christian community, over the strength of these arguments, in particular over whether they can be used to argue for the existence of *God* rather than merely that of some designer or other.

See **design, intelligent; God, arguments for the existence of**

Further reading: Paley 1819; Swinburne 2004

Aristotelianism: Aristotle of Stagira (384–322 BCE) exercised a profound influence on many Christian philosophers, especially **Thomas Aquinas** and his tutor, **Albert the Great**. Aristotle's influence was relatively late, however, in penetrating the Christian world, unlike that of his teacher, **Plato**. This was because only Aristotle's logical works were available in Latin translation (courtesy of **Boethius**) before the thirteenth century. At that point some new translations were made from the Greek and many more from Arabic versions. Aristotle's emphasis on knowledge derived from the senses was to lead the Aristotelian tradition, above all in Thomas Aquinas, to promote empirical proofs of God's existence such as Thomas's famous '**five ways**'. Aristotle's metaphysical views were also extremely influential in the account of form and matter, especially as it relates to the human **soul,** which Aristotelians took to be the form of the body. Aristotle's views in **ethics** also exerted great influence, leading to an attempt to understand morality in terms of **virtues,** albeit with three theological virtues added to the four cardinal virtues of old. Of course, the medievals did not uncritically take over everything that Aristotle said: they were unable, for example, to stomach his doctrine that the world did not have a beginning. Nevertheless, Thomas's great project may well be seen as an attempt to synthesise Aristotelianism and Christianity. Aristotle's influence is still felt in many parts of contemporary Christian philosophy, particularly those parts in the Roman-Catholic tradition, both in his own right and through Thomas Aquinas.

See **Albert the Great; Aquinas, Thomas; Boethius, Anicius Manlius Severinus; empiricism; five ways; soul; virtues**

Further reading: Steenberghen 1970 and 1980

aseity: The word 'aseity' comes from the phrase 'a se' meaning 'from himself'. The doctrine of God's aseity is the doctrine that God does not derive his existence or **nature** from any external source. Traditionally, it has been put somewhat more paradoxically as the doctrine that God derives his existence and nature from himself. The importance of the doctrine lies in the concomitant insistence that aseity belongs to nothing other than God – everything else derives its existence and nature from him.

See **God, nature of**
Further reading: Pohle 1938

atheism: Atheism is **belief** that there is no God. It is sometimes defined as lack of belief in God, but this would include agnostics, who are best kept separate.

See **agnosticism; theism**

Further reading: Berman 1987; Flew 1993; Le Poidevin 1996; MacIntyre and Ricoeur 1969; Russell 1957; Thrower 1971

atonement: The word 'atonement' is derived from 'at-one-ment' and thus refers to the state of being at one with something. The Christian doctrine of the atonement is that Jesus Christ provides for human beings the means to be made one with or reconciled to God, especially through his death on the cross. The doctrine assumes that human beings are alienated from God by **sin** and thus in need of reconciliation. There are two general approaches to the atonement. Subjective theories see the function of the atonement as epistemological (granting us knowledge of God's love and forgiveness) and volitional (motivating us to respond). While this approach is coherent, it seems to lose the unique nature of Christ's work insofar as the life of *any* virtuous individual could grant a comparable understanding of the love of God and motivation to respond to it – why would the crucified one have to be divine? Objective theories view the atonement as a unique work that provides the actual means of reconciliation to God. The philosophical challenge to this view is to explain this work in a metaphysically and morally plausible way. The most famous attempt to do this is found in **Anselm**'s satisfaction theory in *Cur Deus Homo* ('Why God Became Human'). According to Anselm, human sin offends God, whose justice and honour require an infinite recompense. Humanity, however, is unable to provide payment, which leaves infinite (eternal) punishment as the only option. God the Son then becomes incarnate so that, as human, he can justly pay the debt, while, as divine, he is able to pay the debt. Critics object that the image of God paying a debt to himself does nothing to explain the **logic** (or morality) of the atonement. If a rich man were owed money, he might simply forgive the debt, but surely he would not be obliged to pay himself back on the debtor's behalf. Further, while one might find penal substitution to be the more apt analogy, this complicates things even more, for while I may justly pay your fine surely I cannot be justly tortured and killed to fulfil your sentence.

See **Anselm of Canterbury; grace; incarnation; sin**

Further reading: Anselm of Canterbury 2000; Brümmer 2005; Gunton 1989; Hill, Charles 2004; Swinburne 1989a

Augustine of Hippo (354–430): Aurelius Augustinus is usually known in English as 'Augustine of Hippo', since he was bishop of that place and, confusingly, shares his name with Augustine of Canterbury. He was the first major Christian philosopher and remains one of the most influential, thanks to the five million or so words of his that survive. He was born in Thagaste, North Africa, to a pagan father, Patricius, and a devout Christian mother, Monica. He rebelled against his mother's faith and lived with a mistress in Rome and Milan while teaching rhetoric there. He was influenced by **scepticism** and **Manichaeism**, but came through these, and turned vigorously against them in later life. He was converted by reading Romans 13: 13–14, and baptised by his mentor, Ambrose, in Milan cathedral. After being made Bishop of Hippo he spent the rest of his life in writing and in exercise of his episcopal duties. He had wide-ranging philosophical interests: on **time** (of which he famously said that he knew what it was until somebody asked him), memory, language (his views were discussed by **Wittgenstein**) and **ethics** (he wrote a book on the wrongness of lying). What made Augustine a distinctively Christian philosopher was his insistence on thinking through philosophical issues in the light of his faith and the witness of the Bible. He is perhaps most remembered now for his views on more distinctively theological topics. For example, the **nature** and existence of **freedom** vexed him greatly, particularly its compatibility with **predestination** and (more weakly) with **foreknowledge**. It seems that Augustine changed his mind on this issue, and he is now usually taken as a champion of the view that insists that free will is compatible with God's determining our actions. Augustine wrote a classic autobiography, *Confessions*, as well as his theological works, the two most important being *On the Trinity* and *City of God*. This last work draws a firm distinction between the city of pagan culture and the city of Christian thought, which thus marks it out as one of the foundational texts of a distinctively Christian philosophy.

See **foreknowledge and freedom, problem of; language, religious; Manichaeism; predestination; scepticism**

Further reading: Augustine 1877–1902, 1965–, 1990– and Augustine 1991; Battenhouse 1955; Bonner 1986; Brown, Peter 1969; Chadwick 1986; Gilson 1960; Kirwan 1989; Rist 1994; Wills 1999

Augustinianism: Augustine's influence has scarcely waned since he first wrote. In **medieval philosophy**, Augustine's authority was second only to that of the Bible itself, and he influenced all the great thinkers, some, such as **Anselm** and **Bonaventure**, very deeply. At the Reformation, Augustine was claimed by both sides, a process made easier not only by the vast bulk of Augustine's work but also by the fact that he changed his mind on several important issues. Augustine was by no means discarded at the **Enlightenment**, and his influence on **Descartes** and **Malebranche** is well documented. In contemporary philosophy Augustine's ideas are still keenly discussed: his views on language, memory, and the mind are being carefully studied. An 'Augustinian' philosopher is, however, most likely to be committed to the distinctive anti-Pelagian views of

Augustine, that is, his emphasis on the **grace** of God over against human will, and, perhaps, Augustine's concomitant insistence that evil is not a real thing, but merely a defect.

See **Anselm of Canterbury; Bonaventure; Descartes, René; Malebranche, Nicolas; philosophy, medieval; scholasticism**

Further reading: Fitzgerald 1999; Marrou 1957

Ayer, Alfred Jules (1910–89): Ayer, sometime Wykeham Professor of Logic at Oxford, is chiefly of interest to Christian philosophers because of his outspoken attack on religious **belief** in his 1936 classic *Language, Truth and Logic*. In this book he claimed that religious utterances failed not only to be true, but failed even to be meaningful. Ayer argued that this was because they did not meet the **verification principle,** which stipulated that a sentence expressed a meaningful statement if and only if it was either analytic or empirically verifiable, that is, 'not indeed that it should be conclusively verifiable, but that some possible sense-experience should be relevant to the determination of its truth or falsehood' (Preface to *Language, Truth and Logic*). Since, in Ayer's view, religious sentences were neither analytic nor verifiable in this way, they did not express meaningful statements. Some philosophers of religion, such as R. B. Braithwaite, attempted to reformulate **religious language** to meet Ayer's criterion, but the majority of Christian philosophers, with **Alvin Plantinga** being a prime example, argued that Ayer's criterion was either self-refuting or represented a personal decision of Ayer's to record his own way of using the word 'meaningful', which was of little interest to Christians.

See **Plantinga, Alvin; positivism, logical; verification/ verifiability principle**

Further reading: Ayer 1978, 1984, 2001 and 2004; Hahn 1992; Rogers, Ben 2000

Barth, Karl (1886–1968): Barth was not a Christian philosopher but a Christian theologian. Indeed, he rejected any
form of philosophy that he thought exalted itself against
God's self-**revelation**. The acme of this was his famous
review of Emil Brunner's *Nature and Grace*, the substance of which was captured in its one-word title: 'Nein!'
('No!'). For Barth, Christian knowledge always began
with God and his self-revelation in Christ, never with
an autonomous human mind. This led him to reject not
only traditional **natural theology** but also liberal theology.
Barth's voluminous output comprises his famous commentary on Paul's *Epistle to the Romans* and the six million words of his unfinished magnum opus, the *Church
Dogmatics*. Many of Barth's present-day followers reject
Christian philosophy in all its forms, even philosophy applied to thinking through the content of the divine revelation. Barth's own position was more complex, however,
as he delivered the Gifford Lectures (1937–8), and his
later systematic theology softened his earlier ban on natural theology. Interestingly, Barth's brother Heinrich was
a professional philosopher.
    See **revelation; theology, natural**
    Further reading: Barth 1936, 1956–77, 1961, 1965,
1968, 1971– and 2001; Bromiley 1979; Torrance 1962
and 1990; Webster 2000

behaviourism: Behaviourism is the view that mental states are
behavioural states. So, for example, pain is crying out in
a particular manner or flinching in a particular way. The
view has never been popular with Christian philosophers,
not only because of the obvious problems of the stoic
(who suppresses pain-behaviour when pain is felt) and

the actor (who simulates pain-behaviour when it is not felt), but also because it is hard to see that any remotely plausible behaviouristic analysis can apply to God.

See **soul**

Further reading: Clark, Gordon H. 1982; Ryle 1949

belief: To believe a proposition is to think it true. Another, related, use of 'believe' is when one is said to 'believe in' a thing or person. In this sense Christians are said to believe in God. In this context 'believe' means more than just 'believe in the existence of'; rather it also means 'to trust in'.

See **faith**

Further reading: Helm 1973 and 1994; Price 1969; Senor 1995

Berkeley, George (1685–1753): An empiricist philosopher, and Bishop of Cloyne from 1734 to 1752, Berkeley is now known chiefly not for his sermons and ecclesiastical works or even for his strange writings on tar-water, but rather for his philosophical works, in which he defends subjective **idealism**, that is, the view that everything that exists is mental or immaterial. This does not imply that trees (for example) do not exist, for a tree is simply a collection of ideas in the minds of perceivers. Indeed, for Berkeley to exist is to be perceived. But what happens to the tree when we are all soundly asleep – does it then go out of existence, only to reappear when someone wakes up and looks out of the window? No, because God is always watching the tree and everything else. Berkeley comes up with this theory in order to circumvent the atheistic implications he suspected lay in **Locke**'s theory of **substance**, as well as to preserve our knowledge of the world – if we were purely mental and trees were not at all mental then how could we know about them? Few today follow Berkeley down the idealist path, but one cannot ignore his arguments and the problems he raises for other views.

See **empiricism; idealism**

Further reading: Berkeley 1948–57 and 1975; Warnock 1953

Bible, Holy see **revelation, special**

Blondel, Maurice (1861–1949): A French Roman-Catholic philosopher, Blondel worked at a time of intense conflict between his church and modernism. His early work *Action* (1893) focuses on human action as central to human being; here Blondel developed a phenomenology of action focused on the space between the intended goal and the fulfilment of the action. A dialectical tension emerges within this space, but is resolved in the transcendent God, who stands behind every action by **grace**. Blondel is recognised as a leader in the Roman-Catholic revival, and his theological and philosophical work had a deep impact on many subsequent Roman-Catholic theologians including Henri de Lubac, as well as the Second Vatican Council.

See **Rahner, Karl**

Further reading: Blondel 1984 and 1995; Conway 2000; Virgoulay 1992

Boethius, Anicius Manlius Severinus (c. 480–c. 526): Although today best known for his *Consolation of Philosophy*, written in prison while awaiting execution, Boethius also influenced **medieval philosophy** by his translations of Aristotle, his treatise on the **Trinity,** and his work on **logic** and the quadrivium (geometry, arithmetic, astronomy and music). He read **Augustine,** and **Neoplatonism** more generally is reflected in many of his writings. One of his enduring legacies to Christian philosophy is his definition of **eternity** as 'the complete possession all at once of illimitable life' (*Consolation of Philosophy* 5.6). This definition has had considerable influence on the debate about whether God is in **time** or outside time.

See **Augustine of Hippo; eternity; Neoplatonism; philosophy, medieval**

Further reading: Boethius 1882–91, 1973, 1990 and 2000; Chadwick 1981; Marenbon 2003

Bonaventure (c. 1217–74): Born in Tuscany in 1217 or 1221, Bonaventure (John of Fidanza) studied in Paris as a Franciscan friar, and was influenced by his teacher (Alexander of Hales), **Augustine, Neoplatonism** more generally and his friendly rival and contemporary, **Thomas Aquinas**. This last influence was often in the direction of disagreement, for example, over the importance of Aristotle. Bonaventure also differed from Thomas in style, preferring a more mystical approach to his colleague's more rationalistic one. This mysticism, which earned him the nickname 'the seraphic doctor', is reflected in his most famous works, *The Journey of the Mind to God* and his commentary on **Peter Lombard**'s *Sentences*. He also achieved higher ecclesiastical rank than Thomas Aquinas, becoming not just minister-general of the Franciscan order but also a cardinal of the church.

See **Aquinas, Thomas; Augustine of Hippo; Lombard, Peter; Neoplatonism**

Further reading: Bonaventure 1882–1902 and 2002; Gilson 1965

Bouwsma, Oets Kolk (1898–1978): A Christian philosopher in the Reformed theological tradition and a master stylist of the philosophical essay, Bouwsma displayed a unique skill of critiquing his various targets with eloquence and good humour. Among the essays that highlight Bouwsma's inimitable style are 'Descartes' Evil Genius',

'Naturalism' and 'Anselm's Argument'. Bouwsma was a friend of **Ludwig Wittgenstein** and developed Wittgensteinian ideas in his exploration of the nature of religious claims.

See **Wittgenstein, Ludwig Josef Johann**

Further reading: Bouwsma 1965 and 1984; Hustwit 1992

British Society for the Philosophy of Religion: Founded in 1993, the British Society for the Philosophy of Religion represented a broadening of the UK Society of Christian Philosophers to include non-Christian philosophers and discussion of non-Christian philosophy. It is smaller than the American Society of Christian Philosophers and does not have its own journal, but the two societies did come together for a joint meeting in 2003 in Oxford, UK.

See **religion, philosophy of; Society of Christian Philosophers**

Further reading: web site for the British Society for Philosophy of Religion

Buber, Martin (1878–1965): A Jewish philosopher and theologian, Martin Buber exercised some considerable influence on Christian philosophy, particularly through his book *I and Thou*, in which he contrasts the I–it relation that one has with 'objects', that is things that are not **persons** and do not talk back, and the I–thou relation that one should have with persons in order that one may be open to listen to what they have to say. This distinction is, for Buber, similar to the Kantian distinction between using persons as mere means to an end and treating them as ends in themselves. While some circumstances may regrettably entail an I–it attitude to another human, one must never have an I–it relation to God – he is 'the eternal Thou'. Buber has also had an unexpected influence

on some German Christians: they use his translation of
the Hebrew Bible.
   See **Kant, Immanuel**
   Further reading: Buber 1962–4, 1970 and 2001–;
Schilpp and Friedman 1967

Bultmann, Rudolf Karl (1884–1976): A theologian and
   scholar of the New Testament, Bultmann was influenced by neo-Kantianism and the **existentialism** of **Martin
   Heidegger**. As a result, he categorically denied that there
   could be any **miracles**, including the **resurrection** of Jesus.
   Instead, he placed the basis of Christianity in the existential choice for the Christ of **faith**. As such, Bultmann
   defended a 'demythologisation' of the Bible that reinterpreted the gospel in modern existentialist terms shorn of
   supernatural dressing. Critics objected that, once one begins the process of demythologisation, there is no principled means to stop it this side of **atheism**.
   See **Barth, Karl; existentialism; Heidegger, Martin**
   Further reading: Bultmann 1984; Ogden 1962

Butler, Joseph (1692–1752): An Anglican bishop, theologian
   and apologist against **deism**, Butler contributed to both
   philosophy of religion and **ethics**. In his day *The Analogy of Religion* (1736) was a widely celebrated attack on
   deism, which draws an **analogy** between the Bible and the
   natural world, arguing that both show evidence of coming from the same divine hand. Many consider Butler's
   greatest philosophical legacy to be found in his work on
   moral philosophy, particularly in *Fifteen Sermons* (1726),
   in which he critiques psychological hedonism, the view
   that all motives can be traced to the desire for pleasure.
   Instead, Butler argues that pleasure is in fact a by-product
   of primary desires properly sublimated within conscience.
   As such, pleasure can only be completed in objects for

which we have intrinsic regard. Underlying this process is the ultimately perfect coincidence of self-**love** and benevolent love.

See **deism; ethics; God, arguments for the existence of; theology, natural**

Further reading: Butler 1736 and 1900; Penelhum 1985

Calvin, John (1509–64): A French Protestant theologian, Calvin, through his years of reform at Geneva, became the great systematiser of the Reformation while laying the foundations for the theology that would bear his name. While Calvin's background was renaissance **humanism**, he emphasised the comprehensive effect of the fall upon the human will and mind: though humans were created with a **sensus divinitatis** designed to produce **belief** about God within us, its proper function had been corrupted by the fall, leaving humans in ignorance and rebellion. Among Calvin's other themes are a deepened theology of the **Trinity** and an appreciation for sanctification that balanced out Luther's preoccupation with justification. Calvin is most remembered for his emphasis on divine sovereignty, particularly as expressed in the doctrine of double **predestination**. Calvin's great work, the *Institutes of the Christian Religion*, was expanded and revised in successive editions between 1536 and 1559. Many important theologians developed Calvinist themes including Theodore Beza, John Owen, **Jonathan Edwards** and Francis Turretin, thereby creating one of the great Christian intellectual traditions.

See **Calvinism; divinitatis, sensus; Edwards, Jonathan; Kuyper, Abraham**

Further reading: Calvin 1863–1900, 1960 and 1992–; Dowey 1994; Gamble 1992; Helm 2004; Muller 2000; Wendel 1987

Calvinism: A theology developed out of the thought of **John Calvin,** in particular his emphasis on divine sovereignty and **predestination,** Calvinism has been dominant in Reformed and Presbyterian churches. As summarised in the five points of the Synod of Dort (1618), Calvinism provides a logically coherent articulation of divine providence in relation to human salvation: (1) total depravity: original **sin** has distorted every aspect of the human mind and will such that human beings are dead in sin; (2) unconditional election: God elects people for salvation based on his inscrutable will rather than on their foreseen merit; (3) limited **atonement:** Christ died efficiently only for the elect; (4) irresistible **grace:** God's Spirit draws the elect infallibly; and (5) perseverance of the Saints: the elect will persevere in **faith** and not fall away. Some self-confessed Calvinists disagree with one or more of the five points. The most common variation is a four-point Calvinism that rejects 'limited atonement', as in Amyraldianism. Calvinism has facilitated what is probably the most impressive intellectual tradition within Protestantism and has deeply impacted contemporary philosophy in particular through the Dutch Calvinist tradition of **Abraham Kuyper** and **Herman Dooyeweerd.** There are also several institutions committed to a Calvinistic philosophy: Calvin College in the United States, the Institute for Christian Studies in Canada and the Free University of Amsterdam are all examples.

See **Calvin, John; Dooyeweerd, Herman; Edwards, Jonathan; Kuyper, Abraham; Plantinga, Alvin; Wolterstorff, Nicholas**

Further reading: Gamble 1992; Helm 2004; Muller 2003

causa sui: Something is a *causa sui* if it is a cause of itself. This is variously applied to God as (1) God's timelessly causing himself to exist, (2) God's simultaneously causing at every moment himself to exist at that moment, and (3) God's causing at every moment himself to exist at the next moment (assuming there be such) or at every later moment. The last of these is the least controversial philosophically; many philosophers deny that it is possible to be a cause of oneself in any other way.

See **causation**

Further reading: Braine 1987

causation: What is it for one thing to cause another thing to be a certain way, or for one event to cause another event to obtain? Much philosophical ink has been spilt on this question. For Christian philosophers the debate becomes particularly important with reference to the question of whether God can have causal effects in the world and whether he can truly be said to have created the world and with reference to the question of whether the **soul** can have a causal effect on the physical world. Many philosophers talk of the four types of cause, a taxonomy that goes back to Aristotle. The four types are: (1) material cause, that out of which material things are composed; (2) formal cause, the form of the object or the pattern to which it conforms or the manner in which it is organised; (3) final cause, the purpose for which the object was designed or to which something tends; (4) efficient cause, something that brings the effect into being.

See **creation; miracle; soul**

Further reading: Craig and Smith 1995; Ducasse 1924; Sosa and Tooley 1993; Tooley 1997

certainty: There are different sorts of certainty. *Psychological* certainty is the characteristic of someone that believes a proposition with maximal commitment, that is, so strongly that he or she could not believe any proposition more strongly. A proposition is *logically* certain relative to background information if it follows with maximal probability from the background information, that is, if nothing could follow from the background information with greater probability. A proposition is logically certain in itself if it is logically necessarily true. Some philosophers claim that the notions of psychological certainty and logical certainty should coincide, such that one may rationally be psychologically certain only of those propositions that are logically certain in themselves or logically certain relative to those propositions that are logically certain in themselves. Christian philosophers have, especially in the last twenty-five years, resisted this claim, arguing that one may rationally be psychologically certain of propositions that are not logically certain.

See **belief**

Further reading: Klein 1981; Westphal, Jonathan 1995; Wittgenstein 1979

Christ see **incarnation**

Christology see **incarnation**

Clark, Gordon Haddon (1902–85): A pugnacious philosopher from the Calvinist tradition, Clark wrote over forty books and taught philosophy for sixty years. He is best known for his dispute with **Cornelius van Til** over whether there was any content in common between God's knowledge and human knowledge. Clark claimed that the content of some of God's knowledge was the same as that of human knowledge; van Til disagreed. Clark's philosophical system has received the name 'Scriptural-ism' because he insisted that everything we can know can be deduced from Scripture. Clark's influence on contemporary Christian philosophy is largely confined to conservative Calvinism in North America.

See **Calvinism; van Til, Cornelius**

Further reading: Clark, Gordon H. 1957, 1982 and 2004; Crampton 1999; Nash 1968; Robbins 1989

classical theism see **theism, classical**

Clifford, William Kingdon (1845–79): A mathematician and philosopher, Clifford wrote in his oft-anthologised essay 'The Ethics of Belief' this famous statement of **evidentialism**: 'It is wrong always, everywhere, and for anyone, to believe anything on insufficient evidence' (1901: 174). While the essay does not focus on religious **belief** in particular, it is clearly Clifford's primary target. Clifford illustrates the point with the example of a ship-owner that convinces himself – despite the evidence – that his ship is seaworthy. When it sinks and many drown we see the devastation caused by unethical believing. Insofar as religious belief violates the **ethics** of belief, it too is irrational, unethical and potentially harmful. Clifford himself followed these dictates by moving from Roman Catholicism to **agnosticism**. While **William James** offered a famous rebuttal in his essay 'The Will to Believe', more recently philosophers have pointed out that Clifford's principle is self-referentially defeating: he offers no evidence for it, and therefore violates it by believing it.

See **epistemology; epistemology, religious; experience, religious; foundationalism; justification, epistemic; reason; revelation**

Further reading: Clifford 1901; James 1979

compatibilism: Compatibilism about x and y is the doctrine that x and y are compatible, that is, that they may obtain together or be true together or that an individual may possess both. The usual use of this term in philosophy is concerning freedom or moral responsibility on the one hand and **determinism** on the other. The compatibilist claims that freedom or moral responsibility is compatible with determinism, that is, that an individual may be determined by something distinct freely to perform an action for which he or she is morally responsible. The incompatibilist denies this claim, saying that if an individual is determined to perform an action then he or she does not perform it freely and has no moral responsibility for it. Many Christian philosophers are incompatibilists, claiming that God has graciously refrained from determining us in order that we might freely love him. But other Christian philosophers are compatibilists, claiming that if God does not determine everything then he is not sovereign over all. There is also another, rarer, usage of the term 'compatibilism', concerning freedom and infallible foreknowledge. According to this usage, a compatibilist claims that it is possible for an individual, such as God, infallibly to foreknow what an individual will freely do. The incompatibilist in this sense claims that it is not possible for anyone infallibly to foreknow what an individual will freely do. Many incompatibilists in this sense are proponents of **open theism**.

See **foreknowledge and freedom, problem of; theism, open**

Further reading Fischer 1989 and 2005; Kane 2002 and 2005; Tomberlin 2000; van Inwagen 1983

conceptualism: Conceptualism is the view that **universals** are mental concepts of classification rather than objective realities exemplified in the world. As such, this theory takes a middle position on universals, affirming neither **realism** nor **nominalism**. The theory of **divine ideas** can be viewed as a form of conceptualism in which concepts are grounded in the divine mind. **William of Ockham** is often regarded as the leading conceptualist.

See **ideas, divine; nominalism; Ockham, William of; universals**

Further reading: Bacon 1995; Loux 1970; Moreland 2001

conditionals: Conditionals are 'if–then' statements or the propositions expressed by 'if–then' statements. They fall into two main classes: material conditionals, such as 'If Oswald did not kill Kennedy on 22 November 1963 then somebody else did', and subjunctive conditionals, such as 'If Oswald had not killed Kennedy on 22 November 1963 then somebody else would have done.' That these two conditionals are different in meaning is apparent from the fact that most think the first is true but the second false. The 'if' part of the conditional (or the proposition it expresses) is called 'the antecedent' and the 'then' part (or the proposition it expresses) is called 'the consequent'. Counterfactuals are subjunctive conditionals whose antecedents are false (or express false propositions). The standard semantics for counterfactuals, developed by David Lewis and Robert Stalnaker, is, roughly, that a counterfactual is true if its consequent is true in the closest possible world in which the antecedent is true, and that counterfactuals with necessarily false antecedents are vacuously true. Christian philosophers have been interested in this last contention: since God necessarily exists, the statement 'If God had not existed everything else would have been much as normal' is vacuously true on the standard semantics, yet one thinks intuitively that it is false. One project of analytical Christian philosophy is to work on a better semantics for such conditionals, though there is no agreement on such a system of semantics as yet.

See **logic**

Further reading: Beaty 1990; Jackson 1987; Jackson 1991; Lewis, David K. 1986a; Stalnaker 1999

consequentialism: Consequentialism is the view that the moral worth of an action is determined by its consequences, in the popular slogan 'The end justifies the means'. The label was originated by **Elizabeth Anscombe** in her 1958 essay 'Modern Moral Philosophy'. This approach to morality stands in contrast to the approach offered by **deontology**, which sees actions as being intrinsically good or bad irrespective of their consequences. Anscombe herself preferred the approach of **virtue ethics**. The most famous modern consequentialist was John Stuart Mill.

See **deontology; ethics; ethics, virtue**

Further reading: Anscombe 1981c; Darwall 2002a; Scheffler 1988

conservation, divine: The doctrine of divine conservation states that God preserves and upholds **creation** moment by moment. Were God to stop conserving creation it would immediately cease to exist. The doctrine of divine conservation is different from that of **continuous creation** in that if something is conserved in being it itself continues to exist rather than being recreated or replaced by something closely connected. There has been discussion among Christian philosophers as to the relationship between divine conservation and secondary agency.

See **action, divine; creation; creation, continuous**

Further reading: Morris 1988

continental philosophy see **philosophy, continental**

corrigibility: A **belief** is corrigible if it can be corrected, that is can be shown to be wrong from some other source. **Descartes** and his followers thought that beliefs about one's own mental states were incorrigible. For example, it is hard to imagine that I might sincerely think I am in pain and yet accept correction from another on this matter. This may, however, raise questions for the Christian philosopher, since many Christian philosophers think that the only way in which we could gain incorrigible beliefs would be through special revelation, at least since the fall of humankind.

See **certainty; Descartes, René; infallibility**
Further reading: Price 1936

cosmological argument see **argument, cosmological**

counter factual power see **power, counter factual**

creation: 'Creation' refers either to (1) the act by which God brought the contingent universe into being, or (2) the product of that initial act. Christians have long confessed that this creative act was not from a pre-existent plenum but rather *ex nihilo* (out of nothing). Big-Bang cosmology has seemingly confirmed this aspect of the Christian account by positing that the universe was once shrunk down to a mathematical point; this, however, raises a new question, namely, whether it is appropriate to equate $t = 0$ (the moment of origination of the Big Bang) with divine creation. A counterpart of creation out of nothing is the claim that creation was a *voluntary* divine act, a claim that is denied by some Christian philosophers, including advocates of process theology. One might also explore the relationship between God's initial act of creation and his subsequent acts of preservation. While most theologians have recognised a categorical difference between these two acts, some theologians, such as **Jonathan Edwards,** have argued that the subsequent points of creation involve the same act of bringing into being out of nothing. A final issue concerns the nature of creation vis-à-vis abstract objects like **universals.** If these are construed as part of creation, and yet, in accord with our modal intuitions, exist of **necessity,** we are left with the theologically loaded assertion that part of creation exists necessarily with God.

See **conservation, divine; creation, continuous; ideas, divine; science and religion**

Further reading: Copan and Craig 2004; Craig and Smith 1995; Isham, Murphy and Russell 1993; May 1994

creation, continuous: The doctrine of continuous creation is that God continuously creates things moment by moment. This is usually allied with **perdurantism,** the view that objects persist in virtue of having temporal stages, yielding the view that it is God that creates each temporal stage and (usually) unites the parts into a whole. (Note that this sense of 'continuous creation' is to be distinguished from the phrase's scientific use in the now-discredited 'steady-state' cosmological theory.)

See **creation; Edwards, Jonathan; perdurantism**

Further reading: Edwards, Jonathan 1970

creation theology see **theology, creation**

credo ut intellegam: The phrase 'credo ut intellegam' (in English, 'I believe in order that I may understand') was used by **Augustine** and **Anselm** to express the **belief** that **faith** must precede understanding – in other words, one cannot hope to understand the beliefs of the Christian tradition unless one shares them. Some Christian philosophers have enthusiastically embraced this principle, while others have worried about whether it is really possible to believe something without understanding it in order to understand it. Perhaps the best way to apply the principle is to think of there being degrees of belief and degrees of understanding, and that in order to advance in understanding one must first advance in belief.

See **Anselm of Canterbury; Augustine of Hippo**

Further reading: Anselm 2000; Augustine 1990–

defence, free-will: The free-will defence is a response to the **problem of evil,** originally due to **Augustine,** that appeals to the free will (understood according to **libertarianism**) of God's creatures. **Alvin Plantinga** developed a rigorous version of the free-will defence by using the modal logic of possible worlds. He argues that it is for all we know true that, while God could have created a world without evil and suffering, in all possible worlds with free agents some of those agents will freely commit evil acts. Hence, insofar as God desires to create a world where creatures possess freedom, it was not possible to do so without a limited amount of evil. While the free-will defence gives a possible explanation of the existence of moral evil, it has more difficulty explaining natural evil – the evil that arises from natural events like tornadoes and earthquakes. In a controversial move, Plantinga extends the free-will defence to cover natural evil by arguing that such events might be the result of the free acts of demonic agencies.

See **defence, greater-good; evil, problem of; theodicy**

Further reading: Augustine 1990–; Berthold 2004; Plantinga 1974a and 1974b

defence, greater-good: This approach to the **problem of evil,** classically expounded by **Irenaeus,** points out that God might have an overriding reason to allow limited evil in the world, namely, the goal of achieving an overall greater good than would otherwise exist. The primary good, as identified by **John Hick,** is 'soul-making', the maturation of moral agents through suffering and the development of second-order goods like courage and **altruism.** The defence does not answer why God did not simply create mature moral agents at the beginning, though one could perhaps point to the importance of a *moral history*: that is, there may be intrinsic value in agents' developing a moral character and exercising second-order goods over time. Another objection to the theory is that it fails to provide a plausible account of the amount, distribution and duration of evil. While horrific events like the Rwandan genocide often result in some acts of great moral courage and altruism, it may appear implausible (or even offensive) to argue that, on balance, those horrific events are justified in light of a greater good that they achieved.

See **defence, free-will; evil, problem of; Irenaeus; theodicy**

Further reading: Adams, Marilyn McCord 1999; Hick 1977

deism: Deism is the doctrine that, while a divine being exists, it is neither personal nor interested in the world it has created. Deism thus involves the denial of **revelation,** providence, **miracles** and (frequently) **divine conservation.** It arose in seventeenth-century Britain, where deists argued that a perfect God would create a world without need of miraculous intervention, and would make salvific knowledge generally available (through **reason**) rather than concentrated in particular **special revelation.** By the 1740s deism was undergoing sustained attack from both Christians and sceptics. In *The Analogy of Religion* (1736) **Joseph Butler** defended special biblical revelation in analogy with the **general revelation** in **creation,** while **David Hume**'s *Dialogues Concerning Natural Religion* (1779) attacked the arguments of **natural theology** on which deism depended. Devastating though these arguments were, the final downfall of deism may be due as much to its own inability to inspire religious devotion or to forestall the slide into practical, and then dogmatic, **atheism.** In recent years deism has been revived among notable scientists such as Carl Sagan and E. O. Wilson.

See **Butler, Joseph; creation; Hume, David; miracle; theology, natural**

Further reading: Byrne 1989; Gay 1968; Sturch 1990; Toland 1999

deontology: Deontology is the approach to **ethics** that concentrates on duty. More generally, it is the approach to ethics that holds that the fundamental bearers of moral properties are actions (or the will to perform certain actions), with states of affairs and agents bearing moral properties only derivatively. Much Christian moral philosophy, particularly in the Protestant tradition, has been deontological. Discussion among Christian philosophers has centred on the question of whether the deontological tradition is superior to both the **consequentialist** tradition and to the **virtue** tradition, and on the question of whether all our duties are derived from God or not.

See **consequentialism; dilemma, Euthyphro; ethics; ethics, virtue**

Further reading: Darwall 2002b; Fried 1978; Kant 1959

Derrida, Jacques (1930–2004): A French philosopher of Jewish descent well known for his 'philosophy of deconstruction', Derrida came to prominence in 1966, when he delivered a paper that advocated a *de*construction of the structuralist movement. Derrida then widened his target to include the general tendency in philosophy to construct systems of thought by privileging one term in a set of binary oppositions such as internal/external, universal/particular and good/evil. Through analysis Derrida sought to undermine this method by identifying how the marginalization of the excluded term is arbitrary and ineffectual. Underlying this challenge is Derrida's attack on 'logocentrism', the belief in a substantial word present in communication, and the 'metaphysics of presence' that it assumes. Derrida's unfruitful dialogue with John Searle illustrates the continued division between **continental philosophy** and **analytical philosophy**. Christian philosophers are deeply divided in their assessment of Derrida's work: some see his denial of the 'real presence' in various media (music, art, literature) as nihilistic, while others see Derrida's deconstruction as targeting not meaning or God, but rather our own inadequate grasp of these realities.

See **ontotheology; philosophy, continental; postmodernism; Westphal, Merold**

Further reading: Caputo 1997; Derrida 1998; Derrida 2001; Rayment-Pickard 2003

Descartes, René (1596–1650): French philosopher René Descartes challenged **scepticism** and **scholastism** while creating a body of work sufficient to earn him the title 'Father of Modern Philosophy'. This title refers to his emphasis upon individual **reason** and **certainty**, as developed particularly in *Discourse on Method* (1637) and *Meditations on First Philosophy* (1641). Living in a time of political and social turmoil and growing scepticism, Descartes became increasingly preoccupied with the certainty of mathematics as a model for knowledge. To meet scepticism on its own terms he accepted for the sake of the argument the most extreme scepticism, facilitated by his hypothesised 'evil demon', who could lead us to think incorrectly even about the most elementary mathematical truths. In the midst of a sea of doubt, Descartes then establishes an 'Archimedean point' of certainty in his argument: 'I think. Therefore, I exist' (*Cogito, ergo sum*). Having established this certain **belief**, Descartes then finds an idea in his mind, that of a most perfect being, which, owing to its perfection, must exist in reality. Descartes reasons from this **ontological argument** that a perfect God would not deceive us, and so we can trust our senses. As Arnauld pointed out, however, if an evil demon can deceive one to hold erroneous beliefs about basic mathematics and **logic**, surely it could deceive Descartes at every step of this argument, a dilemma that leads to the infamous Cartesian circle. Descartes's influence is also found in his forceful rejection of the scholastic world of substantial forms and final causes in favour of a mechanistic universe, a move that paved the way for modern **science**. Finally, Descartes's dualistic contrast between world (extended substance) and mind (thinking substance) has been enormously influential, while in recent decades it has joined his foundationalist epistemology (that is, his view that every item of our knowledge is either deservedly foundational or solidly built on foundations) as a target of sustained criticism. Of particular interest to Christian philosophers, apart from his ontological argument for God's existence, is Descartes's understanding of God's power as unlimited even by the laws of logic.

See **certainty; dualism; Enlightenment; epistemology; foundationalism; Locke, John; Malebranche, Nicolas; scepticism; soul**

Further reading: Cottingham 1992; Descartes 1969–75, 1979 and 1984–91; Gaukroger 1995; Wilson 1982

design, argument from/to see **argument from/to design**

design, intelligent: So-called 'intelligent design' is a version of the **argument from design** which has been developed by critics of dysteleological **evolution,** including Philip Johnson, Michael Behe and William Dembski. Dembski argues that the two traditional types of explanation in **science, necessity** and blind contingency (chance), need to be supplemented by the third explanation of directed contingency (design). Indeed, directed contingency is already essential to many scientific disciplines including cryptography and forensics; Dembski thus commends it likewise to the natural sciences. There are three criteria necessary to warrant the design inference: contingency, complexity and specified function. Hence, if a biological structure (such as DNA) is contingent, sufficiently complex and has a specified function, we can legitimately conclude that it has been designed. While critics dismiss intelligent design as another way to introduce God into science, it does not explicitly address whether the designer is supernatural or merely superintelligent.

See; **argument from/to design; God, arguments for the existence of**

Further reading: Behe 1996; Dembski 1998 and 1999; Pennock 2001

determinism: Determinism concerning human beings is the thesis that every action performed by a human is determined, that is, antecedently caused or fixed, by something else. The something else might be another agent, one's genes, one's upbringing, a prior state of the universe, God, or some combination of these factors. Most Christian philosophers that have been determinists have been theistic determinists, that is, have regarded human actions as being ultimately determined by God. Most non-Christian philosophers that have been determinists have held that human actions are determined by the prior states of the universe and the laws of nature. There has been a variety of opinion among Christian philosophers over exactly who is determined: whether it is (1) all unregenerate humans, (2) all humans with original **sin** (that is, excluding Jesus and Adam before the fall), (3) all nondivine humans (that is, excluding Jesus), (4) all creatures (that is, including angels), or (5) everything (including God, who is determined by his own **nature**). The major questions concerning determinism are (1) is it true? and (2) if determinism is true does it follow that those determined are not free? Those that answer 'yes' to (1) and (2) are called 'hard determinists', and those that answer 'yes' to (1), but 'no' to (2), are called 'soft determinists'. Those that answer 'no' to (1) and 'yes' to (2) are often called 'libertarians'. In general, those that answer 'no' to (2) are called 'compatibilists', those that answer 'yes' to (2) are called 'incompatibilists'.

See **compatibilism; freedom**

Further reading: Earman 1986; Helm 1993; van Inwagen 1983

dilemma, Euthyphro: The Euthyphro dilemma is the question, classically posed by **Plato** in his dialogue the *Euthyphro*, concerning the relative priority of God's will and moral properties. For example, are actions morally right because God commands them, or does God command actions because they are morally right? While the Roman-Catholic tradition has tended to take the second horn of the dilemma, many Christian philosophers from the Protestant tradition have tended to take the first horn. One objection to the second horn is that it apparently establishes a moral realm separate from God and outside his power; an objection to the first horn is that it seems to make morality arbitrary and to evacuate of all content the believer's praise for God's **perfect goodness**. Attempts have also been made to escape between the horns of the dilemma by arguing that morality is a reflection of the **nature of God**, but that God's nature is unalterable, even by God himself.

See **ethics; ethics, divine-command theory of**

Further reading: Adams, Robert Merrihew 1987; Hare 2001; Helm 1981; Plato 1977 and 1981

divine-command theory see **ethics, divine-command theory of**

divinitatis, sensus: The phrase 'sensus divinitatis' (Latin for the 'sense of the divine') was used by **John Calvin** to identify a human cognitive faculty designed to produce **belief** in God with a naturalness and immediacy parallel to that of our five senses. **Sin** has adversely affected our sensus divinitatis, however, thereby inhibiting our awareness of God, his **nature** and purposes. **Alvin Plantinga** and other advocates of **Reformed epistemology** have taken up this idea as a foundational epistemological basis for belief in God. That is, forming beliefs about God is part of our properly functioning cognitive apparatus, and, thus, to do so is perfectly rational. There is some discussion among historians of doctrine over whether this is a correct use of the concept as understood by Calvin.

See **Calvin, John; epistemology, Reformed; Plantinga, Alvin**

Further reading: Dowey 1994; Plantinga 2000

Dooyeweerd, Herman (1894–1977): A Dutch Reformed philosopher of law, Dooyeweerd is now noted not so much for his particular interest in jurisprudence as for his more general and systematic view of reality that expanded from his legal theory. He studied at the Calvinistic Free University of Amsterdam, and then worked for the Dr Abraham Kuyper Foundation, before returning to the Free University as Professor of Legal Philosophy. Dooyeweerd saw himself as implementing **Kuyper**'s dream of a fully Christian and Reformed philosophy on a scale to match **Kant**'s. To this end Dooyeweerd wrote over 200 separate titles thinking through the principles underlying a wide range of academic subjects; these titles varied in length from a few pages in the case of some shorter articles to several thousand pages for the major works, such as the three-volume work *The Philosophy of the Cosmonomic Idea*, published in 1936, also known under the title *A New Critique of Theoretical Thought*. Dooyeweerd is perhaps best known today for his theory of aspects, in which he isolates fifteen categories into which everything can be fitted. Dooyeweerd's philosophy has had influence not only in his native Netherlands, but also in Canada, the United States and South Africa. The Dooyeweerdian school of thought is often known as 'reformational philosophy'.

See **Calvinism; Kuyper, Abraham**

Further reading: Clouser 2005; Dooyeweerd 1975; Hart 1984; Kalsbeek 2002

dualism: Dualism is the doctrine that, in a certain respect, there are two things or two sorts of thing. The most common use of the word now among Christian philosophers is to refer to the doctrine (properly 'substance dualism') that the human person is made up of two sorts of parts: physical (the body) and non-physical (the soul/mind); 'substance dualism' is also used to refer to the subtly different doctrine that a human person is a soul/mind using a body. A weaker version of this thesis is property dualism: the view that a person is a substance of but one kind (physical), but having both physical and non-physical properties. 'Substance dualism' is also used more generally to refer to the doctrine that substances come in two sorts in the world: mental substances and physical substances. This version of dualism allows for God (and perhaps angels and demons) to be the only mental/spiritual substances. An older usage of 'dualism' is for the idea that there are two principles, one good and one evil, fighting for the control of the universe. Dualism of this sort is reflected in **Manichaeism**, Zoroastrianism and *Star Wars*.

See **Descartes, René**

Further reading: Descartes 1984–91; Robinson 1993; Swinburne 1997

Duns Scotus, John (c. 1266–1308): A Scottish-born Franciscan scholastic philosopher and theologian, Duns Scotus died before he could produce a *Summa Theologiae* or even revise his existing works, such as his commentaries on **Peter Lombard**'s *Sentences*. He is known for his views that the will could go against the intellect, that God had to become incarnate irrespective of **sin** and that the moral law was decreed by God, but necessarily so decreed. He also argued for a **univocal** account of language about God and creatures, defended **realism** against **nominalism** concerning **universals**, and claimed that different individuals could share every property except *haecceity* (and entailed properties). He was nicknamed 'the subtle doctor', but a less positive appreciation of him is detectable in the origin of our word 'dunce'. His work exercised considerable influence on the Franciscan order because of its forthright move away from a strict **Thomism** and reversion to a more old-fashioned **Augustinianism**.

See **philosophy, medieval; scholasticism**

Further reading: Cross 1999 and 2004; Duns Scotus 1950–, 1987 and 1997–; Williams, Thomas 2003; Wolter 1990 and 2003

Edwards, Jonathan (1703–58): A congregational minister in colonial New England, Edwards was a leader in the Great Awakening and was important both as a philosopher and as a theologian. While his impact on theology has been great, sustained interest in his philosophical achievements only began in about the 1950s. Edwards's philosophical theology is dominated by a conception of the absolute sovereignty and aesthetic perfection of God. To this end Edwards defends a strong sense of divine **determinism** coupled with **occasionalism**. Like **Malebranche**, Edwards believes that any indeterminacy beyond God's immediate causal control impinges upon the divine majesty. In *Freedom of the Will* he argues that the libertarian conception of **freedom** leads to an absurd infinite regress of self-causation for each allegedly self-determined act. Further, he defends **compatibilism** by noting that the only plausible criteria for free actions are desire and absence of constraint. Edwards also (apparently independently) developed a version of **idealism** similar to that of **Berkeley**. Like Berkeley, he rejects **Locke**'s distinction between primary and secondary qualities, arguing rather that all sensory input derives not from external objects, but rather as a direct communication of God's divine thoughts. Edwards so stressed dependence upon the divinity that he saw God as divinely creating everything anew each moment in the same way as the initial **creation**. Based on these beliefs Edwards developed novel treatments of a number of doctrines including original **sin**. Edwards also composed an important psychological and epistemological study in *Religious Affections* and a powerful discussion of divine Trinitarian aesthetics. At his untimely death he left behind 60,000 pages of written text.

See **Berkeley, George; Calvinism; creation, continuous; determinism; occasionalism**

Further reading: Edwards, Jonathan 1970, 1971 and 1974; Helm and Crisp 2003; Lee 2005; Lesser 1981 and 1994; Marsden 2003; Smith, Stout and Minkema 1995; Stein 1996

empiricism: Empiricism is the doctrine that some or all of our knowledge or concepts come from experience. The version of empiricism with respect to concepts is often known as 'concept empiricism' and the version of either that says that *all* our knowledge or concepts come from experience is often known as 'extreme empiricism', with the version that says that *some* (but not all) of our knowledge or concepts come from experience being often known as 'moderate empiricism'. On these definitions, **Locke, Berkeley** and **Hume** were moderate empiricists, and Mill an extreme empiricist.

See **rationalism**

Further reading: Atherton 1999; Aune 1970; Berkeley 1948–57; Garrett and Barbanell 1997; Hume 1974; Kenny 1986; Locke 1975–; Mill 1963–

endurantism: Endurantism is the doctrine that persistent things persist in virtue of existing wholly at more than one time. Christian philosophers that are endurantists include **Geach, van Inwagen**, Oderberg and Merricks.

See **perdurantism**

Further reading: Chisholm 1976; Lewis, David K. 1986b; Merricks 2001; Oderberg 1993; Van Inwagen 1990

Enlightenment: A broad philosophical and cultural movement in Europe and North America (c. 1650–1789), the Enlightenment was characterised by an exaltation of universal human **reason,** autonomy and individualism, coupled with a distrust of tradition. Heralded by Francis Bacon's defence of scientific induction and **Descartes's** emphasis on individual reason and proof, the spirit of the movement is most memorably captured in **Kant's** famous essay 'What is Enlightenment?' in which he challenged all to 'Have courage to use your own reason!'. Many contemporary Christian philosophers consider, however, the Enlightenment to have had a largely negative influence on philosophy, given its distrust of Christian tradition and **revelation.** It is true that thinkers like **John Locke** attempted to defend Christianity according to Enlightenment strictures, but it is questionable whether these attempts did more harm or good, since their effect was to place Christian dogma, and even minimalist **theism,** in a defensive posture that left theologians increasingly preoccupied with prolegomenal questions of **epistemology** and method.

See **Butler, Joseph; deism; Paley, William; reason; theology, natural**

Further reading: Cassirer 1955; Gay 1973; Israel 2001

epistemic justification see **justification, epistemic**

epistemology: Epistemology is the study of the nature of knowledge, **epistemic justification** and rational **belief.** Traditionally knowledge has been defined as 'justified true belief', but this definition has been sharply disputed in recent decades. Among the other topics considered in epistemology are the nature of noetic (belief) structures, the relation between justified belief and knowledge, the nature of particular sources of belief including perception, memory and **religious experience,** and the problem of **scepticism.** Ever since **Descartes's** 'turn to the subject', epistemology has often been treated as 'first philosophy', a position that had previously belonged to **metaphysics**. Within recent **analytical philosophy**, however, there has been a growing shift to seeing philosophy of language as first philosophy.

See **belief; certainty; corrigibility; epistemology; epistemology, Reformed; experience, religious; fallibilism; foundationalism; reason; revelation**

Further reading: Audi 2003; BonJour 2002; Kim and Sosa 2000; Van Til 1969a and 1969b; Wolfe 1982; Wood 1998

epistemology, Reformed: A theory of **epistemology** that defends the thesis that religious (specifically Christian) **beliefs** may be properly basic and even constitute knowledge, Reformed epistemology derives its name from the Christian Reformed theological tradition, and in particular the views of theologians like **John Calvin** and **Abraham Kuyper**. Not surprisingly, the main philosophers to have developed this theory are either from this tradition (**Alvin Plantinga, Nicholas Wolterstorff**) or are sympathetic to it (**William Alston**). Among the criticisms of Reformed epistemology is the 'Great-Pumpkin Objection': if belief in God can be properly basic, then it is rational to believe in anything, including the Great Pumpkin. Since this is absurd, Reformed epistemology must be rejected. In response, advocates of Reformed epistemology point out that the rationality of properly basic beliefs is prima facie. Hence, if there were defeaters for belief in God (or the Great Pumpkin) such belief would become irrational until the defeater could itself be defeated. As such, the position can distinguish between rational and irrational forms of belief. Further, many of those beliefs that one deems to be properly basic are held within a particular doxastic community, and there is no reason why Christians cannot thus accept their beliefs as prima facie properly basic rather than, say, following an atheistic doxastic community in saying that they are not.

See **Alston, William Payne; divinitatis, sensus; epistemology, religious; fideism; foundationalism; Plantinga, Alvin; Wolterstorff, Nicholas**

Further reading: Alston 1993; Dooyeweerd 1975; Plantinga 2000; Plantinga and Wolterstorff 1983

epistemology, religious: Religious epistemology is the branch of **epistemology** concerned with **beliefs** of a specifically religious nature, and the specific epistemological issues that they raise including the relationships among **revelation, faith** and **reason**. Since the **Enlightenment** there has been an inordinate amount of attention paid to the epistemological evaluation of religious beliefs, in particular the extent to which they meet (or fail to meet) the strictures of classical **foundationalism**. In recent years this assumption has been sharply criticised by defenders of **Reformed epistemology**.

See **Alston, William Payne; Clifford, William Kingdon; epistemology, Reformed; experience, religious; faith; fideism; foundationalism; James, William; Plantinga, Alvin; reason; revelation; Wolterstorff, Nicholas**

Further reading: Alston 1993; Geivett and Sweetman 1993; Penelhum 1971; Senor 1995; Yandell 1994

equivocal: A word is used equivocally in two contexts when it has a totally different meaning in one context from the meaning that it has in the other. Some suggest in the debate concerning **religious language** that words used both of God and creatures are used equivocally in the two contexts.

See **analogical; language, religious; univocal**

Further reading: Cole and Lee 1994; Ramsey 1957 and 1971

eternity: Christian thinkers have traditionally described God as 'eternal', but what precisely does this mean? There are two main schools of thought: the traditional, 'atemporalist', school, which thinks that God is outside **time,** and the more innovative, 'temporalist', school, which thinks that God is everlasting within time. Stump, Kretzmann, **Leftow** and **Helm** are representatives of the first school; Pike, **Wolterstorff** and the 'open theists' are representatives of the second school. There are also hybrid views, such as Craig's view that God is in time with **creation** and outside time *sans* creation, and **Swinburne** and Padgett's that God is in his own, unmetricated, time. The issue of God's relationship to time is of great importance to Christian philosophers since it is closely connected with other issues: many atemporalists claim that if God is omniscient he must be timeless, whereas many temporalists claim that if God is a **person** that relates to us humans then he must be in time. The doctrine of the **incarnation** also raises questions here, since it seems that Christians are committed to the claim that Jesus was divine and the claim that he was (and is) in time.

See **Helm, Paul; Leftow, Brian; time; Wolterstorff, Nicholas**

Further reading: Hasker 1989; Helm 1988; Leftow 1991

ethics: Ethics may be defined as the study of morality (though some, such as Bernard Williams, distinguish differently between the two). It is traditionally divided into three areas: (1) meta-ethics, concerned with the meaning of moral terms ('good', 'bad', 'right', 'wrong', etc.) and whether moral values are objective, subjective or something else; (2) normative ethics, concerned with what sorts of things are the primary bearers of moral properties – actions, states of affairs, or agents – and in virtue of what they bear them – conformity to the will of God, maximising happiness, or being 'brute facts' etc.; and (3) applied ethics, concerned with certain practical dilemmas that arise in life. Certain aspects of (3) have grown into disciplines in their own right: business ethics and medical ethics, for example.

See **consequentialism; ethics, divine command theory of; ethics, virtue**

Further reading: Baron, Pettit and Slote 1997; Holmes 1984; MacIntyre 1985 and 2002; Williams, Bernard A. O. 1985

ethics, divine-command theory of: The divine-command theory of ethics views the ground of moral laws as deriving from the divine command or will. This is one response to the ancient **Euthyphro dilemma:** is something good because God commands it, or does God command it because it is good? Since to choose the latter option seems to place ethics outside God, the divine-command theory chooses the former option and so bases ethical laws on the divine will or command or, perhaps, the divine nature itself. Many able philosophers have defended this position including **William of Ockham** and, recently, **Robert Merrihew Adams** and Philip Quinn. Critics claim that the theory faces the problem of arbitrariness insofar as God could have decreed that it would be morally good to torture fuzzy kittens and immoral to help old ladies cross the street. Another objection is that the theory undermines the meaning of God's **perfect goodness,** for if the good simply derives from the will of God then God is good simply in virtue of following his own will.

See **argument, moral; ethics**
Further reading: Harris 2003; Helm 1981; Quinn 1978

ethics, virtue: Virtue ethics is the approach to **ethics** that sees the fundamental bearers of moral properties as being agents rather than actions or states of affairs. The supporters of this approach tend to see it as a return to a medieval ethics harking back to Aristotle. It has been championed in recent years by many Christian philosophers, initially **Elizabeth Anscombe** and, lately, Linda Zagzebski. Virtue ethics involves a rejection of the deontological idea that there are rules determining the moral worth of actions. The question to ask is 'what would the virtuous person do in this situation?', and these answers may well not conform to any clear rule. Two key Aristotelian concepts for the virtue ethicist, beside the concept of virtue itself, are *eudaimonia* or well-being, and *phronesis* or practical wisdom. The renaissance of virtue ethics has also had the effect of increasing awareness of the agent in other ethical theories, and various deontologists and consequentialists have tried to refine their theories to take account of some insights from virtue theory.

See **Anscombe, Gertrude Elizabeth Margaret; ethics; virtues**

Further reading: Anscombe 1981c; Crisp and Slote 1997; Darwall 2002c; Murphy, Kallenberg and Nation 1997; Statman 1997; Zagzebski 2004

Euthyphro dilemma see **dilemma, Euthyphro**

evidentialism: Evidentialism is the epistemological theory that the **epistemic justification** of a **belief** depends on the evidence one has for it. **John Locke** developed an influential version of the theory with his claim that belief should always be proportioned to the evidence. Advocates of the view differ as to the level of evidence required to make a belief rational and the extent to which one must possess or grasp the evidence as opposed to knowing some who do (or did). But, wherever the evidence resides, evidentialists commonly assume that such evidence must have a public, demonstrable component. Evidentialism is closely aligned with classical **foundationalism**, and has often been used as a means to judge religious belief as irrational.

See **Clifford, William Kingdon; epistemology; epistemology, Reformed; epistemology, religious; faith; fideism; foundationalism; reason**

Further reading: Audi 2003; Konyndyk 1986; Wykstra 1989

evil, problem of: The problem of evil occurs in many forms. Philosophical discussion has eschewed the practical and pastoral problems of evil, and concentrated on the logical and evidential/probabilistic problems. The logical problem of evil is the problem that it appears that the proposition that evil exists logically implies the proposition that God does not exist. The argument goes roughly thus:

1. Evil exists.
2. If God exists then he will prevent all evil that he can prevent and knows about, thanks to his perfect goodness.
3. If God exists then he can prevent all evil that he knows about, thanks to his omnipotence.
4. If God exists then he knows about all evil that exists, thanks to his omniscience.
5. God does not exist.

Many Christian philosophers have striven to show that appearances deceive here, and that the argument is not logically sound. There are two broad defences against the argument, both denying (2): the **free-will defence** and the **greater-good defence**. The free-will defence takes its lead from **Augustine**'s early works. Its leading contemporary exponent is **Alvin Plantinga**, who claims that, for all we know, God cannot create a world in which everybody freely refrains from evil. Moreover, a world in which some people freely do good and some do evil may well be better than one in which everybody is forced to do good. The greater-good defence takes its lead from **Irenaeus**. Its leading contemporary exponent is **John Hick**, who claims that suffering evil is necessary to make our **souls** adult souls rather than childish, immature souls. In other words, we should be spiritually impoverished if we did not have the experience of struggling through adversity. The evidential or probabilistic problem of evil is the problem that the proposition that evil exists makes more likely the proposition that God does not exist. Debate has ranged furiously over the past thirty years or so over who bears the burden of proof: the Christian philosopher to explain why it's quite likely that God permits evil or the atheist to explain why it isn't likely. There are various refined versions of the problem of evil, such as the problem of natural evil (suffering not inflicted by humans), the problem of horrendous evils (addressed in particular by **Marilyn McCord Adams**), and the problem of why God allowed the fall (that is, the first **sin** of his creatures).

See **Adams, Marilyn McCord; Augustine of Hippo; defence, free-will; defence, greater-good; goodness, perfect; Hick, John; Irenaeus; omnipotence; omniscience; Plantinga, Alvin**

Further reading: Adams, Marilyn McCord 1999; Hick 1977; Lewis, C. S. 1940; Plantinga 1974a; Rowe 2001; Swinburne 1998; Whitney 1998

evolution: 'Evolution' generally describes any gradual process of change. It is used more specifically to describe any theory that explains biological diversity through gradual change derived from initial commonality. There have been many theories of this type (for example, Lamarckianism). Finally, it is used to refer to Charles Darwin's theory of evolutionary development through natural selection, a picture that was later completed with the discovery of genetics and thus the mechanism of inherited random mutations. Scientists and philosophers disagree sharply on the propriety of extending Darwinian theory to explain non-biological spheres including human psychology and social and economic relationships. One particularly contentious issue concerns eugenics: if we are evolving is it not licit, even morally obligatory, to take control of our own evolution? Philosophically, evolution raises a number of issues including the viability of traditional conceptions of **creation** and original **sin**. Another hotly debated issue in the **science and religion** arena is whether evolution is inherently *dysteleological* such that no agent, not even God, can direct the 'random' mutations that occur, or whether God could be providentially directing each step of the process.

See **creation; design, intelligent; science; science and religion; sin**

Further reading: Beilby 2002; Dennett 1996; Haught 2000; Hull 2001; Melsen 1965; Midgley 2002

existentialism: A diverse philosophical movement, existentialism is characterised by a stress on the individual, freedom of choice and, in many cases, the 'absurdity' of the universe. **Kierkegaard** is usually thought of as the first existentialist; he led a reaction against the abstract rationalism of **Hegel**'s philosophy – instead of focusing on the 'absolute consciousness' Kierkegaard wanted to focus on the subjective and personal side of the life of the individual. The movement is called 'existentialism' because of the special use of the word *existenz* ('existence') to describe a 'distinctively human mode of being'. Existentialism also involves the rejection of the view that humans have pre-existing essences; existentialists insist that existence is ours to work out how we wish – in **Sartre's** slogan, 'existence precedes essence'. Existentialism developed in two separate directions, one atheistic and one religious. The best-known atheistic existentialists were **Heidegger** (though he denied the label 'atheist'), Sartre and Camus. The last two were also great stylists, both being offered the Nobel Prize for Literature. The best-known religious existentialists are Kierkegaard, **Marcel**, **Jaspers** and **Buber**, though many theologians, most famously **Bultmann**, were also influenced by existentialist thought.

See **Buber, Martin; Bultmann, Rudolf Karl; Heidegger, Martin; Jaspers, Karl Theodor; Kierkegaard, Søren Aabye; Marcel, Gabriel; Sartre, Jean-Paul**

Further reading: Blackham 1997; Guignon and Pereboom 2001; Sartre 1948

experience, religious: An experience is religious if the individual undergoing it takes it to involve an encounter with a transcendent divine reality. While such experience is generally believed to contrast with mundane non-divine experience, **Schleiermacher** rejected the notion of special **divine action** and instead viewed religious experience as a component of all human experience. Assuming that we demarcate the range of religious experience as less than the totality of experience, we can then enquire into its specific epistemological status. **William James** argued pragmatically in *The Varieties of Religious Experience* that putative religious experience can be accepted at face value owing to its positive effects on the percipient. Recently, **William Alston** has argued in *Perceiving God* that 'mystical perception' can serve as an epistemological ground for **belief** in God analogous to the ground sense perception provides for knowledge of the world. The argument from religious experience reasons that the **existence of God** provides the simplest explanation for the widespread distribution and nature of reports for special religious experience.

See **epistemology, religious**

Further reading: Alston 1993; Archer, Collier and Porpora 2004; Baillie 1962; James 1920; Yandell 1994

F

faith: Within **analytical philosophy** 'faith' is an epistemological term referring to **belief** in a proposition in the absence of evidence due (at least in part) to trust in the source of that belief. Faith thus involves both cognitive apprehension and personal commitment. In this sense, one can have faith in many circumstances, including the testimony of another **person** or of one's own sense faculties. The call to have faith, so essential to Christian belief, raises some important epistemological questions. For instance, the fact that those that believe the **resurrection** without seeing receive commendation (John 20: 29) seems to stand in tension with epistemic intuitions that **scepticism** in the absence of evidence is commendable. One resolution is to see Doubting Thomas as maintaining scepticism despite adequate testimony or evidence to make faith in Jesus a rational epistemic alternative. Another possibility is to reject the demand for rationality as a primary good, and instead see faith as an irrational, but ultimately commendable, decision. As such, one can say that rationality is not the only, or even primary, epistemic virtue. The existentialist tradition has picked up on this theme, with **Kierkegaard** famously discussing 'a leap of faith' that one has to make in embracing religious commitment. **Pascal**, from whom Kierkegaard drew some inspiration, took faith as being a virtue of the **practical reason**, rather than of the theoretical reason.

See **credo ut intellegam; epistemology; epistemology, Reformed; epistemology, religious; existentialism; fideism; fides quaerens intellectum; Kierkegaard, Søren Aabye; Pascal, Blaise; reason; reason, practical; revelation**

Further reading: Adams, Robert Merrihew 1987; Penelhum 1995; Senor 1995; Sessions 1994; Swinburne 2005

fallibilism: Fallibilism is the position that some or all of our **beliefs** are liable to error and thus lack the maximum **epistemic justification** of **certainty**. Most philosophers today recognise fallibilism at least as regards some class of beliefs. Fallibilism stands in direct opposition to the Cartesian demand for the grounding of all knowledge in certainty as in classical **foundationalism**. Fallibilism has been influential among scientists that adopt a critical realist stance, for they believe that scientific theories are approximating reality to a greater or lesser extent, and, thus, that theories are open to being revised or rejected in accord with new data. Fallibilism can likewise appear attractive for the theologian that recognises that theological formulation is always open to revision and further emendation. Indeed, such a view is central to the theology of **Wolfhart Pannenberg**, who views all theological claims as hypotheses liable to **falsification** prior to Jesus' second coming.

See **epistemology; falsification principle; foundationalism; Pannenberg, Wolfhart; reason**

Further reading: Audi 2003; Polanyi 1974

falsification principle: Suggested by Karl Popper, the falsification principle distinguishes scientific statements from non-scientific statements in virtue of their conceivable falsification. A highly influential application of the principle to religion is found in **Antony Flew**'s contribution to the essay 'Theology and Falsification'. Flew presents a scenario, taken from John Wisdom, where two individuals enter a forest clearing, one convinced that it is tended by a gardener, the second remaining a sceptic. Through successive attempts by the sceptic to falsify the **belief** – for instance by waiting in the bushes and erecting an electric fence to catch the gardener – the other keeps revising the attributes of the gardener, for example, he is invisible and can walk through fences. Clearly the belief in the gardener does not meet the principle of falsification. The gardener is of course meant as an **analogy** for belief in God, equally rendering such belief, and theological reflection on it, unscientific or even vacuous. Even if this did apply to a minimally defined **theism**, it would appear not to work for a religion like Christianity, which could conceivably be falsified either by empirical evidence (for example, historical evidence that the **resurrection** of Jesus was a hoax) or by demonstrating the incoherence of a central Christian belief (for example, the **Trinity**). A more basic difficulty for the principle is that it does not accurately describe the nature of scientific statements. As Imre Lakatos argued, a scientific hypothesis need not ever be falsified, so long as one adds supplementary hypotheses to explain prima facie contrary data. The real fate of unsuccessful scientific theories is not falsification but increased degeneracy until they are finally abandoned. As such, theological assertions are no more infinitely adaptable to countervailing evidence than scientific ones, and so theological statements are none the worse if they are not falsifiable.

See **Flew, Antony; science; science and religion; verification/verifiability principle**

Further reading: Diamond and Litzenburg 1975; Flew and MacIntyre 1955; Popper 1996; Rosenberg 2000

Feuerbach, Ludwig (1804–72): Initially a Christian, Feuerbach felt increasing tension between orthodoxy and the Hegelian philosophy he encountered in university, such that by the early 1830s he had become a left-wing Hegelian and abandoned the Christian faith. Feuerbach became famous or infamous in 1841 upon the publication of *The Essence of Christianity*, an inverted Hegelian interpretation of Christianity. On his view it was not God that becomes self-conscious through **creation**, but rather human beings that become self-conscious through God, or rather the *idea* of God. Now that we are mature we can reject this idea and thus embrace **atheism** and **materialism**. Feuerbach's was the first projection theory of religion, an approach that would deeply influence later thinkers like Karl Marx and **Sigmund Freud**.

See **atheism; Freud, Sigmund; Hegel, Georg Wilhelm Friedrich; materialism**

Further reading: Feuerbach 1967–; Feuerbach 1997; Wartofsky 1977

fideism: From the Latin *fides*, fideism is the position that religious **belief** is grounded in **faith** rather than **reason** or evidence. Fideists disavow any attempt to provide rational grounds for religious belief and may even heighten paradox to attack reason. Identifying fideists is difficult, particularly since it is doubtful that many of the theologians often associated with the position in fact held it. For instance, while **Kierkegaard** and **Tertullian** are often cited as fideists, it is more likely that each was rejecting a particular construal of reason rather than reason per se.

A clearer example would be Pierre Bayle, who claimed that the more irrational one's faith was, the better.

See **epistemology, religious; faith; reason**

Further reading: Adams, Robert Merrihew 1987; Evans 1998; Hester 1992; Penelhum 1983; Plantinga and Wolterstorff 1983

fides quaerens intellectum: This, 'faith seeking understanding' in English, is the unofficial slogan of the contemporary revival in Christian philosophy, derived from **Augustine**, by way of **Anselm**. It refers to the process of rationally thinking through what one already believes, as opposed to trying to strip oneself of all one's religious beliefs and starting again to reconstruct them from scratch.

See **Anselm of Canterbury; Augustine of Hippo; philosophy, medieval; scholasticism**

Further reading: Barth 1960

Finnis, John Mitchell (1940–): A Roman Catholic philosopher at the universities of Oxford and Notre Dame, Finnis is widely considered one of the world's leading moral philosophers and **natural-law** theorists. Finnis has helped develop a reinvigorated natural-law alternative to deontological and consequentialist ethics. To this end, Finnis seeks to identify the first principles of **practical reason** that guide our ethical action to the end of achieving seven intrinsic goods that are knowable per se (in themselves). Among these goods are (1) human life, (2) justice and friendship, and (3) religion and holiness. Finnis believes that the good of human life renders contraception unacceptable, and he charges that Roman-Catholic ethicists that accept contraception are in danger of embracing a proportionalist ethic. Finnis has worked to develop his natural-law framework in a way appreciable by non-theists, a project that has opened him up to charges of compromise. Among his many influential works is *Natural Law and Natural Rights* (1980).

See **ethics; law, natural; Thomism**

Further reading: Covell 1992; Finnis 1980 and 1983

five ways: 'The five ways' is a familiar name for the five arguments for the **existence of God** that **Thomas Aquinas** presents in *Summa Theologiae* (Ia, q2, a3). Thomas believes that human **reason** can come to knowledge of the existence of God by reasoning from the effect to the necessary cause. In the first way he begins with the fact of movement in the world (being in Act), which requires a first mover. In the second way he argues that the existence of efficient **causation** requires a first efficient cause. According to the third way, things that exist contingently do not exist at all points in **time**. But then (Thomas claims) if we retroject backwards far enough, we should come to a time when nothing existed. But if there were a time when nothing existed, then, without a necessary being to bring everything into existence, nothing would have ever come to exist. Each of these ways can be seen as a form of the **cosmological argument**. The fourth way looks to a maximum good as necessary as a standard and ground for the relative finite goods that we experience. This parallels some forms of the **moral argument**. Finally, the fifth way identifies the ends to which objects in **creation** work as evidence for a final causal ground of order and design. This final way is a form of the **argument to design**. Each of these arguments has found its share of criticism. For instance, Thomas's reasoning on the third way is not convincing: why is it impossible that it might have been that at any given time of the past there was at least one contingent entity? Further, Thomas has been critiqued for his easy move from each argument to the conclusion 'and this everyone knows to be God'. Finally, some object that in Thomas these arguments appear like a prolegomenal **epistemic justification** of theology, but that is to misread him in light of contemporary issues of **foundationalism**.

See **Aquinas, Thomas; argument, cosmological; argument, moral; argument from/to design; Thomism**

Further reading: Aquinas 1963–80; Jay 1946; Kenny 1969b

Flew, Antony (1923–): An English philosopher, Flew, though son of a well-known Methodist theologian, achieved lasting influence as a leading atheist through his essay 'Theology and Falsification', in which he compares **belief** in God to belief in an invisible gardener. In his article 'The Presumption of Atheism' Flew argues that the term **atheism** should not be understood as meaning belief in the absence of God but rather an absence of belief in God. Flew has also been well known for his debates with leading theists like Gary Habermas and William Lane Craig. In recent years Flew has undergone a much-publicised conversion to belief in God, for which he cites his **scepticism** over the account given by naturalism of the evolution of life. Flew's belief in God is, however, purely philosophical, and he remains sceptical of claims to **special revelation**.

See **atheism; falsification principle**

Further reading: Flew 1966 and 1993; Flew and Habermas 2004

foreknowledge and freedom, problem of: Either I'll stay in tomorrow or I'll go out tomorrow. Suppose that I shall stay in tomorrow. Then God, who has perfect knowledge, surely knows now that I shall stay in tomorrow. But then how can I be free to go out tomorrow, since if I were to go out I should undo the past by making God not have known that I'd stay in after all, which surely is impossible.

This is the problem of freedom and foreknowledge. It depends on God's having infallible forebelief of free actions (not necessarily of humans: the problem also arises concerning his own free actions if he is in **time**). The notion of freedom employed here is that of **libertarianism**, which is usually glossed as *having the power to the contrary*, that is, having the power to perform the action in question and the power to refrain from performing it. Many solutions have been offered to this problem:

1. Denial that we have **freedom** on the libertarian conception. This is the strategy of theistic determinists, prominent among whom are those of a Calvinistic bent. This strategy by itself leaves the problem of God's foreknowledge of his own free actions untouched.
2. Denial that God is in time. This entails that God has no forebelief or foreknowledge, and so the problem does not get off the ground. This does not address the problem of prophets in time, however.
3. Denial that God has knowledge of future free actions. This is the strategy of the 'open theists', who variously claim, with regard to free actions, that there is no future to know, or that there is, but it is just plain impossible to foreknow it (**Swinburne**). This leaves prophecies of events requiring the performance of specific free actions looking fallible, however.
4. Affirmation that we have **power over the past**. This strategy claims that we can bring it about now that God knew something in the past. Most advocates of this position deny that we have causal power over the past, but claim we have **counterfactual power** over it.
5. Ockhamism. This is the view that God's foreknowledge and, indeed, forebelief, are 'soft facts' and so not accidentally necessary and so do not endanger the freedom of future actions.

6. **Molinism**. This is the view that God's foreknowledge is based on his knowledge of what free agents would do in various situations and of the situations they will in fact be in.

See **compatibilism; determinism; freedom; freedom, counterfactuals of creaturely; infallibility; knowledge, middle; Molina, Luis de; Molinism; necessity, accidental; Ockham, William of; omniscience; past, power over the; theism, open**

Further reading: Fischer 1989; Zagzebski 1991

foundationalism: The epistemological theory that noetic (**belief**) structures include two types of justified belief: (1) properly basic beliefs, which confer **epistemic justification** on other beliefs, but do not require it themselves, and (2) properly non-basic beliefs, which derive their epistemic justification from an appropriate doxastic/discursive relation to properly basic beliefs (for example, deduction). As such, foundationalism is an affirmation that the chain of epistemic justification must be finite (*pace* infinitism) and that some beliefs are not justified by other beliefs (*pace* coherentism). In popular parlance 'foundationalism' is often used to refer to one historically influential and particularly contentious subset of foundationalist theories derived from **Descartes** and **Locke**. This theory, more properly called 'classical' or 'strong' foundationalism, demands that all properly basic beliefs be self-evident, evident to the senses, or incorrigible. While classical foundationalism has long been taken (though not by Descartes and Locke) to deny rationality to religious beliefs, consistent application of its overly rigorous criteria would also undermine the rationality of most other putative sources of basic belief including memory and testimony. Classical foundationalism has been dogged by the problem of self-referential defeat since the proposition that 'all justified beliefs are self-evident, evident to the senses, or incorrigible or derived from beliefs that are' does not itself meet these criteria: hence, if classical foundationalism is true, we are not justified in believing it. Some philosophers (for example, Richard Rorty) take the failure of classical foundationalism as warrant to reject all forms of foundationalism. In contrast, many others (for example, Alvin Goldman, Ernest Sosa and **Alvin Plantinga**) have in recent years developed modest forms of foundationalism that retain the distinction between properly basic and non-basic beliefs, while broadening the criteria for proper basicality to something more closely approximating our common-sense intuitions.

See **epistemology; epistemology, Reformed; epistemology, religious; justification, epistemic; reason**

Further reading: Audi 2003; DePaul 2001; Rockmore 2004

four-dimensionalism see **perdurantism**

free will see **freedom**

free-will defence see **defence, free-will**

freedom: The question of freedom or free will is one of the thorniest in Christian philosophy. Almost all Christian philosophers agree that humans have free will; the disagreement is over what free will is and whether it is compatible with **determinism** – those that hold that it is so compatible are termed 'compatibilists' and those that deny it are termed 'incompatibilists'. (Confusingly, 'compatibilist' is also a designation for one that thinks that free will and *foreknowledge* are compatible, and 'incompatibilist' for one that thinks they are incompatible.)

Those incompatibilists that uphold free will (and therefore deny determinism) are also called 'libertarians'. The
classic incompatibilistic definition of free will is to say that
an agent freely performs an action if that agent could have
refrained from performing that action, all prior states remaining the same. This is often known as 'the liberty of indifference' or 'contra-causal freedom' or 'agent-causation
freedom'. The classic compatibilistic definition of free
will is to say that an agent freely performs an action if
that agent desired to perform that action. This is often
known as 'the liberty of spontaneity'. It is an oversim-
plification to hold that Christian philosophers from the
Roman-Catholic tradition uphold the liberty of indifference, whereas those from the Protestant tradition uphold
the liberty of spontaneity: some Roman-Catholic philosophers, such as the followers of Bañez, are compatibilists,
and many Protestant philosophers, **Alvin Plantinga** being
one example, are incompatibilists. Philosophical discussion centres around which of the two concepts of free will
is the correct one, and theological discussion centres on
two issues: (1) whether the compatibilist's understanding of free will is consistent with our notions of moral
responsibility, and (2) whether the incompatibilist's understanding of free will is consistent with the traditional
understanding of divine providence and **grace**.

See **compatibilism; freedom, counterfactuals of creaturely; grace**

Further reading: Fischer 1989 and 2005; Kane 2002
and 2005; Lucas 1970; Tomberlin 2000; van Inwagen
1983

freedom, counterfactuals of creaturely: The notion of counterfactuals of creaturely freedom seems to have been
introduced first by Pedro da Fonseca (1528–99), a
Portuguese Jesuit philosopher and theologian, and his

disciple **Luis de Molina**. Latterly it has been revived by **Alvin Plantinga** and his followers. A counterfactual of creaturely freedom is a sentence or proposition that describes what a creature (such as a human) would freely do if he or she were placed in certain circumstances. What makes this an important notion is that the understanding of **freedom** presupposed in the discussion is that of libertarianism, that is, the liberty of indifference, not the liberty of spontaneity. The notion of counterfactuals of creaturely freedom has its theological application in the idea of **middle knowledge,** which is simply the idea that God knows all the true counterfactuals of freedom prevolitionally, that is, God knows them but does not make them true. This middle knowledge, then, according to the follower of Molina ('the Molinist'), enables God to exercise meticulous providential government of the world while still allowing for human responsibility. Critics of **Molinism** allege that the doctrine is incoherent either because there are no true counterfactuals of freedom (perhaps because there could be no truthmaker for them – the 'grounding objection') or because nobody can know them in advance without imperilling free will.

See **freedom; knowledge, middle; Molina, Luis de; Plantinga, Alvin**

Further reading: Dekker 2000; Flint 1998; Hasker, Basinger and Dekker 2000; Plantinga 1974b

Freud, Sigmund (1856–1939): A Viennese psychologist, Freud was the father of psychoanalysis. While it is not correct to say that Freud discovered the unconscious, he did develop the notion that aspects of the unconscious can be repressed leading to mental illness, to overcome which pathology he developed the method of psychoanalysis. Freud added an element of scandal to his thought with the claim that much mental illness originates in the repression of taboo sexual desires that originate in infancy. Critics argue that Freud's goal of developing a **science** of the mind was a failure and that psychoanalysis has been only marginally successful as a therapy for mental illness. Freud was a life-long critic of **theism** (describing himself as a 'godless Jew'), believing that **science and religion** are inimical. He extended his theories to **religion** by claiming that theism arises from a projection of divine meaning onto a hostile universe (wish fulfilment), an idea he developed in *The Future of an Illusion* (1927). His final book, *Moses and Monotheism* (1939), argues rather fancifully that Moses was Egyptian and the religion of the Jews an Egyptian import; Freud then constructs an imaginative explanation for the origins of the conception of Christ as a crucified redeemer. Freud's projective interpretation of religion, while asserted rather than argued, has been enormously influential in shaping attitudes toward religion in twentieth-century Western culture.

See **atheism; Feuerbach, Ludwig**

Further reading: Freud 1928; Freud 1953–74; Lear 2005; Nicholi 2003

game, language see **language game**

Geach, Peter Thomas (1919–): An English Roman-Catholic philosopher known for his firm views and trenchant expression of them, Geach has contributed greatly to the establishment in the UK of analytical Thomism, that is, a re-expression of the views of **Thomas Aquinas** in the manner of contemporary **analytical philosophy** and without much of the metaphysical and logical baggage of **medieval philosophy**. Most of Geach's work has been in **logic**, philosophy of mind, or **philosophy of religion**, in which he has defended the traditional doctrine of **Hell**, but argued for something like **open theism** in his denial that there is any future now for God to know now. He has also proposed a novel interpretation of the doctrine of the **Trinity** in terms of relative identity. He was married to **Elizabeth Anscombe**.

See **Anscombe, Gertrude Elizabeth Margaret; Aquinas, Thomas; Hell; philosophy, medieval; theism, open; Trinity, doctrine of the**

Further reading: Geach 1977a, 1977b, 1980 and 2000; Gormally 1994; Lewis, Harry A. 1991

Gifford, Adam (Lord) (1820–87): A Scots lawyer, Lord Gifford is chiefly known today for his generous bequest, which funds prestigious lecturerships, research fellowships and occasional conferences at the four ancient Scottish universities (St Andrews, Edinburgh, Glasgow and Aberdeen). The bequest stipulates that the lectures and fellowships should be for 'Promoting, Advancing, Teaching, and Diffusing the study of **Natural Theology**', but this has been so broadly construed as to allow **Karl Barth** and even atheists (as long as they were, in Lord Gifford's words, 'able, reverent men, true thinkers, sincere lovers of and earnest inquirers after truth') to give lectures. Other famous Gifford lecturers include **William James, Alvin Plantinga**, and **Alfred North Whitehead**, and even the former British Prime Minister, Arthur Balfour.

See **James, William; Plantinga, Alvin; theology, natural; Whitehead, Alfred North**

Further reading: web site of the Gifford Lectures; Jaki 1995; Witham 2005

God, arguments for the existence of: Arguments for the existence of God are arguments that purport to prove, or provide rational grounds to believe in, the **existence of God**. Of these types of arguments there are two basic divisions: **a posteriori** and **a priori**. The **ontological argument**, which is rooted in pure conceptual reflection, is the most famous a priori argument. A posteriori arguments reason to the existence of God from some aspect of the world, such as the existence of contingency (**cosmological argument**), purpose and order (**argument to design**), morality (**moral argument**), or **religious experience** (argument from religious experience). In the nineteenth and twentieth centuries these arguments began to be dismissed by sceptics because they failed to establish their conclusion with the rigour of a universally compelling proof, but then it has been pointed out that no philosophical argument of any interest accomplishes this lofty standard. One might also consider arguments purely for the rationality of theistic **belief** under this rubric, of which the most famous example is probably **Pascal**'s Wager. In an unpublished paper, entitled 'Two Dozen (or so) Theistic Arguments', **Alvin Plantinga** challenged other Christian philosophers to exercise more creativity in exploring new arguments for God's existence.

See **a posteriori/a priori; argument, cosmological; argument, moral; argument, ontological; argument from/to design; experience, religious**

Further reading: Barnes 1972; Braine 1987; Craig and Smith 1995

God, existence of: While the question of *whether* God exists appears innocent enough, some philosophers charge that the assumption that one can predicate *existence* of God is contentious, even false. The primary genesis of this criticism is found in **Neoplatonism**, which views God as transcending the category of being. This hyper-transcendental conception has influenced theologians ever since, down to the work of **Paul Tillich**, who carefully refers to God as the *Ground* of being while warning that discussion of the *being* or *existence* of God is a blasphemous objectification of the divine that leads ultimately to **atheism**. Critics cannot find sense in any claim that God transcends existence, and counter instead that it is Tillich, with his denial of divine existence, that is in danger of atheism.

See **atheism; Neoplatonism; ontotheology; theism; Tillich, Paul**

Further reading: Mavrodes 1993; Plotinus 1956; Tillich 1951–63

God, nature of: It is not surprising that the nature of God has been of great interest and concern to Christian philosophers, who have devoted considerable time and energy to expounding what can be known of the divine nature and rebutting atheistic objections to it. Perhaps three broad approaches can be identified: (1) **perfect-being theology,** which seeks to analyse the divine nature in the light of the single defining attribute of perfection or '**maximal greatness**'; (2) **creation theology,** which seeks to postulate as features of the divine nature those features that we can see reflected in, or are needed to explain, the world around us; and (3) purely biblical theology, which seeks to attribute to the divine nature only those features that are attributed to God in **special revelation**. Attributes traditionally held to be part of the divine nature are **omnipotence, omniscience, omnipresence, perfect goodness** and **eternity.** Much philosophical discussion has gone into the explication of these attributes, their defence against atheistic objections, and arguing for the existence of a being that possesses them. One of the other attributes traditionally ascribed to God is **divine simplicity**. In its strongest form the doctrine of divine simplicity asserts that each of God's attributes is identical with each of his attributes, and that God himself is identical with this attribute. In other words, God is his nature. Indeed, on this approach it may seem as if the very word 'nature' is inappropriate when we are talking of God. Many modern philosophers (such as **Alvin Plantinga**), however, see no need to embrace the doctrine of divine simplicity in such a strong form, insisting that our intuitions about the unity of the divine nature can be satisfied by thinking of a single attribute, such as maximal greatness, as somehow determining the other, distinct, attributes.

See **eternity; goodness, perfect; nature; omnipotence; omnipresence; omniscience; simplicity, divine; theology, creation; theology, natural; theology, perfect-being**

Further reading: Hill, Daniel J. 2005; Kretzmann 1997; Morris 1991; Swinburne 1993a; Wierenga 1989

goodness, perfect: God's perfect goodness is his being unsurpassable in morality. Sometimes this is called 'omnibenevolence', but that label would seem rather to refer to the different doctrine that God is benevolent in every way to every one. Obviously discussions of God's perfect goodness inherit the general problems of discussions in **ethics**. A deontologist, for example, would tend to define God's perfect goodness as that he always does the best action (because it is the best action) if there is one, and if there isn't one then he does a good action (because it is a good action) if there is one, and he never does a bad action. A virtue ethicist would claim that God's perfect goodness consists in his having the greatest possible combination of virtues. A consequentialist would claim that God always actualises the best possible state of affairs (because it is the best one) if there is one, and if there isn't one then he actualises a good one (because it is a good one) if there is one, and he never actualises a bad one. Perfect goodness, however, is usually held to go beyond this and to have a modal component, such that God's perfect goodness consists in its being *impossible* for him to be less than good. Various questions then arise in connection with this assertion that God *cannot* **sin**: (1) can he then be truly praiseworthy for not sinning? (2) does this not compromise his perfect freedom or **aseity**? (3) is this consistent with God's **omnipotence**? Christian philosophers have devoted much time to discussing these questions; the most plausible answer to (1) and (2) seems to be that God's perfect goodness is something from within his own nature, rather than an external constraint, and that this does not compromise his freedom or praiseworthiness. The question about omnipotence has traditionally been answered by denying that sinning is an action of the kind with which power is concerned.

See **aseity; ethics; omnipotence**

Further reading: Hill, Daniel J. 2005; Morris 1991

grace: God's grace is his undeserved favour. Christian philosophers disagree about whether in order to be perfectly good God must dispense his grace equally to all. The Calvinist/Augustinian tradition claims that God does not give all his grace equally to all – he gives his saving grace to the elect only, and it is by itself sufficient to effect their salvation. In contrast, the Arminian tradition upholds the view that saving grace is distributed equally to all or, at least, all that hear the gospel; saving grace is, however, for the Arminian not sufficient in itself to effect salvation. Calvinist philosophers wrestle with the objection that on their view God's grace overrides free will; Arminian philosophers wrestle with the objection that their view underplays God's sovereignty. Most Christian philosophers do, however, agree that God's grace is primary in salvation, and humans merely respond to it.

See **Augustinianism; Calvinism**

Further reading: Edwards, Jonathan 1971; Garrigou-Lagrange 1939; Helm 1993; Oman 1931; Pinnock 1975 and 1989; Pinnock, Rice, Sanders, Hasker and Basinger 1994

great-making property see **property, great-making**

greater-good defence see **defence, greater-good**

greatness, maximal: 'Maximal greatness' is a technical term roughly corresponding to 'absolute perfection'. The difference is twofold: (1) a being that is absolutely perfect is generally held to have every **great-making property** to the highest degree, whereas a being that is maximally great is generally held only to be such that no possible being is greater (thus allowing for it to be impossible to have every great-making property to the highest degree); and (2) it is generally held that, by definition, there can be only one absolutely perfect being, whereas it is not true *by definition* that there can be only one maximally great being.

See **property, great-making**

Further reading: Hill, Daniel J. 2005; Morris 1991

guilt, original see **sin**

hard-fact/soft-fact debate: The debate among Christian philosophers over hard facts and soft facts is bound up with the **problem of foreknowledge and freedom**. There is not even agreement among Christian philosophers as to the definition of the terms 'hard fact' and 'soft fact', however, let alone as to the existence of these facts. The intuition behind the distinction is that there are some facts that obtain entirely in virtue of the state of the world at one single time (hard facts), and there are other facts that obtain in virtue of the state of the world at different times (soft facts). An example of a hard fact might be the fact that the Battle of Hastings was fought in 1066: this fact obtains purely in virtue of what happened in 1066 (the fact that it wasn't called 'the Battle of Hastings' till later is irrelevant). An example of a soft fact would be the fact that the media correctly guessed in 2004 the result of the 2005 UK elections. This fact obtains not just in virtue of the fact that the media made a certain guess in 2004 but also in virtue of the results of the 2005 UK elections (had they been different the media's guess would have been wrong). The debate impinges on the debate over foreknowledge and freedom because it is contended that God's foreknowledge is a soft fact about the past, since the fact that God foreknew in the distant past that Judas would betray Christ obtains partly in virtue of the fact that Judas did later betray Christ. Further, God's forebelief is also claimed to be a soft fact, since the fact that God forebelieved in the past that Judas would betray Christ obtains partly in virtue of the fact that Judas did later betray Christ: God would have had a different **belief** had Judas not done so. The importance of the claim that God's forebelief is not a hard fact about the past is that it is claimed that only hard facts about the past are necessary and outside our power in the present. It follows that God's forebelief does not endanger the freedom of our future actions just in virtue of its pastness. The strategy of attempting to solve the **problem of foreknowledge and freedom** by invoking the distinction between hard facts and soft facts is known as 'Ockhamism' after **William of Ockham**. This distinction was reintroduced into the modern debate by **Marilyn McCord Adams**.

See **Adams, Marilyn McCord; foreknowledge and freedom, problem of; Ockham, William of; Plantinga, Alvin**

Further reading: Fischer 1989; Ockham 1983; Zagzebski 1991

Hartshorne, Charles (1897–2000): A leading process theologian and philosopher, Hartshorne taught for years at the universities of Chicago and Texas. Through his long career Hartshorne developed a sustained attack upon **classical theism** by developing an alternate philosophical theology, which he called 'neoclassical theism'. Hartshorne developed his work in dialogue with the **process philosophy** of **Alfred North Whitehead,** though his initial philosophical development was independent of Whitehead's work. Hartshorne held to panexperientialism, the view that all reality from matter to mind is on the same continuum of process. His conception of God is temporal and bipolar, encompassing both supreme becoming and supreme being. This also leads to a form of panentheism, where God exists eternally with the world and fully experiences everything in it, though he is not reducible to it. Hartshorne remained philosophically unfashionable for much of his career, arguing vigorously for the rationality of **theism,** defending the ontological argument, and developing a robust **metaphysics** even in the leanest years of **logical positivism**. As with Whitehead's philosophical theology, that of Hartshorne has had little impact upon **analytical philosophy,** but it has been very influential upon process theologians such as John Cobb and David Ray Griffin.

See **philosophy, process; theism, classical; theology, process; Whitehead, Alfred North**

Further reading: Hartshorne 1948, 1965 and 1976

Hegel, Georg Wilhelm Friedrich (1770–1831): A German idealist philosopher, Hegel has had an influence on modern continental philosophy perhaps surpassed only by **Kant**. Hegel's early work was highly critical of traditional Christianity and expressed a longing for a return to natural **religion** such as he saw in the ancient Greeks. Beginning with his 1801 move to Jena, however, he began to focus on Kant's critical philosophy and to develop what would become *Phenomenology of Spirit*, a sprawling and eclectic description of the human race moving toward self-knowledge. At this point Hegel returned to Christianity as a repository for key concepts to express his philosophy, arguing that humanity can be thought of as a collective subject, which he called *Geist* (Spirit). This collective subject is coming to self-consciousness through the myriad individual conflicts of history, each of which is incorporated into the final resolution. Hegel termed the conclusion to this process of self-knowledge 'Absolute Spirit'. This process is explicated through the **doctrine of the Trinity** by seeing God beginning as pure consciousness. But consciousness requires an object, and so God creates the world, which is the object of divine consciousness. The relationship of God to the world is symbolised in the **person** of Jesus Christ. Then, when the world returns to God, the process is completed in Spirit and God becomes self-conscious. It is not clear whether Hegel's Trinitarian categories can be wholly collapsed into the **immanence** of secular history or whether they point to the emergence of a pantheistic divine **transcendence**. Karl Marx would opt for the former interpretation, thereby creating his philosophy of dialectical **materialism**. The latter interpretation of Hegel would have a great influence on Christian theology down to contemporary theologians like **Wolfhart Pannenberg** and Jürgen Moltmann.

See **Feuerbach, Ludwig; Kant, Immanuel; Kierkegaard, Søren Aabye; Pannenberg, Wolfhart**

Further reading: Beiser 1993 and 2005; Desmond 2003; Fackenheim 1968; Hegel 1968–, 1977 and 1984; Houlgate 1998; Inwood, Michael 1983; MacIntyre 1972

Heidegger, Martin (1889–1976): Among the most revered and controversial of modern philosophers, the German existentialist Martin Heidegger spent his career exploring the meaning of Being. While **Leibniz** believed the fundamental question was 'Why is there something rather than nothing?', Heidegger views this question as committing the error of **ontotheology** and so failing to bring us to the **nature** and **truth** of Being. Indeed, this is but one example of the distortion of Being in the history of Western philosophy. In his magnum opus, *Being and Time* (*Sein und Zeit*, 1927), Heidegger assays an analysis of Being through the phenomenon of human being (*Dasein*). Human being is unique, owing to its openness to Being, which is expressed in the ability to ask questions of its own being, and face 'thrownness', the brute fact of existence. In contrast to the Cartesian view of the disembodied self, *Dasein* is not separated from the world, but rather immediately involved within it. Anxiety at our situation provides the means to authenticity. There is, however, no *essence* of the **person** to speak of, but only a collection of interpretations. Not surprisingly, Heidegger's analysis, both in *Being and Time* and in his subsequent essays and lectures, continues to evoke strong reactions. Adding to the controversy, Heidegger was involved with Nazism until 1945, and after the Second World War he never clearly denounced this past involvement. Nonetheless, he has had a great impact on **continental philosophy** and numerous modern theologians including **Karl Rahner, Paul Tillich** and **Rudolf Bultmann**. Heidegger is often accused of **atheism,** but in fact he repudiated the label. Nevertheless, Heidegger was committed to doing his philosophy without any reference to God: 'Philosophy, in its radical self-positing questioningness, must be in principle atheistic.'

See **existentialism; ontotheology; postmodernism**

Further reading: Caputo 1986; Dreyfus 1990; Edwards, Paul 2004; Guignon 1993; Heidegger 1975–, 1977 and 2002

Hell: The moral problem of Hell for Christian philosophers is that the Bible teaches that God is loving (for example, 1 John 4: 8) and that God sends some people not to Heaven, but to Hell (for example, Matthew 25). Hell is a place of suffering for those in it and nobody leaves Hell for Heaven. The traditional view is that Hell is everlasting, that is, that those sent to Hell remain there forever. A more moderate view is that those in Hell suffer for a specified period and then are annihilated (annihilationism, or conditional immortality). Some think that Hell is empty, with the finally impenitent ceasing to exist with physical death, and everybody else going to Heaven. The universalist thinks that everybody goes to Heaven, though it is not always clear quite how widely 'everybody' is to be taken here, that is, whether it is restricted to humans or whether it also includes the Devil (as it does for **Origen**). Roman-Catholic dogma also includes belief in Purgatory, as a place of purification for those that die but are not ready to go straight to Heaven, but this is not (as is sometimes mistakenly thought) a substitute for Hell, but rather a third possible post-mortem destination. The philosophical problems thus arising for the traditional doctrine of Hell include whether retributive **punishment** is justified, whether it is possible for a finite agent to deserve infinite punishment, whether the continuing presence of evil in Hell will spoil the bliss of the redeemed in Heaven, whether God can and should forgive the finally impenitent, and whether God's infliction of eternal punishment can be justified on the basis of the misuse of our **freedom**.

See **freedom; punishment**

Further reading: Kvanvig 1993; Walls 1992

Helm, Paul (1940–): The last to hold (as originally endowed) the Chair in the History and Philosophy of Religion at King's College, London, and the first to hold the J. I. Packer Chair in Philosophical Theology at Regent College, Vancouver, Paul Helm has written in defence of **classical theism**, and, in particular, **Calvinism**. He has defended the view that God is outside **time**, and also attacked the libertarian view of human **freedom**, insisting that it undermines the doctrine of God's sovereignty. Helm has also done historical work on the philosophy of **John Calvin** and **Jonathan Edwards**, and on the continuity of Calvin's ideas with those of the English Puritans. He has also played a role in encouraging the development of Christian philosophy in the UK.

See **Calvin, John; Calvinism; Edwards, Jonathan; theism, classical**

Further reading: Helm 1988, 1993, 1998 and 2004

Hermeneutics: Hermeneutics is (1) the theory of interpretation, a systematic articulation of the principles that underlie the interpretation of texts, (2) an approach to philosophy that begins with issues of interpretation. The history of hermeneutics has seen (2) gradually emerge from the development of (1). Initially hermeneutics arose with a concern for the appropriate exegesis and interpretation of religious texts (especially the Bible). Medieval biblical hermeneutics was dominated by the 'Quadriga' – the alleged four levels of meaning in each biblical passage:

literal, allegorical, tropological (or moral) and anagogical (or eschatological). With the Reformation turn to the literal sense, the development of modern hermeneutics began, coming fully to birth with **Friedrich Daniel Ernst Schleiermacher**, who argued that we come to understand the text both with relation to the grammatical form and the psychological condition of the writer. Through the work of philosophers like Wilhelm Dilthey, **Martin Heidegger** and Hans-Georg Gadamer, hermeneutics in the second sense has gradually emerged. Hence, Gadamer viewed hermeneutics in the broadest sense as encompassing everything interpretable, from texts to people to events. Moreover, he stressed the absence of transhistorical criteria of interpretation, which leads to the hermeneutical circle, a recognition that understanding comes only through tacit foreknowledge. The interpretation of texts thus involves a fusion of horizons between the interpreter and text. This has proved very influential for such Christian philosophers as **Paul Ricoeur**.

See **Heidegger, Martin; Ricoeur, Paul; Schleiermacher, Friedrich Daniel Ernst**

Further reading: Gadamer 2003; Ricoeur 1981, 1991, 1996 and 2004; Shapiro and Sico 1984; Thiselton 1992

Hick, John Harwood (1922–): An English theologian/philosopher, Hick, despite beginning his career as a conservative Christian, later adopted a religious pluralism where all major religions share an ethical core that seeks to move the devotee from being self-centred to other-centred. Hick has since developed the most philosophically sophisticated defence of pluralism. He refers to the centre of religious concern as 'the Real' and argues that while major religions aid a turning to the Real, this ultimate reality transcends all doctrinal statements except for those that are formal (trivially applying to everything) and negative (**via negativa**). Critics claim that, contrary to pluralist intentions, Hick's view is elitist, effectively saying that all religions are wrong while he is correct. Further, given Hick's denial of any positive knowledge of the Real, his claim that it is emulated in the move to being other-centred rather than, say, in being self-centred, appears to be arbitrary. Among Hick's other work is a defence of religious **belief** against **logical positivism** based on the possibility of eschatological verification (*Faith and Knowledge*, 1957), an influential Irenaean 'soul-making' **theodicy** (*Evil and the God of Love*, 1966), and an important study of death, reincarnation and **resurrection** (*Death and Eternal Life*, 1976).

See **defence, greater-good; language, religious; pantheism; transcendence**

Further reading: Hick 1957, 1976, 1977 and 1989

Hippo, Augustine of see **Augustine of Hippo**

Hobbes, Thomas (1588–1679): Hobbes traced his life-long fear of disorder to his premature birth when his mother heard of the advance of the Spanish Armada. This fear of disorder exhibits itself not only in the subject matter of Hobbes's books, in particular his insistence on the necessity of an absolute sovereign to give strong government, but also in the rational form of their composition: Hobbes's attempt to demonstrate his conclusions in the geometrical manner. His most important philosophical works were in the philosophy of politics and law, culminating in the publication in 1651 of his magnum opus, *Leviathan* (the title being taken from Job 41: 1, and being a metaphor for the absolute sovereign). Hobbes's political work in fact fell between two stools: it displeased the Parliamentarians because of its advocacy of absolute sovereignty, and it failed to satisfy the Royalists because Hobbes founded the unconditional obedience he wanted for the sovereign not on divine right but on a primitive social contract made to escape the state of nature in which lives were 'solitary, poor, nasty, brutish, and short'. Hobbes also defended a thoroughgoing **materialism** and **determinism** in a three-volume Latin work, *Elementa Philosophiae*: the first volume of which, *De corpore* (published in 1655), focused on how one's bodily actions were determined by basic principles of motion. The second volume, *De homine* (published in 1658), applied the principles of motion to the life of the mind (which Hobbes of course thought material). The third volume, *De cive* (appearing before the others in 1642), applied these same principles to man's organised social life and what is necessary to get a state with staying-power (as opposed to one that will collapse into civil war, Hobbes's great fear). Hobbes was accused of **atheism,** but he was in fact an unorthodox theist that thought that God was a physical being. This and his doctrine that humans were rarely, if ever, motivated by true **altruism** earned him the unflattering nickname 'the beast of Malmesbury'.

See **determinism; materialism**

Further reading: Hobbes 1839–45; Martinich 1995 and 2005; Sorrell 1996

humanism: Humanism is the view that human beings are of unique or supreme value. While the Renaissance's fascination with the human form and the glories of Greek and Roman civilisation reveals a humanistic impulse, modern humanism arose in the **Enlightenment** with the elevation of human **reason** and an increasing **scepticism** over the claims of **religion**. Today most self-declared humanists defend a secular **worldview** in which human flourishing in the world is of the utmost importance while religion is either marginalised or rejected. Occasionally there have been attempts to define humanism more rigorously as in the 'Humanist Manifesto' (1933).

See **atheism; materialism**

Further reading: Herrick 2003; Kurtz 1997

Hume, David (1711–76): Although his first book, *A Treatise of Human Nature*, received a bad reception on its publication between 1739 and 1740, Hume did not let this prevent him from publishing *An Enquiry Concerning Human Understanding* in 1748. This contained the notorious Section X, 'Of Miracles'. The year 1751 saw the publication of *An Enquiry Concerning the Principles of Morals*, which Hume later took to have been his best book. It was followed by *The Natural History of Religion* in 1757. Having retired to revise for posthumous publication *Dialogues Concerning Natural Religion*, Hume died in 1776, apparently facing death with atheistic equanimity, which provoked the admiration of Adam Smith, but the bafflement of Boswell and the scepticism of Dr Johnson. Hume has had a considerable impact on Christian philosophy in two ways. First, he has cast doubt on the effectiveness of traditional **arguments for the existence of God**: in *Dialogues Concerning Natural Religion* Philo, Hume's mouthpiece, and a sceptic concerning the existence of God, attempts to punch holes in the arguments for the existence of God, particularly the **argument to design**, and to use the existence of evil to buttress a sceptical position. Hume's attack on **belief** in the miraculous, which is defined as 'violation of the laws of nature' (*An Enquiry Concerning Human Understanding*: X. i), is based on his principle that a wise person 'proportions his belief to the evidence' (X. i) and the view that 'no testimony is sufficient to establish a miracle, unless the testimony be of such a kind, that its falsehood would be more miraculous, than the fact, which it endeavours to establish' (X. i). Christian philosophers have met Hume's objections either directly by trying to show that the evidence for God's existence and the occurrence of miracles is compelling, or indirectly by claiming that Hume's probabilistic arguments are not relevant to Christian belief. Hume's influence, which first aroused **Kant** from 'his dogmatic slumbers', still lives on, however.

See **argument from/to design; evil, problem of; God, existence of; miracles; theology, natural**

Further reading: Hall 1978; Hume 1874–5 and 1974; Stroud 1981

idealism: Idealism about something in philosophy is the doctrine that it is 'ideal', that is, mind-dependent. There are three main forms of idealism: (1) subjective idealism, which holds that what we think of as physical things exist only because they are perceived by minds; (2) transcendental idealism, which holds that physical things have the properties they do because of the way in which our minds conceptualise them; and (3) absolute idealism, which holds that behind the physical world of appearances lies the Absolute. **Berkeley** is a representative of (1); **Kant** of (2); and **Hegel** and Bradley of (3). Each of (1)–(3) has been combined with Christianity, but most Christian philosophers have turned against both idealism and **materialism**. (In addition, there is a somewhat rarer form of idealism in which everything apart from God is held to be an idea in the mind of God; **Jonathan Edwards** held something close to this.)

See **Berkeley, George; Edwards, Jonathan; Hegel, George Wilhelm Friedrich; Kant, Immanuel; materialism**

Further reading: Berkeley 1948–57; Edwards, Jonathan 1974; Ewing 1961; Hegel 1968–; Kant 1992–; Vesey 1982

ideas, divine: The word 'idea' has been used with two basic senses in English-language philosophy: (1) as a reference to Plato's Forms (**universals**); (2) in the eighteenth century as a broad (even indeterminate) term to refer to mental events including sense data and concepts. The phrase 'divine ideas' relates only to the first sense, as a theory that seeks to reconcile the existence of universals with **theism** by explaining them as divine thoughts/concepts (hence a theory of divine **conceptualism**). This theory has a history in the work of theologians from **Augustine** to **Thomas Aquinas**. The challenge for the theist is to reconcile the intuition of divine sovereignty/**aseity** – that God alone is independent in his existence – with the intuition that universals exist eternally and of **necessity**. Thomas Aquinas' attempt to overcome this problem through **divine simplicity** is at best controversial. Another problem concerns the modal necessity of universals. The challenge here, taken up by advocates of theistic actualism, is to explain how some divine thoughts can be logically necessary (for example, $7 + 5$ *must* equal 12), presumably as God thinks them true in every possible world, and yet to maintain that they have a causal dependency in virtue of being God's thoughts. Some advocates of divine ideas have found it natural to view human cognition of divine concepts in terms of **divine illumination**.

See **conceptualism; creation; illumination, divine; universals**

Further reading: Davis, Richard 2001; Plantinga 1980; Wippel 1993

illumination, divine: The theory of divine illumination is the theory that human cognition is supplemented by

divine action. The idea can be found among the Greek philosophers such as in **Plato**'s theory of recollection and Aristotle's discussion of the active intellect (*De Anima*: III, 5). Subsequent interpreters of Aristotle differed on whether he conceived an ongoing divine supplementation of the human mind or a divinely infused capacity. **Augustine of Hippo** adopted the former interpretation, noting that Christ is the light that lightens every man (John 1: 9). While Augustine's interpretation was to be defended by many Christian philosophers, including **Bonaventure**, **Thomas Aquinas** took the latter interpretation, viewing this illumination as infused from birth. While this amounted to an affirmation of innate illumination, it heralded the demise of both types of theory, though a novel form arose later in the work of **Malebranche**. To be sure, the phenomena that the theory seeks to explain, including concept acquisition and synthetic **a priori** knowledge, remain as puzzling as ever, but to most people today an appeal to divine illumination smacks of an appeal to the 'God of the gaps' that is at least as mysterious as the phenomena it attempts to explain.

See **Augustine of Hippo; ideas, divine; Malebranche, Nicolas; reason; revelation**

Further reading: Marrone 2001; Pasnau 1997; Thompson, Silvanus Phillips 1907

immanence see **transcendence**

immortality: Immortality is the property of not being subject to death. Traditionally, Christian philosophers have not hesitated to attribute this property to God. Nevertheless, there is a problem with so doing: Christians believe that Jesus was divine and was yet subject to death. One can claim that he gave up his immortality, or that he was immortal in his divine **nature** but not in his human nature, but perhaps the most satisfactory answer is to say that

God cannot die in the sense of 'go out of existence alto-gether', but that God can die in the sense of 'take a body to himself only for that body to stop functioning at some later time'. Immortality, in a certain sense, has also been attributed to humans. Christian philosophers have not, of course, thought that humans would never die, but have insisted that there is life after the death of the body and that humans (or those in Heaven, at least) will never go out of existence. One task here for Christian philosophers is to respond to Bernard Williams's objection that such a life would be boring.

See **incarnation**

Further reading: Penelhum 1970 and 1973; Williams, Bernard A. O. 1973

immortality, conditional see **Hell**

immutability: Immutability is the divine property of being un-changeable, meaning that God cannot undergo change that is real or intrinsic to his being. **Plato** argued that since God is a perfect being, any change would be a move away from perfection; but it is impossible that God cease to be perfect and therefore impossible that he change. This argument fails to consider the possibility of change that does not deviate from perfection, like walking on a mountain ridge rather than stepping off the peak. Strict immutability also follows from both **divine simplicity** and atemporal **eternity**, however. While immutability is an important aspect of **classical theism**, it appears to stand in tension with the Christian claims that God cre-ates and then, as the Son, becomes incarnate, both of which suggest intrinsic divine change. In order to recon-cile these claims **Thomas Aquinas** argued that God lacks any real relation to **creation**. Instead, the change God ex-periences with creation is analogous to the change a father experiences when his son grows taller than he is. While he loses the property of being taller than his son and gains the property of being shorter than his son, the father does not undergo any intrinsic change. Regarding the **incarnation**, defenders of immutability have claimed that the change it brings about is limited to the human **nature** of Christ while the divine nature timelessly experiences all that the incarnation involves. Some Christian philosophers have advocated a weaker version of immutability in which, while God's essential nature remains unchanging, God undergoes intrinsic change as he interacts with creation. Such a view implies a rejection of atemporal eternity for a sempiternal or everlasting view.

See **eternity; impassibility; incarnation; nature; simplicity, divine; theism, classical; theology, perfect being**

Further reading: Dorner 1994; Weinandy 1985

impassibility: Impassibility is the divine property of being incapable of being externally acted upon and, thus, of being immune from suffering. Of all the properties of God in **classical theism**, impassibility is probably the most controversial and widely repudiated today. Theologians widely reject the attribute as irreconcilable with the biblical portrait of God as a being that suffers, paradigmatically in the **person** of Jesus Christ. One strong argument against impassibility is drawn from the **incarnation**: if Christ suffers and Christ is God, then God suffers. Moreover, the impassibilist's response that predicates impassibility of Christ's divine **nature** and possibility of the human nature, appears to many to be Nestorian. Another argument is based on the assumption that impassibility entails an absence of **love**, but that is to misunderstand the attribute in classical theism. Though derived from the Aristotelian concept of Pure Act, the Christian understands impassibility not to mean that God is aloof and uncaring, but rather that he is *more* loving *because* he does not suffer. In short, impassibilists reason that those that suffer will necessarily have some concern for their own suffering and so cannot be fully available in love for another. Since God *is* fully available in love for another, it follows, by this argument, that he does not suffer.

See **immutability; incarnation; theism, classical; theology, perfect being**

Further reading: Creel 1985; Moltmann 1974; Weinandy 2000

incompatibilism see **compatibilism**

incarnation: An incarnation is literally a *becoming flesh*, specifically the Christian doctrine that the second person of the **Trinity** became a human being (John 1: 14). The central problem of the incarnation is concerned with the fact that God seems to exemplify attributes that are incompatible with being a human **person**. Take for instance the attribute of **omniscience**. How can it be that the Son is divine and so essentially omniscient, but that, apparently, he is ignorant and learns in the incarnation? The traditional response that the Son is omniscient *qua* divinity but of limited knowledge *qua* humanity sounds suspiciously as though it is invoking two subjects of predication, which would seem to imply Nestorianism. The more radical approach of kenoticism (as held by, for example, Charles Gore) involves denying that the Son essentially exemplifies whatever divine attributes would conflict with an incarnation. Hence, at the incarnation the Son ceases to exemplify attributes like omniscience, **omnipotence** and **omnipresence** – at least until the glorified state. Attractive though it may be, kenoticism presents us with a dilemma: either we deny the strong intuitions that God essentially exemplifies these attributes, or we deny that in the incarnation Christ is fully God.

See **atonement; sin**
Further reading: Cross 2002; Davis, Stephen 2004; Morris 1986; Sturch 1991; Torrance 1978

indifference, liberty of see **freedom**

ineffability: Ineffability is the property of being unable to be truly spoken of. When one describes God as ineffable one means that God surpasses attempts to describe him: with God such sentiments as 'words cannot express our gratitude' are literal **truth**. Some Christian philosophers affirm that God is totally ineffable, that is, that there is no true description of him. This approach is problematic, however, since 'God is totally ineffable' then appears to be a true description of God. A more moderate doctrine of ineffability is that God cannot be totally described. Almost all Christian philosophers assent to this, but it may well be that mere humans (or even the flavour of coffee) cannot be totally described either. How to strike a happy medium between these two unsatisfactory versions has proved so difficult that some wits have exclaimed that even the very property of ineffability is itself ineffable.
See **God, nature of; language, religious**
Further reading: Scharfstein 1993

infallibility: Infallibility is the attribute of being unable to be wrong. Christian philosophers attribute it first and foremost to God. Not only is God never wrong, it is impossible for him ever to be wrong. Not only is God infallible in his **beliefs**, but he is infallible in his **revelations** too, since he cannot lie. For this reason Christians have traditionally treated the Bible as infallible. Some Christians in addition allow tradition and the Pope infallible status as regards faith and morals since they think they are also vehicles for God's revelation. Philosophical problems arise with squaring God's infallible forebelief with human **freedom,**

and over our fallible apprehensions of God's infallible revelation.

See **foreknowledge and freedom, problem of**

Further reading: Küng 1994; Stonehouse and Woolley 1967

Irenaeus (fl. 180): Bishop of Lyons and a biblical theologian, Irenaeus had little time for formal philosophy. His work *Against Heresies* (177) is concerned with the refutation of Gnosticism, a polymorphous movement that threatened to undermine Christianity with its rigorous **dualism** between matter and spirit and its view of salvation through secret knowledge. To counter this threat, Irenaeus emphasised the unity of the Old and New Testaments as the work of one God revealed in Jesus Christ and the Spirit. Irenaeus developed a Trinitarian theology of mediation, describing the Son and Spirit as God's 'two hands' in the world. In *Proof of the Apostolic Preaching* he refutes Gnostics that claim to possess a secret knowledge from the Apostles by his appeal to the *public* teachings of orthodoxy in the apostolic succession traceable through the Roman bishops. Among his other arguments is an influential conception of humans as created imperfect, a theory that would influence eastern theology and later be used by **John Hick** for a modern 'soul-making' **theodicy**.

See **Justin Martyr; Origen of Alexandria; theodicy; Trinity**

Further reading: Grant 1996; Irenaeus 1883–4 and 1992

James, William (1842–1910): An American psychologist philosopher and brother to novelist Henry, William James did his early work primarily in psychology, culminating in *The Principles of Psychology* (1890). Following C. S. Peirce, James is also known for his defence of **pragmatism**. But, while Peirce invoked a pragmatic principle for the application of ideas as a rule for meaning, James controversially argued for a pragmatic theory of **truth** (the theory that something is true if and only if it would be useful to believe it), a view for which he has been roundly criticised. James also made important contributions to religious thought. In *The Will to Believe* (1897) James counters **W. K. Clifford**'s claim that religious **belief** is irrational because of lack of evidence. On the contrary, James argues, in certain circumstances we face a genuine (rational) option for belief even in the absence of evidence, so long as the hypothesis is living (possibly true for the person), forced (such that one must choose for or against it) and momentous (of great implication). The choice between **theism** and **agnosticism** represents such a choice. In his Gifford Lectures (1901–2), *The Varieties of Religious Experience*, James chronicles numerous vivid first-hand accounts of **religious experience** that he uses to establish his thesis that **religion** is justified by its transformative effect on individual human lives.

See **Clifford, William Kingdon; epistemology, religious; experience, religious; pragmatism**

Further reading: James 1920, 1975–, 1979 and 1981

Jaspers, Karl Theodor (1883–1969): The most famous German existentialist after **Heidegger**, Jaspers, who started out in medicine before turning to philosophy, distanced himself from his illustrious predecessor. His magnum opus was the three-volume *Philosophy* (1932), in which he distinguished three modes of being for the human subject: (1) being-there as an empirical subject for examination (*Dasein*); (2) being self-conscious as a thinker (*Bewusstsein überhaupt*); and (3) being free in the authentically human mode of freedom, particularly in confronting what he called 'limit situations' such as struggling, suffering, death and guilt. For this mode Jaspers, like the other existentialists, was fond of the term *existenz* and the term *Geist* for its subject. Jaspers also wrote about the psychological nature of encounters with God.

See **existentialism; Heidegger, Martin**

Further reading: Jaspers 1969–71, 1971 and 2000; Schilpp 1981

Jesus see **incarnation**

justification, epistemic: One is epistemically justified in holding a **belief** if one cannot be blamed for holding it, even if it turns out to be false. Common suggestions for what epistemic justification entails include possessing adequate evidence and being able to rebut counter-evidence. While it was once widely believed that justified true belief was both necessary and sufficient for knowledge, in a famous paper Edmund Gettier undermined the latter assumption by identifying justified true beliefs that do not appear to be knowledge. Gettier's argument initiated a period of intense debate among epistemologists regarding the nature of epistemic justification and the possibility of yet a *fourth* criterion for knowledge. Among the other items up for debate has been the term 'justification' itself, which **Alvin Plantinga** has advocated abandoning since it implies a contentious deontological **epistemology**.

See **epistemology; reason**

Further reading: Alston 1989b; Audi 2003; Gettier 1963; Swinburne 2001

Justin Martyr (c. 100–c. 165 CE): A Christian philosopher, theologian and the most notable of the second-century apologists, Justin, a convert from paganism, came to view Christianity as a more perfect philosophy. His *First* and *Second Apology* develop the concept of a *logos spermatikos* (seminal word) embedded in pagan philosophy that is fulfilled in Christ, who is the Logos of the Father. While defending Christianity as the fulfilment of pagan **truth**, Justin also defended it against charges of **atheism** and immorality, and pleaded that Christians be treated with justice. Justin's third extant writing, *Dialogue with Trypho*, is a fascinating defence of Christian belief to an educated Jew. Here too Justin appeals to the Logos doctrine to defend Christ as the fulfilment of Old Testament **revelation**. Justin's apologetic approach stands at the head of a tradition coming down to modern exponents such as **Paul Tillich** that seeks points of contact with non-Christian **worldviews**. Further, his Logos Christology represents the nascent steps toward a Trinitarian theology that moves beyond the bare confession of scripture. Justin was martyred in Rome.

See **apologetics**; **incarnation**; **Irenaeus**; **theism, classical**; **Trinity, doctrine of the**

Further reading: Barnard 1967; Justin Martyr 1861, 1876–81 and 2003

kalām cosmological argument see **argument, cosmological**

Kant, Immanuel (1724–1804): The founder of critical philosophy and one of the greatest philosophers of modern times, Kant began as a conventional 'pre-critical' philosopher building on the work of **Leibniz** and his main interpreter Christian Wolff. His monumental *Critique of Pure Reason* (1781; 2nd edn 1787), however, introduced

Kant's critical phase. In this work Kant seeks to reconcile the rationalist and empiricist philosophical traditions by asking how synthetic **a priori** judgements (in mathematics) are possible. Kant's answer is found in his 'Copernican Revolution', where he argues that knowledge does not involve the mind's adequation to the world, but rather the world's adequation to the mind. Kant thus defends a form of conceptual antirealism in which synthetic a priori knowledge relates to the human categories in the mind rather than the world per se. Kant's revolution effectively undermined all knowledge of the noumena (*ding an sich*), including traditional **metaphysics** and theology. Kant then sought in the *Critique of Practical Reason* (1788) to re-establish belief in ethical synthetic a priori knowledge (with belief in God) through our ethical sense or **practical reason**. Kant defends a universal moral law, the *categorical imperative*, that is binding upon all people. God is then reintroduced as a practical postulate to ensure that in the next life all will receive due punishment and rewards. In *Religion within the Limits of Reason Alone* (1793) Kant turns to address specifically Christian **revelation**. While he maintains an appreciation for 'radical evil' that is unusual for a late-**Enlightenment** thinker, the life of Jesus is reduced to being an ethical example, which is not surprising, since Kant's critique of metaphysics forbids our saying that Christ is God. Kant has had a profound and wide-ranging influence on Christian philosophy: some have focused on his arguments against the traditional **arguments for the existence of God,** others have picked up on Kant's desire to base **religion** on morality, while others have, under his influence, attempted to see religion in purely symbolic or moral terms, or, at best, to become agnostic about the **nature of God.**

See **Enlightenment; foundationalism; realism**

Further reading: Caygill 1995; Guyer 1992; Kant 1902–44, 1956, 1959, 1960 and 1992–

Kenny, Sir Anthony John Patrick (1931–): Once a Roman-Catholic priest, now an agnostic, Kenny has exercised considerable influence on Christian philosophy, particularly in the UK (where he has worked), through pointing out the problems that a Christian philosopher has to address. In particular, he has argued that none of the traditional **arguments for the existence of God** works as a proof, and that the traditional concept of God is inconsistent in any case. He has written much on the history of philosophy, particularly in connection with **Thomas Aquinas, Descartes**, Frege and **Wittgenstein**. He has also contributed to the philosophy of mind and action, the **philosophy of religion** and **ethics**. Kenny has also engaged in non-philosophical academic work, including translating some books of the Bible and composing a statistical study of the language of the New Testament.

See **Aquinas, Thomas; Descartes, René; Wittgenstein, Ludwig Josef Johann**

Further reading: Kenny 1969b, 1979, 1985, 1992, 1997 and 2004

Kierkegaard, Søren Aabye (1813–55): A Danish philosopher, considered by many to be the first philosopher of **existentialism**, Kierkegaard vociferously attacked what seemed to him two false conceptions of Christianity: **Hegel**'s rationalistic dialectic of history and the Christendom of his native Denmark. Against this he emphasised the tenuous nature of existence and the demand of **faith** and commitment. As a result, Kierkegaard stresses the individual subjectivity in each moment rather than the rational grasp of a totalising system. In *Either/Or* (1843) he highlights the centrality of choice by contrasting ethical and aesthetic (hedonistic) lifestyles. In *Philosophical Fragments* (1844), a jarring title for any Hegelian, Kierkegaard attacks the rational, timeless approach to Christ with the Christ of history, who, he points out, is contemporaneous with us today. *Concluding Unscientific Postscript* (1846) carries the irony farther with a direct challenge to Hegel's 'scientific' philosophy. Within this context, the famous phrase 'truth is subjectivity' identifies not relativism, but the primacy of commitment. *Fear and Trembling* (1843) develops these existentialist themes by bringing us into the agonising moment of Abraham's decision to sacrifice Isaac, an event that suggests a troubling 'teleological suspension of the ethical'. Throughout his writings, Kierkegaard stressed the primacy of the will and the choice of faith apart from **reason**, particularly in the light of God's infinite qualitative difference from humanity. Kierkegaard's own life was punctuated by tragedy, including the untimely death of his mother, father and three of his siblings. Moreover, Kierkegaard's ill health, his choice to break off his engagement with Regine, and his visible attacks on the state church guaranteed his role as a social outcast, granting his writing a deepened authenticity. His work has had a far-reaching effect on twentieth-century existentialism, as well as on Christian theology, beginning with **Karl Barth**'s break with liberalism in the 1920s.

See **Barth, Karl; dilemma, Euthyphro; existentialism; faith; fideism; Pascal, Blaise**

Further reading: Hannay and Daniel 1997; Hong, Hong and Prenzel-Guthrie 2000; Kierkegaard 1962–4, 1978–, 1985, 1992 and 2000; Shakespeare 2001; Westphal, Merold 1996

knowledge see **epistemology**

knowledge, free: God's free knowledge is his knowledge, conceptually posterior to his act of will, of what will actually happen. This depends on his will because it is up to God what, if anything, to create.

See **knowledge, middle; knowledge, natural**

Further reading: Molina 1988

knowledge, middle: God's middle knowledge is his knowledge of what agents would freely do if placed in certain circumstances. It is so-called because it comes logically in between God's **natural knowledge** (of absolute possibilities) and his **free knowledge** (of what will contingently happen because he so wills). Whether God has middle knowledge has always been hotly controversial; the first to suggest that he did was Pedro da Fonseca, though it was his disciple **Luis de Molina** that invented the phrase *scientia media*. In recent years **Alvin Plantinga** reinvented the doctrine of middle knowledge, and it is once again the focus of much disagreement. The importance of the doctrine, often called **Molinism**, is that it apparently offers hope of reconciling a strong view of divine providence with libertarianism concerning human **freedom**.

See **knowledge, free; knowledge, natural; Molina, Luis de; Molinism; Plantinga, Alvin**

Further reading: Dekker 2000; Flint 1998; Hasker, Basinger and Dekker 2000; Molina 1988; Plantinga 1974b

knowledge, natural: God's natural knowledge is his knowledge, conceptually prior to his act of will, of all the possible states of affairs that he could bring about.

See **knowledge, free; knowledge, middle**

Further reading: Molina 1988

Kuyper, Abraham (1837–1920): A Dutch statesman, Prime Minister of the Netherlands (1901–5), educator, Reformed theologian and leader of a break-away denomination from the Dutch state church, Kuyper developed a systematic appeal for a Christian **worldview** in his Stone Lectures (delivered at Princeton in 1898) on **Calvinism**. In contrast to other Calvinists like Charles Hodge, who, following the Princeton tradition of common-sense philosophy derived from **Thomas Reid**, emphasised the continuity between the reasoning of non-Christians and Christians, Kuyper believed that there was a sharp divergence between the two owing to their very different worldview presuppositions and the noetic effects of regeneration. Kuyper sought to realise these convictions when he founded the Free University of Amsterdam by including in its constitution (changed in the 1960s) the principle that all dimensions of scholarship would be developed in accord with the principles of Calvinism. Kuyper's views influenced Dutch-Reformed philosophers **Herman Dooyeweerd, Alvin Plantinga** and **Nicholas Wolterstorff**, all of whom argued for the importance of reflecting philosophically from a Christian perspective and for Christian interests.

See **Calvinism; Dooyeweerd, Herman; Plantinga, Alvin**

Further reading: Dooyeweerd 1975, Kuyper 1932 and 1998; Plantinga 2000

L

language, religious: Religious language is language that refers to what is believed to be the ultimate nature of reality or its relationship to us. While religious language appears grammatically and syntactically like non-religious language, the unique **nature** of its subject suggests that they could differ radically in deeper ways. For instance, while the phrases 'Mother spoke to me' and 'God spoke to me', or 'The doctor healed me' and 'God healed me', appear to differ only in their subject, this surface similarity may well conceal important differences beneath. While there certainly seem to be cases where the religious and non-religious use of language is **univocal** (for example, 'God exists' and 'My mother exists'), many Christian philosophers have argued that most religious language depends on **analogy** between the religious and non-religious reality. Insofar as one views human concepts as inadequate for describing divine reality one could follow the **via negativa** or, more radically, lapse into an apophatic, mystical silence.

See **analogy; equivocal; God, existence of; ineffability; univocal; via negativa**

Further reading: Alston 1989a; Sherry 1976a; Sherry 1976b

language game: The term 'language game' was introduced by **Wittgenstein** in *Philosophical Investigations* to refer to the different uses of language. Wittgenstein purposely leaves the concept open, but it can be identified indirectly by the enumeration of examples including asking questions, issuing orders, guessing and joking. The 'game' involves the appropriate use of the language within the rules of a particular context rather than the transmission of some mysterious hidden-away 'meaning'. Moreover, different games are self-contained such that it is incorrect to transfer the language of one into another. This concept has appealed to some Christian theologians and philosophers (for example, **D. Z. Phillips**), who see in it a means to establish the autonomy of Christian belief over against classical **foundationalism**. Critics object that this conception loses the realist reference of philosophical and theological language, and thus that meaning cannot be replaced by a consideration of usage.

See **language, religious; realism; Wittgenstein, Ludwig Josef Johann**

Further reading: Baker and Hacker 1984; Kerr 2002; Kripke 1982; Wittgenstein 1958

law, natural: Natural-law theories in **ethics** are theories that the moral standards that govern human behaviour are derived from the **nature** of rational creatures. These theories take their origin from **Thomas Aquinas,** who defines natural law as the rational creature's participation in the eternal law, which Aquinas says is God's way of government. The natural law also constitutes the basic principles of **practical reason** for all rational creatures, binding on, and knowable to some degree by, all. Aquinas states that the first precept of the natural law is that good is to be done and pursued, and evil is to be avoided; and that every action has goodness in so far as it pursues the good, whereas it is lacking in goodness, and thus is said to be evil, in so far as it is lacking in pursuit of the good. It is possible to group together the various ways in which actions might pursue or fail to pursue the good; these classifications will then yield the types of action that are good and the types that are bad. There are also natural-law theories in the philosophy of law; these hold that the law gets its authority from the fact that many of its demands are codifications of moral demands. A leading contemporary theorist in both domains is **John Finnis.** Critics have charged that natural-law theories commit the 'is'/'ought' fallacy, that is, the (alleged) fallacy of moving from purely factual premises to an evaluative conclusion.

See **Aquinas, Thomas; ethics; Finnis, John Mitchell**

Further reading: Aquinas 1963–80; Finnis 1980; Lisska 1996; Oderberg and Chappell 2004

Leftow, Brian (1956–): A Yale-educated medievalist, metaphysician and philosopher of religion, Leftow is the current (and first non-British) holder of the Nolloth Chair in the Philosophy of the Christian Religion, in succession to **Richard Swinburne**. He has written in defence of **classical theism**, particularly the doctrine that God is outside **time**, and has also developed a trenchant critique of social theories of the **Trinity**. His spiritual autobiography is included in Morris 1994.

See **eternity; philosophy, medieval; theism, classical; Trinity**

Further reading: Davies and Leftow 2004; Davis, Kendall and O'Collins 1999; Leftow 1991; Morris 1994

Leibniz, Gottfried Wilhelm (1646–1716): A German polymath, Leibniz made original contributions to mathematics (co-inventing the differential calculus), jurisprudence, theology and philosophy. While he interacted with leading philosophers such as Samuel Clarke, **Malebranche,** Arnauld and **Spinoza,** he published little of his philosophy during his lifetime, having been occupied with other pursuits, including his duties as librarian to the Duke of Brunswick. Among his philosophical works are *New Essays on Human Understanding* (a response to **Locke's** *Essay*), *Essays on Theodicy* and the compact *Monadology* (1714), a systematic attempt to discern the basic metaphysical structure of the universe. The foundation of Leibniz's rational system is the **principle of sufficient reason**, which insists on a necessary criterion of explanation for every event. Leibniz appeals to a **cosmological argument** to explain the ground of all existence. In response to the question of why God created this world rather than another, Leibniz asserts that God, by his **nature,** must of rational **necessity** create the best of all possible worlds. Hence, it follows that this is the best of all possible worlds, a claim that Voltaire would ridicule in *Candide*. Leibniz and his disciple Christian Wolff would become the main targets of **Immanuel Kant**'s *Critique of Pure Reason*, and would be further marginalised by the strong empiricism among English-speaking philosophers. Indeed, Leibniz's philosophical influence would remain slight until the twentieth century. Since then, his philosophy has elicited great interest, especially his treatment of possible worlds, which provides the framework for current work in modality.

See **Enlightenment; Locke, John; Malebranche, Nicolas; sufficient reason, principle of**

Further reading: Adams, Robert Merrihew 1994; Hooker 1982; Jolley 1994 and 2005; Leibniz 1923–, 1965, 1969, 1985 and 1998; Woolhouse 1994

Lewis, Clive Staples (1898–1963): A literary critic, novelist (The Chronicles of Narnia, a seven-book sequence of children's stories, is an allegory of the Christian faith), and the foremost British Christian apologist of the twentieth century, Lewis was for some years an atheist, but gradually made a pilgrimage back to Christianity, a choice that he described in *Surprised by Joy* and defended in *Mere Christianity*. This influential apologetic work includes a popular form of the **moral argument** as well as his oft-quoted 'liar, lunatic, or lord' trichotomy faced by those considering the claims of Christ. Lewis's powerful **theodicy** was presented in *The Problem of Pain* and supplemented by other works such as *The Great Divorce*, which addresses the problem of **Hell**. Finally, *Miracles* develops a penetrating critique of naturalism, and includes Lewis's important argument from **reason**. In this argument Lewis points out that the naturalist's picture of the world allows only for efficient **causation**. But this excludes the possibility of belief from rational causes, which undermines the **epistemic justification** for our beliefs, including belief in naturalism. Lewis is famous for his vivid writing in which he persuasively puts forward the case for Christianity while ably criticising alternatives. As a result, he has influenced a whole generation of Christians including important popular apologists like Harry Blamires and Francis Schaeffer.

See **apologetics; God, arguments for the existence of; theology, natural**

Further reading: Christopher and Ostling 1975; Duriez 2002; Lewis, C. S. 1940, 1947 and 1952; Reppert 2003; Yolton 1993

libertarianism see **compatibilism**

liberty of indifference see **freedom**

liberty of spontaneity see **freedom**

Locke, John (1632–1704): Perhaps the greatest English philosopher, Locke, a rationalist Protestant, deeply influenced **metaphysics**, philosophy of language, political philosophy and **epistemology**. While he pioneered work in religious freedom and the social-contract basis of society, even more important for Christian philosophy is Locke's work in **religious epistemology** in his *Essay Concerning Human Understanding* (1690). It is here that Locke laid out an **ethics** of **belief** that he believed provided a means of establishing societal stability and unity in light of the novel religious toleration of William and Mary's England. Locke saw this role as being fulfilled by the universal appeal to **reason**, which 'must be our last judge and guide in everything' (*Essay*: 4.19.4). This set the stage for a pervasive **evidentialism** concerning the claims of **religion**, which

Locke sought to meet in *The Reasonableness of Christianity* (1695). This method led Locke to regard Christian **special revelation** with a diffidence that spurred the growth of **deism**, however. Among Locke's other contributions is an intriguing **argument for the existence of God** from consciousness (*Essay*: 4.3.28), in which **divine action** is invoked as the means by which primary and secondary qualities are associated in consciousness. A similar argument has been defended in recent years by **Robert Merrihew Adams**. Locke also wrote a commentary covering most of the epistles of the apostle Paul.

See **Enlightenment; epistemology; foundationalism; reason; revelation**

Further reading: Ayers 1993; Chappell 1994; Locke 1975– and 1999; Lowe 2005; Wolterstorff 1996

logic: Logic is the study of the correct way of reasoning. It is a prescriptive discipline rather than a merely descriptive one (psychology describes how we actually do **reason**). The two main methods for describing how we should think are the propositional calculus and its extension the predicate calculus. There are also other systems such as modal logic, temporal logic, and so on. Frequently the question is asked whether God is 'subject to' logic. This question in fact betrays a misunderstanding: logic prescribes a way of *reasoning*, and so no individual is 'subject' to it. The question may be pressed as to whether God can perform logically impossible actions. But 'a logically impossible action' is not an action at all; what is meant is that we have a form of words that seems to denote an action until we realise that it does not make logical sense. There is nothing for God to fail to do. One might ask instead whether God follows the laws of logic when he reasons. Most Christian philosophers, including **Aquinas**, have, however, denied that God reasons (since he already knows whatever the conclusion of the reasoning would be). Finally, if the question is asked whether God's **beliefs** form a logical whole the answer is that insofar as they can be said to form a whole they do: God does not have inconsistent beliefs, since all his beliefs are true.

See **truth**

Further reading: Flew 1998; Geach 1972; Hodges 2001; Moreland and Craig 2003

Lombard, Peter (c. 1100–60): Lombard's main achievement was in compiling the *Sentences*, four books of extracts from the Bible and the Church Fathers arranged systematically, with the first book on the **Trinity**, the second on **creation**, the third on the **incarnation** and the fourth on the sacraments. The *Sentences* enjoyed a central position in the medieval academy: it was the compulsory text to be commented on in order to become a master of theology. Among those that commented on it are **Aquinas, Bonaventure, Ockham, Duns Scotus** and Luther. The importance of the *Sentences* in the medieval tradition led to Lombard's being given the title 'the master of the *Sentences*'. There is not much original matter in the *Sentences*, though Lombard does offer some solutions of apparent disagreements among authorities, and the work acquired its place in the canon through the judicious choice of authorities to be compared.

See **Aquinas, Thomas; Bonaventure; Duns Scotus; Ockham, William of**

Further reading: Colish 1994; Lombard 1971–81; Rosemann 2004

Lonergan, Bernard J. F. (1904–84): A Roman Catholic theologian and philosopher, Lonergan is best known for his transcendental **Thomism,** in which he seeks an analysis of the human subject by identifying transcendental conditions of the possibility of thought and action that will reveal the **nature of God** in every act of cognition. Lonergan intends this type of analysis to provide a pre-theological foundation for theological discourse. He develops this analysis of human subjectivity in the massive work *Insight* (1957), while in *Method in Theology* (1972) he applies his philosophy of human knowing to theological methodology. While some have praised Lonergan's work as an impressive attempt to engage modernity on its own terms, others have questioned the value of meeting **Enlightenment** principles of **reason** and **foundationalism** that are widely repudiated today.

See **foundationalism; Rahner, Karl; Thomism**

Further reading: Lonergan 1957; Lonergan 1972; Meynell 1991

love: The nature of love is an important topic for Christian philosophers for two reasons: (1) Scripture teaches that God is love (1 John 4: 16), a love shown supremely in the **incarnation**; (2) love for God and for each other is commanded of all people (Luke 10: 27). Concerning (1), philosophical discussion has revolved around the question of whether God must love everyone maximally, or whether it is possible for him to have a special degree or kind of love for selected individuals; those Christian philosophers that believe in the **impassibility** of God have also had to explain how God's love may be squared with his lacking passions, and those that believe in **Hell** have had to explain how his love may be reconciled with sending some to permanent damnation. Concerning (2), Christian philosophers have debated what precise type of love is commanded of Christians. **C. S. Lewis** famously isolated four different types of love: *eros, storge, philia* and *agape*, with the last of these being the one that

Christians must show to all, even if the first three loves are definitely lacking. A supplementary question is this: if love is an emotion how can it be commanded?

See **goodness, perfect; Hell; impassibility; incarnation; Lewis, Clive Staples**

Further reading: Carson 2000; Geisler 1973; Kierkegaard 1995; Lewis, C. S. 1947; Nygren 1982; Singer 1984–7; Vanhoozer 2001

MacIntyre, Alasdair Chalmers (1929–): A British Roman-Catholic moral philosopher working in America, MacIntyre has exercised a profound influence on many Christian philosophers and theologians. In particular, he has defended **virtue ethics** and a return to **Aristotelianism,** arguing that much current **ethics** is so rootless as to be useless and nonsensical. In 1955, during his Marxist phase, MacIntyre co-edited with **Antony Flew** a collection of essays in **philosophy of religion,** but since then his work has been in moral and political philosophy, or on the history of these. MacIntyre gave the Gifford Lectures at the University of Edinburgh in 1988.

See **Aristotelianism; ethics; ethics, virtue**

Further reading: Flew and MacIntyre 1955; Horton and Mendus 1994; Knight 1998; MacIntyre 1959, 1985, 1988 and 1990; Murphy, Mark C. 2003; Murphy, Kallenberg and Nation 1997

Malcolm, Norman (1911–90): An American philosopher that studied under **O. K. Bouwsma** and **Ludwig Wittgenstein,** Malcolm was particularly influenced by the latter, and himself became a leading Wittgensteinian. Malcolm painted an enigmatic portrait of Wittgenstein in *Ludwig Wittgenstein: A Memoir* (1958). He also did important work on the private-language argument and, in keeping with a Wittgensteinian sense of the autonomy of different **language games,** he was an astute critic of scientific reductionism, and a defender of the rationality of religious **belief.** Malcolm also published an important work of philosophical psychology on dreaming and defended a version of the **ontological argument.**

See **language game; Wittgenstein, Ludwig Josef Johann**
Further reading: Malcolm 1959 and 1963

Malebranche, Nicolas (1638–1715): Long under-appreciated in the English-speaking world, Malebranche was an innovative French philosopher/theologian that developed an original philosophy built on the thought of **Augustine** and **Descartes.** Malebranche's chief work, *The Search After Truth* (1674–5), develops two striking doctrines: **occasionalism** and the vision in God. Occasionalism depends on divine omnicausality and was posited as a response to the formidable problem of causal interaction presented by Cartesian **dualism.** Further, Malebranche believed that the existence of secondary **causation** would diminish God's greatness. Malebranche's critique of causation was later taken up by **David Hume,** albeit shorn of its theistic framework. His emphasis on the vision in God (according to which we perceive not physical objects but **divine ideas**) follows on from this, for if we cannot have any direct interaction with anything, then the content of our conscious life must result from a direct impression of divine ideas upon the human mind. All that would be required to turn this theory into the **idealism** of **Berkeley** would be the elimination of extended **substance.** While sharing some parallels with the Augustinian theory of **divine illumination,** Malebranche's theory is unique. Not surprisingly, both these doctrines have come under heavy criticism: one standard charge is that Malebranche so emphasises the divine sovereignty that his view is in danger of collapsing into **pantheism**.

See **Augustine of Hippo; Descartes, René; ideas, divine; illumination, divine; occasionalism**

Further reading: Easton, Lennon and Sebba 1992; Malebranche 1958–84, 1980a and 1980b; Nadler 2000; Pyle 2003; Sebba 1959

Manichaeism: A syncretistic religion, Manichaeism is based on the revelations of the Babylonian prophet Mani (216–77 CE), which combined themes from Judaism, Christianity, Greek mystery religions, Buddhism and a striking Zoroastrian **dualism**. Mani taught a mythological vision of two eternal kingdoms, God's kingdom of light and Satan's kingdom of darkness, locked in an eternal, cosmic struggle. Building on a Gnostic theme, the human **soul** is captured in embodiment but can be freed through secret knowledge and rigorous asceticism. In retrospect, a young **Augustine** would be the sect's most illustrious adherent, though he grew intellectually dissatisfied with it and later viewed it as a Christian heresy.

See **Augustine of Hippo; dualism; Neoplatonism**

Further reading: Lieu 1994; Mirecki and BeDuhn 2001

Marcel, Gabriel (1889–1973): A French existentialist philosopher and playwright who converted to Roman Catholicism in 1929, Marcel sought to address the issues of **existentialism** as a Christian. His philosophy in such works as *Metaphysical Journal* (1927) and *Being and Having* (1935) is written in journal form. In the latter work, Marcel distinguishes between the two ways of encountering the world: as object, something we can have, and as subject, something that we are. The pre-eminent example is one's own body, which can either be possessed as an object or lived as a being. Marcel also developed the distinction between problem and mystery. A problem is rooted in an object that stands before one, requiring reduction and ultimate elimination through technique, while a mystery is an inexplicable and ineliminable reality within which an individual personally participates. Marcel castigated other existentialists for their bleak perspectives, and sought to demonstrate the centrality of God to each moment in the lives we are given. His sober but optimistic philosophical work carries through into his plays, e.g. *The Broken World*. Marcel delivered the Gifford Lectures in 1949–50, later published as *The Mystery of Being*.

See **existentialism**

Further reading: Lapointe and Lapointe 1977; Marcel 1965 and 2001; Moran 1992

Maritain, Jacques (1882–1973): A wide-ranging French neo-Thomist philosopher, Maritain wrote over eighty monographs, some popular and some scholarly. He also maintained a vigorous interest in politics and social affairs, serving for four years as French ambassador to the Vatican. Maritain thought that there were various different forms of reality that could not be reduced to each other, for example, the physical and the spiritual, and he expounded in his *The Degrees of Knowledge* (1932) the various different corresponding forms of knowing reality, of which **science** and religious **faith** were just two.

See **Thomism**

Further reading: Allard and Germain 1994; McInerny 1988; Maritain 1944, 1948, 1955, 1982– and 1995–

Martyr, Justin see **Justin Martyr**

Marxism: The philosophy of Marxism (often called, follow-ing Engels, 'dialectical **materialism**') was, according to Engels, 'the science of the general laws of motion and development of nature, human society and thought', and, in particular, the law of the transformation of quantity into quality, the law of the unity and interpenetration of opposites, and the law of the negation of the nega-tion. Marx's own attitude to philosophy, however, is per-haps best summed up in his famous dictum 'the philoso-phers have only interpreted the world in various ways; the point is to change it'. The main influence of Marxism on Christian philosophy has been the naturalistic account of **religion** that Marx put forward. Marx said that 'the critique of religion is the foundation of all critique' and famously described religion as 'the opium of the masses'; that is, he thought that religion was a tool used by the ruling classes to keep the others submissive. Critics have claimed, however, that this position is simply assumed, rather than argued for, by Marx and his followers, and, even if it were true, that fact would not imply that the religion itself were false. Nevertheless, some Christian philosophers have taken the social and economic critique of capitalism seriously and endeavoured to construct a Christian version of it. Liberation theology is one such result.

See **materialism**

Further reading: Carver 1991; Kolakowski 1981; Mac-Intyre 1953 and 1995

materialism: Materialism is a philosophy of the ultimate con-stituents of reality that generally postulates either (1) all that exists is material, or (2) all that exists is either material or dependent upon the material. The first view has an ancient pedigree in Greek atomism, but has al-ways struggled with the 'location problem' for putative non-material entities such as **universals** and mental events. In this regard, the second view is appealing insofar as it allows non-material entities such as mental events, so long as they depend upon physical states. Both (1) and (2) raise the question of **epistemic justification**: why believe that everything is material or dependent upon the material?

Sometimes 'naturalism' is used as a synonym for 'materialism'. Naturalism is also occasionally distinguished as the view that all reality will be finally explicable in a completed natural science. This view avoids the further worry that a future **science** might do away with concepts of the material altogether in favour of (say) forces or some heretofore unconceived reality. Even so, naturalism raises the same question of epistemic justification: why think that natural science is the standard of all knowledge? Is this not a case of unjustified scientism? While materialism is commonly associated with **atheism**, both **Tertullian** and **Thomas Hobbes** held a form of materialism, as do Mormons today.

See **Hobbes, Thomas; Tertullian, Quintus Septimius Florens; Russell, Bertrand; science; science and religion**

Further reading: Beilby 2002; Brown, Murphy and Malony 1998; Craig and Moreland 2000; Papineau 1993; Rea 2002

maximal greatness see **greatness, maximal**

meaning see **hermeneutics**

medieval philosophy see **philosophy, medieval**

metaphor: A metaphor is a statement of a certain sort that is not meant to be taken literally. When the Bible describes God as 'a rock' it does not mean to be taken literally;

1020

rather it means to be taken as affirming of God some of
the attributes of a rock, such as stability, permanence, de-
pendability and so on. Some Christian philosophers claim
that all talk about God is metaphorical, but this view
is problematic: surely there must be some literal truth
underlying the metaphor, as there would seem to be in
the case of describing God as 'a rock'. Nevertheless, it
is certainly the case that metaphor plays an important
part in the Bible's description of God and this is entirely
understandable, since many of our words are intended
primarily for discussion of finite physical things rather
than for God.

See **language, religious**

Further reading: Black 1962; Ramsey 1957 and 1971;
Ricoeur 1977; Soskice 1985

metaphysics: Metaphysics (or 'first philosophy') is the study
of ultimate reality and its structure. It involves **ontology**
or the study of what exists (the dispute between **atheism** and **theism** is primarily an ontological one, about
whether God exists) and the study of how the fundamental components of reality are fundamentally related, such
as the relations of identity and **causation**. Metaphysical
issues for the Christian philosopher apart from the **existence of God** are: what God is like; how God is related
to **creation**; what humans are like; what the other parts
of creation are like; whether there are other creatures in
creation than animals, vegetables, and minerals; and the
other metaphysical questions that vex Christian and non-
Christian alike.

See **God, nature of; theism**

Further reading: Hasker 1983; Mackinnon 1974;
Moreland and Craig 2003

middle knowledge see **knowledge, middle**

miracle: Two significant ways of defining 'miracle' are (1) 'an event that has God as primary cause but has no secondary cause' and (2) 'a divinely originated interruption in natural law'. Both of these definitions raise the interesting question of how miracles relate to **science**. For instance, with regard to the law of the conservation of energy, does a miracle constitute the addition of new energy into the universe, which would be, in principle, scientifically detectable? At a more basic level, **David Hume** raised an influential epistemological objection to our ability ever to identify miracles in the sense of (1) and (2). According to Hume, given the scarcity of miracles and the concrete reality of human fallibility and scheming, it is always more plausible to conclude that the testifier to a miracle report is either mistaken or lying. One can critique this argument by countering that its **a priori** judgement is simply unjustified. For instance, one could argue that there are adequate grounds to conclude that Jesus was miraculously resurrected based on evidence for the empty tomb, post- **resurrection** appearances, and the origin and spread of the Christian faith. One could also define 'miracle' without recourse to special **divine action** as in (3) 'an event of divine origination that serves as a special sign for God's action/purpose in the world'. Picture a farmer who is facing drought and is distraught to hear a forecast with no rain. He prays for rain and within an hour it rains just the right amount. According to (3), this event could be considered a miracle if it was a divine response to **prayer** even though a meteorologist might give a fully 'natural' account of these same events.

See **Hume, David; science and religion**

Further reading: Geivett and Habermas 1997; Lewis, C. S. 1947; Swinburne 1989b

Molina, Luis de (1535–1600): A leading sixteenth-century Spanish scholastic and Jesuit, Molina is today chiefly remembered for the doctrine of **middle knowledge** that he developed from the teachings of his master, Pedro da Fonseca (1528–99). In his *Liberi arbitrii cum gratiae donis, divina praescientia, providentia, praedestinatione et reprobatione concordia* (1588) Molina uses this doctrine to reconcile the libertarian understanding of **freedom** and divine foreknowledge, since God knows what I shall do tomorrow by knowing in what circumstances I shall find myself tomorrow and what I should do were I in those circumstances; and to reconcile free will and **predestination**, since God predestines me to Heaven by putting me in circumstances in which he knows I shall freely accept the gifts of his **grace**. Molina also wrote on ethical and political questions, including his five-volume work, *De Justitia et Jure* (posthumously published in 1614), a defence of free-market economics and an attack on the contemporary practice of the slave trade.

See **foreknowledge and freedom, problem of; knowledge, free; knowledge, middle; knowledge, natural; omniscience; predestination; scholasticism**

Further reading: Molina 1953 and 1988

Molinism: Molinism is the doctrine, named after its principal inventor, **Luis de Molina,** that God has **middle knowledge,** that is, pre-volitional knowledge of what free agents would do if they were placed in certain circumstances.

See **Molina, Luis de; knowledge, middle**

Further reading: Dekker 2000; Flint 1998; Hasker, Basinger and Dekker 2000; Plantinga 1974b.

moral argument see **argument, moral**

moral philosophy see **ethics**

morality see **ethics**

natural theology see **theology, natural**

naturalism see **materialism**

nature: While the word 'nature' has multiple meanings, perhaps its commonest use in philosophy is to identify the set of kind-essential properties, a *kind essence*, that make something what it is. For instance, to be human is to exemplify a human nature (that is, the necessary set of properties that jointly make something human).

One might think it is not possible to have more than one nature, but Christian theologians have commonly agreed that in the **incarnation** Jesus Christ exemplifies two natures – the divine nature necessarily and the human nature contingently. The existence of natures has multiple repercussions for theology, and not just for Chalcedonian orthodoxy. For instance, in theological anthropology one often hears discussion of a 'fallen human nature'. Taken literally, however, this would mean that fallen humans belong to a different kind essence from redeemed humans, and thus that a human being becomes of a different kind at redemption or glorification. While many philosophers are sceptical of the existence of natures – often dismissing them as linguistic constructs – the biblical claim that humans are made in the divine image is interpreted by many Christian philosophers as implying that there is a mind-independent human nature.

See **conceptualism; universals**
Further reading: Forbes 1985; Plantinga 1974b

nature, divine see **God, nature of**

necessity: If a being is necessary then it is impossible that it should not have existed. God is held by many Christian philosophers to be a necessary being. There are, however, different types of necessity, and there is some dispute over precisely which apply to God. The strongest type is that of logical or conceptual necessity, that is, that God has to exist as a matter of logic. It is often held that this is demonstrated by **Anselm**'s **ontological argument**. Some Christian philosophers, however, disagree with this assessment, often holding that the notion that something exists of logical necessity makes no sense. Many of these suggest that the **existence of God** is necessary in a weaker way: that God's existence is ontologically or metaphysically necessary. On this view, God's existence is not a truth of logic, but a truth of metaphysics. This means that while **atheism** is necessarily false, it cannot necessarily be shown to be false using purely logical means. Among other sorts of necessity are **accidental necessity**, which crops up in discussions of **foreknowledge and freedom**, and physical necessity, which is very much in view in discussions of **miracles**.

See **argument, ontological; logic; metaphysics; necessity, accidental; ontology**

Further reading: Ducasse 1924; Hintikka 1973; Kripke 1981; Plantinga 1974b

necessity, accidental: A proposition is true of accidental necessity at a certain time if it is outside causal reach at that time, that is, if it cannot be caused to be true or caused to be false at that time. It is alleged in the problem of **foreknowledge and freedom** that God's forebelief yesterday that I shall stay in bed tomorrow is now accidentally necessary, and that since it is now true of accidental necessity that if God forebelieved yesterday that I'd stay in bed tomorrow then I'll stay in bed tomorrow, it follows that it is now true of accidental necessity that I'll stay in bed tomorrow, whence it follows, so the argument goes, that my staying in bed tomorrow will not be an action arising from free will.

See **foreknowledge and freedom, problem of; Ockham, William of**

Further reading: Fischer 1989; Molina 1988

neo-Thomism see **Thomism**

Neoplatonism: A philosophical movement that developed out of Middle Platonism, Neoplatonism flourished in different schools in the years 250–529 CE. The father of Neoplatonism was **Plotinus,** and the second most influential Neoplatonist, his disciple, Porphyry. Their thought had an enormous impact on Christian theology despite Porphyry's writing a book entitled *Against the Christians*. Other schools of Neoplatonism were the school of Pergamum, of which Emperor Julian the Apostate was a member, and the school of Alexandria, established by Ammonius, which included **Origen** as a member. Later Christians influenced by Neoplatonism to some degree include **Augustine, Boethius** and Pseudo-Dionysius, who in the fifth century CE combined Neoplatonism with adherence to the **via negativa** and a strong sense of the hierarchy of **creation**. These three and others formed a conduit for the influence of Neoplatonism on **medieval philosophy**. When Marsilio Ficino translated the *Enneads* into Latin in 1492, the influence of Neoplatonism was able to spread yet further. One group of Christian philosophers on whom Plotinus thus had a strong influence was the group known as 'the Cambridge Platonists', which was active from the 1630s to the 1680s. This group, composed of Ralph Cudworth, Nathaniel Culverwell, Henry More, John Smith and Benjamin Whichcote, attempted to develop a distinctively Christian, though rather mystical, version of Neoplatonic philosophy. Even in recent decades Neoplatonism has influenced Christian philosophers such as Stephen Clark and theologians such as **Paul Tillich**.

See **Augustine of Hippo; Origen of Alexandria; Plotinus; Tillich, Paul; transcendence**

Further reading: Armstrong and Markus 1960; O'Meara 1982; Rist 1985; Wallis 1995

Nietzsche, Friedrich Wilhelm (1844–1900): The son of a Lutheran clergyman who died insane in 1848, Nietzsche began his academic life by studying theology in his native Prussia, but then switched to a study of the classics, and was appointed Professor of Classical Philology at the University of Basel at the age of just 24. Nietzsche attacked Christianity for promoting a morality of the serf and the weak, and for preferring the spiritual over the physical. This attack can be seen in such works as his masterpiece *Thus Spake Zarathustra* (1883–5), *The Twilight of the Idols* (1889) and *The Antichrist* (1895); Nietzsche was also responsible for the phrase, picked up by a later generation of theologians, 'God is dead' in his *The Gay Science* (1882). Nietzsche not only rejected God and traditional morality, which he thought should be supplanted by a new morality invented by the *Übermensch*; he also rejected the idea of facts and objective **truth**. Nietzsche had in early life a close friendship with Richard Wagner, but the friendship broke down in 1879 as Nietzsche accused Wagner of propping up a degenerate culture. Nietzsche went mad at the age of 44, apparently over the sight of a horse's being flogged, and he was nursed until his death by his domineering sister, Elisabeth.

See **atheism**

Further reading: Magnus and Higgins 1996; Nietzsche 1909–13, 1967–, 1968, 1977, 1980, 1995 and 1995–; Schacht 1983

nihilism: Nihilism is literally the belief in nothing, that is, the rejection of everything. Few Western philosophers believe that nothing exists at all, though this view is attributed to some Eastern philosophers; 'nihilism' is usually used to denote the rejection of all moral values. Some have claimed that **Nietzsche** was a nihilist in this sense, but it seems in fact that Nietzsche did not reject all possible moral systems; he wanted a new morality to be invented. Some Christian philosophers have alleged that all atheistic **worldviews** are bound to collapse into moral nihilism, but this is not a logical consequence. Some nihilists have found nihilism to lead to despair; others have claimed that it provides true **freedom**. Christian philosophers, by contrast, claim that true freedom can be found only in a relationship with Jesus Christ, who not only brings freedom but also repels despair. Christian philosophy thus stands in sharp contrast to nihilism.

See **worldview**

Further reading: Edwards James C. 1990; Löwith 1995; Rosen 1969

nominalism: Nominalism is the view, opposed to **realism** (also called 'Platonism'), that **universals** (such as **truth,** beauty and goodness) do not have a mind-independent existence, but are merely linguistic items. The debate between nominalism and realism preoccupied much of **medieval philosophy,** and it has latterly re-entered **analytical philosophy.** The distinctive problems that arise for Christian philosophers are: (1) if universals have a real mind-independent existence are they created by God and within his power, or independent of him? (2) if universals are, in contrast, merely linguistic items, how are we to describe God's power and other attributes, which far outstrip our finite powers of expression? **Abelard** and Roscelin (who described universals as mere 'flatus vocis' – 'breath of the voice') were representatives of the nominalist school; **Aquinas, Bonaventure** and **Duns Scotus** were realists. **Ockham** held a mid-way position called **conceptualism**: that universals have a mental reality over and above their linguistic representation but not outside the mind (though this position is frequently also loosely described as 'nominalistic').

See **Abelard, Peter; Aquinas, Thomas; Bonaventure; conceptualism; Duns Scotus, John; Ockham, William of; realism; universals**

Further reading: Moreland 2001; Oberman 1983; Tooley 1999

non-realism see **realism**

objectivism: Objectivism about something is the doctrine that that thing is mind-independent, absolute and non-relative. For example, the relativist about **truth** holds that no proposition is true absolutely, but propositions are true or false only relative to a certain framework: a framework of times possibly, or, according to some followers of **postmodernism**, a framework of **persons**. The objectivist, by contrast, holds that at least some propositions are true absolutely, that is, they are not true 'relative to' anything. Many philosophers that are not relativists about all truths are still relativists about certain truths. For example, the ethical relativist holds that no ethical proposition is true absolutely, but that they are all true or false relative to times, cultures or subjects. The ethical objectivist denies this, and holds that some ethical propositions are absolutely true.

See **ethics; postmodernism**

Further reading: Helm 1987; Hill, Daniel J. 2005; Nagel 1986; Rorty 1991; Wright 1987

occasionalism: Occasionalism is the doctrine that there is no efficient **causation** within **creation**. As such, whatever appears to be a case of efficient causation (for example, fire's roasting flesh) is really just the coincidence of events (the fire burns, the flesh roasts). Occasionalism has periodically been advocated by theologians based on the intuition that divine omnicausality ensures the sovereignty of God while non-divine efficient causality detracts from it (see for instance **Nicolas Malebranche** and **Jonathan Edwards**). Occasionalism has also been advocated for philosophical reasons, in particular the failure of **Descartes** and his heirs to posit a plausible means of mind–brain interaction. **David Hume** also adopted occasionalism for empiricist reasons. Whatever its attractions in the seminar room, occasionalism is very implausible for anyone granting common sense any philosophical standing, while, theologically, its denial of non-divine efficient causation intensifies the **problem of evil**.

See **causation; Edwards, Jonathan; Malebranche, Nicolas; miracle**

Further reading: Fakhry 1958; Nadler 1993

Ockham/Occam, William of (c. 1285–1349): Having been born in Ockham, Surrey, William joined the Franciscan order, and was educated at Greyfriars in London, and at Oxford. He was summoned to the papal court in Avignon to respond to a charge of heresy, but fled in 1328 before the verdict could be given; he was excommunicated for his pains. Ockham spent the rest of his life under the protection of Emperor Lewis of Bavaria. He acquired the nicknames of 'the invincible doctor' and 'the more-than-subtle doctor'. Ockham took a mediating position between **nominalism** and **realism** regarding the problem of **universals**. This position became known as **conceptualism**. This led him to the claim that morality depended to a very large extent on God's arbitrary commands. Ockham is perhaps best known today for his 'razor': the doctrine that entities (or types of entities) should not be multiplied beyond **necessity**. Perhaps, however, his contribution of most interest to present-day Christian philosophers is his solution to **the problem of foreknowledge and freedom**. This he accomplished by denying that **accidental necessity** accrues to God's beliefs about future contingents since his beliefs are **soft facts**. Ockham also leant more heavily on **revelation** than on **reason** for theological knowledge, rejecting the traditional arguments of **natural theology** for the **existence of God**. Ockham's argument with the Pope led to his writing much on the relationship between church and state, which he thought should be one of independence.

See **foreknowledge and freedom, problem of; philosophy, medieval; necessity, accidental; scholasticism**

Further reading: Adams, Marilyn McCord 1987; Ockham 1967–88, 1974, 1980, 1983 and 1990; Wolter 2003

Ockhamism see **Hard-fact/soft-fact debate**

omnipotence: One naively assumes that omnipotence is the power to do anything. But this definition immediately runs into trouble: God is omnipotent and yet there appear to be actions that God lacks the power to do – God does not have the power to learn or to make himself non-existent. One popular way that Christian philosophers have employed to get round this problem is to define God's omnipotence in terms of states of affairs, saying that God has the power to bring about any state of affairs. But this is also problematic, as we may see by considering the state of affairs of Peter's freely denying Christ. This state of affairs was brought about by Peter, but it seems that God did not have the power to bring it about, for it seems that if God had brought it about that Peter denied Christ Peter would not have done so freely. So it seems that Peter has a power that God lacks. The traditional response to this has been to claim that this is not a real power, though opinions vary over precisely why it is not. There is also debate among Christian philosophers over whether the second person of the **Trinity** kept his omnipotence in the **incarnation**.

See **freedom; God, nature of**

Further reading: Brink 1993; Hill, Daniel J. 2005; Urban and Walton 1978

omnipresence: Omnipresence is the property of being present everywhere in at least some sense of 'present everywhere'. Christian philosophers do not believe that God is physically present everywhere in the way that we are physically present in the space occupied by our bodies. Rather, Christian philosophers believe that God is present everywhere in the sense that God knows what is happening everywhere (thanks to his **omniscience**) and is able to act anywhere (thanks to his **omnipotence**). It is fair to term this 'omnipresence' because we mere humans know what is happening and are able to act only through our bodies, which determine where we are present. Christian philosophers have debated whether the second person of the **Trinity** remained omnipresent throughout the **incarnation**.

See **God, nature of**

Further reading: Aquinas 1963–80; Brom 1993; Quinn and Taliaferro 1997

omniscience: Omniscience is easily defined as the knowledge of all **truth** (though we should also add that God has personal knowledge of everything). Christian philosophers have wrestled, however, with various problems that have been posed: one is the famous **problem of foreknowledge and freedom**, another is the problem of indexicals – can God know what I know when I know that I am sitting here now? The point is that it is not merely an arbitrary matter of expression that I report what I know by the words 'I am sitting here now'; no, this reflects part of my knowledge, since I might have forgotten my name and know myself only as 'I'. It appears that only I can know myself this way (God knows only himself as 'I') and, consequently, it appears that there are truths that I, but not God, can know. One response to these problems is to say that an agent is omniscient if and only if that agent knows all that it is possible for him or her to know, but this is unsatisfactory since it appears that there are many truths that it is impossible for us to know (for example, about God's nature) and one naturally assumes that, even if we knew everything possible for us to know, this ignorance would still be enough to prevent us from being correctly counted as omniscient.

See **foreknowledge and freedom, problem of; God, nature of**

Further reading: Craig 1987 and 1991; Hill, Daniel J. 2005; Rudavsky 1985

ontological argument see **argument, ontological**

ontology: Ontology is the branch of **metaphysics** that studies what exists. The key ontological questions for Christian philosophers, apart from the **existence of God**, concern the existence of the **soul**, and the existence of immaterial beings, such as angels, that are neither human nor divine.

See **metaphysics**

Further reading: Hasker 1983; Moreland and Craig 2003; van Inwagen 2002

ontotheology: **Heidegger** coined the term 'ontotheology' to refer to his identification of ontology (study of being) with theology (study of God). According to Heidegger, Western philosophy has been adversely impacted by the linking of the study of beings with the Supreme Being. The result is that the distinct emphases of each have been conflated, such that Being (the object of theology) is erroneously conceived of as *a* being. This fallacious conflation produces the God of the philosophers, an objectification of the absolute that is appropriately rejected. Christian theologians that adopt Heidegger's analysis see it as presenting a criticism of the conflation of philosophical conceptions of God with the God of biblical revelation. **Perfect-being theology** is an example of the approach that Heidegger targets since philosophers of this approach treat God as an object under the general category of perfection. Perfect-being theologians reply that one can recognise the provisional nature of theological reflection while also recognising that God is the greatest conceivable being and thus in some sense *a* being.

See **Heidegger, Martin; philosophy, continental; theology, perfect-being; Tillich, Paul**

Further reading: Ruf 1989; Westphal 2001

open theism see **theism open**

Origen of Alexandria (c. 185–c. 254 CE): Considered by many theologians to be the first world-class Christian philosopher, Origen was a biblical scholar, theologian and philosopher that died of wounds sustained in the Decian persecution. His approach to theology typifies the 'Alexandrian School', which emphasised the divine **nature** of Christ in the **incarnation** and the allegorical interpretation of Scripture. Origen's *On First Principles* presents a systematic vision of Christian theology powerfully (if problematically) adapted to middle-Platonist philosophical assumptions. As such, he argues that human beings pre-existed physical embodiment as spirits (*logika*), which became embodied only after falling away from God. Further, Origen defended universalism, arguing that even the devil would finally be reconciled to God. At the same time, his commitment to free will led Origen to admit that there could be another fall and a repetition of the cycle of reconciliation. Complicating things further, Origen's conception of the **Trinity** is subordinationist, with the Father being the supreme deity, and the Son and Spirit descending derivations. Finally, Origen argued that one of the *logika* (that of Jesus) remained united with the Word when all others fell away. According to Origen, the **incarnation** just is this intimate unity of Word and Jesus, an explanation that surely appears adoptionistic. Hence, while Origen's theology is an impressive intellectual achievement, it ranges far from what would become the standards of orthodoxy. Among Origen's other achievements are the *Hexapla*, a landmark in textual criticism, and *Against Celsus*, an impressive apologetic response to a leading pagan critic of the Church.

See **Augustine of Hippo; creation; incarnation; Neoplatonism; Trinity**

Further reading: Origen 1857, 1878, 1936 and 1980; Trigg 1998

original sin see **sin**

P

Paley, William (1743–1805): An Anglican bishop and apologist, Paley, while not an original thinker, was gifted in the art of writing popular presentations of **apologetics**, as in *A View of the Evidence of Christianity* (1794), which was required reading at Cambridge University for decades. Today Paley's most discussed work is *Natural Theology* (1802), which includes his famous defence of the **argument to design**. As Paley puts it, if you are walking across a heath and encounter a watch, you would surely conclude that it had been designed. But the human eye is an even more exquisite example of craftsmanship and therefore likewise requires an inference to a designer. Paley's argument would receive a sharp challenge from the purported elimination of teleology in Darwinian **evolution** as captured in Richard Dawkins's memorable book title *The Blind Watchmaker*.

See **argument from/to design; evolution; God, arguments for the existence of; theology, natural**

Further reading: Paley 1819, 1825 and 1849

panentheism see **pantheism**

Pannenberg, Wolfhart (1928–): A Lutheran theologian whose overriding concern has been the reestablishment of the rationality of Christianity in the light of the challenge of the **Enlightenment**, Pannenberg sees **Barth**'s response as inadequate and so has reinterpreted **revelation** as public and historical in nature (*Revelation as History* (1961)). This reveals one aspect of the Hegelian influence in Pannenberg's thought. Further, he denies that **faith** can produce knowledge; instead, knowledge of the risen Christ must come through textual criticism and historical research

(*Jesus – God and Man* (1968)). Indeed, Pannenberg views all claims to knowledge as provisional hypotheses prior to the end of history. On these grounds he seeks to establish the provisional rationality of theology. This method leads to Pannenberg's anthropological study, which seeks to establish the innate human capacity to receive revelation. While interpretations of Pannenberg as holding to **evidentialism** seem plausible, the oft-stated criticism that his views of knowledge and **epistemic justification** are foundationalist is misguided as he is probably better understood as holding a form of coherentism. Pannenberg's three-volume *Systematic Theology* (1991–8) is among the most important theological works of recent decades, though his most philosophical work is his *Theology and the Philosophy of Science* (1976).

See **Barth, Karl; evidentialism; foundationalism; reason; revelation**

Further reading: Pannenberg 1968, 1976, 1985 and 1991–8; Shults 1999

pantheism: Although pantheism may be characterised roughly as the view that God is everything, the word 'pantheism' in fact refers to two separate positions: (1) everything is a part of God and God is identical with the totality of what exists; (2) everything is identical with God. The second view, a form of absolute monism, is paradoxical if not incoherent, and is held by some religious traditions, most notably the Hindu tradition of Advaita Vedanta. A closely related concept is pan*en*theism, the view that God is *in* everything. This view sees all things as divine, but denies that God is identical with the world, seeing it rather as a proper part of God, analogous to the relation of a body to the human **person**. Panentheism is found in **process theology** as well as in the writings of a number of theologians today working in feminism and **science and religion**. Pantheism and panentheism are not always easy to distinguish: **Hegel**, for instance, has been identified with both.

See **creation; Hegel, Georg Wilhelm Friedrich; miracle; philosophy, process; theology, process**

Further reading: Hunt 1970; Jantzen 1984; Leslie 2001; Levine 1994

particulars see **universals**

Pascal, Blaise (1623–62): A French mathematician, philosopher and Christian apologist, Pascal became a defender of the Christian faith and, in particular, of its Jansenist form (against the Jesuits) after a **religious experience** in 1654 turned his primary focus from mathematics and **science** to theology and **apologetics**. While never completed, his defence of the Christian faith, posthumously collected as the *Pensées* (*Thoughts*) (1670), provides a very different approach from the dominant Cartesianism of the day. Rather than seek **certainty**, Pascal stressed the tenuous nature of existence, referring to man as but 'a thinking reed'. He also recognised the challenge of **scepticism** and argued that the proofs for the **existence of God** fail to be compelling. Even so, he believed that Christianity has superior explanatory power, as in the doctrine of original **sin**, which captures both the dignity and tragedy of human existence. His apologetic brilliance is found in the famous Wager, a trailblazing model of modern decision theory. In the Wager, Pascal argues that even if the evidence for and against Christianity is equal, we ought to believe in God because if we lose, we lose nothing, but if we win, we gain infinite happiness. While this argument has faced its share of criticism, it continues to be defended today. Pascal also believed that we can know through **reason** of the heart in a way that anticipates **Reformed epistemology**. His philosophy has had an enormous impact, from atheistic **existentialism** to Christian apologetics.

See **Descartes, René; epistemology, Reformed; Kierkegaard, Søren**

Further reading: Kreeft 1993; Morris 1992; Pascal 1965 and 1998–

past, power over the: One solution to the **problem of fore-knowledge and freedom** is to say that we have power over the past, in particular over God's past forebeliefs about what others would freely do in the future. It follows that I have the **freedom** to stay in bed tomorrow and the freedom to get up tomorrow since I have the power to bring it about that God believed yesterday that I'd freely stay in bed tomorrow and the power to bring it about that God believed yesterday that I'd freely get up tomorrow. Christian philosophers disagree over how exactly 'bring it about that' is to be understood. Most, though not all, Christian philosophers do not want to affirm that we can now cause God to have had certain **beliefs** in the past. Many Christian philosophers do, however, want to affirm that we have **counterfactual power** over the past. Others deny that it is possible to have any sort of power over the past, thus leaving the problem unsolved. Like many other areas of contemporary discussion in Christian philosophy, this has its root in **medieval philosophy**.

See **foreknowledge and freedom, problem of; power, counterfactual**

Further reading: Fischer 1989; Flint 1998; Hill, Daniel J. 2005

perdurantism: Perdurantism, or four-dimensionalism, is one answer to the question 'How do things persist through time?'. Perdurantism says that they persist through time by having different temporal parts or stages ('perdurance'). None of the stages themselves actually persists, but each exists only at an instant. Perdurantism is opposed to **endurantism,** which says that persistent things exist wholly at more than one time ('endurance'), that is, that they do not have temporal parts. **Jonathan Edwards** was one Christian philosopher to embrace perdurantism.

See **Edwards, Jonathan; endurantism**

Further reading: Edwards, Jonathan 1970; Lewis, David K. 1986b; Noonan 1980; Sider 2001

perfect-being theology see **theology, perfect-being**

perfection, absolute see **greatness, maximal**

person: 'What is a person?' is an enduring philosophical question. It is made more acute for the Christian philosopher by three considerations: (1) the orthodox Christian belief in the **resurrection** of the dead, which means that persons can survive the death of the body; (2) the doctrine of the **incarnation,** according to which the second person of the **Trinity** became human (as well as remaining a divine person); (3) the view that God is a person or a community of three persons, in whose image human persons are made. The reason why these considerations make the problem more acute is that they place more constraints on what an analysis of personhood has to be to be successful, or demand the use of **analogy** in postulating several different but related meanings to the word 'person'.

See **soul; Trinity, doctrine of the**

Further reading: Baker 2000; Chisholm 1976; Lowe 1996; Merricks 2001; Parfit 1984; Swinburne 1997

Phillips, Dewi Zephaniah (1934–): A British philosopher of religion heavily influenced by **Wittgenstein** and

Wittgenstein's disciple Rush Rhees, D. Z. Phillips has held professorships in both his native Wales and the USA. A prolific author, he has written some twenty monographs and many articles, including analyses of **immortality** and **prayer,** in which his radical Wittgensteinian approach to **religion** has led him to argue that even believers do not think that religious **beliefs** are true or that prayer involves communication with God. In all his work his concern to treat religion as a separate form of life and **religious language** as a separate **language game** is apparent.

See **language game; prayer; Wittgenstein, Ludwig Josef Johann**

Further reading: Phillips 1965, 1970, 1988 and 1993

Philosophers, Society of Christian see **Society of Christian Philosophers**

philosophy, analytical: Analytical philosophy is an approach to philosophy that emerged in the late nineteenth and early twentieth centuries with the work of Gottlob Frege, **Bertrand Russell** and **Ludwig Wittgenstein,** and that has since been dominant in British and North-American philosophy. Analytical philosophy involves no particular school or doctrine beyond the belief that analysis, the clarification of concepts and attention to the logical structure of language are essential for philosophical progress. As Russell said, 'I have sought solutions of philosophical problems by means of analysis; and I remain firmly persuaded, in spite of some modern tendencies to the contrary, that only by analysing is progress possible' (1959: 11). Typically analytic philosophers shy away from synthesis, the construction of systems of thought, instead limiting their work to a piecemeal postulation and assessment of philosophical claims. While analytical philosophers have often been at best ambivalent about Christianity, a growing number of Christians have adopted this method. While Christian analytic philosophers initially focused their efforts on defences of the rationality of theistic belief and the **arguments for the existence of God**, more recently attention has increasingly shifted to the analysis and defence of particular Christian doctrines (for example, **Trinity** and **incarnation**), and practices (for example, **prayer**). Critics complain that analytical philosophy falls prey to the dangers of over-analysis, which become even more egregious when it is directed toward essentially ineffable theological mysteries. Analytical philosophers counter that the method gives helpful assistance in working for clarity in our use of concepts and language.

See **Alston, William Payne; Plantinga, Alvin; positivism, logical; Russell, Bertrand; Wittgenstein, Ludwig Josef Johann; Wolterstorff, Nicholas**

Further reading: Biletzki and Matar 1998; Dummett 1993; Gross 1970; Hales 2002; Martinich and Sosa 2001

philosophy, continental: The term 'continental philosophy' identifies the separation of philosophy on the European mainland from that of the UK and North America (**analytical philosophy**) in the early twentieth century. Continental philosophy developed out of the phenomenology of Husserl (though it increasingly abandoned his search for a scientific philosophy), and developed through existentialist, hermeneutical, structuralist and deconstructionist phases (**Jacques Derrida**). While analytical philosophers focus on technical analysis, continental philosophers view their practice in greater continuity with other disciplines in the humanities such as literature, history and, to some extent, the social sciences. As such, their philosophical style is more parabolic, narratival, and heuristic than propositional, expository and rational. Some Christian philosophers have seen these trends as in accord with a biblical humility serving as a fitting critique to the pretensions of **ontotheology**; critics reject continental philosophy as lacking in intellectual rigour and, at its worst, perpetuating obfuscation. Christian critics also worry that anti-Christian and even atheistic assumptions are embedded in this approach.

See **Derrida, Jacques; existentialism; Heidegger, Martin; hermeneutics; ontotheology; postmodernism; Ricoeur, Paul**

Further reading: Kearney 2003; McNeill and Feldman 1998; Schroeder 2005; Solomon and Sherman 2003

philosophy, medieval: In some ways the medieval period was the high point for Christian philosophy: the vast majority of (Western) philosophers were Christians and all were theists. There was no professional disciplinary boundary between theology and philosophy, and it was not only permissible, but expected, that philosophers should appeal to the **truth** of the Christian faith in their work in other areas. Indeed, for many the philosophical impulse *was* the impulse to understand the faith and defend it. Anselm's phrase '**fides quaerens intellectum**' ('faith seeking understanding') sums up the spirit of much medieval philosophy. It is somewhat arbitrary where to begin the epoch of medieval philosophy: **Augustine** (354–430) and **Boethius** (c. 480–c. 526) are often used as starting points, but perhaps they are best viewed as belonging to antiquity rather than to the Middle Ages, and it is perhaps best to think of **Anselm** (1033–1109) as the first great medieval philosopher. The greatest period of medieval philosophy was in the thirteenth century, which saw not only the greatest medieval philosopher, **Thomas Aquinas** (c. 1225–74), but also **Bonaventure** (c. 1217–74) and, towards the end of the century, **Duns Scotus** (c. 1266–1308).

The major event to which Christian philosophers in the Middle Ages responded was the rediscovery of Aristotle's works; Aquinas represents the acme of the synthesis of Christianity and **Aristotelianism**. In the century after him **William of Ockham** (1285–1349) expounded a more nominalistic version of medieval philosophy (**conceptualism**). The rest of the fourteenth century saw a gradual decline towards Renaissance philosophy in the fifteenth century. Francisco Suárez (1548–1617) bears the traditional title of 'the last of the scholastics', though his work occurred during a brief revival of the spirit of medieval philosophy after the Middle Ages proper were over.

See **Anselm of Canterbury**; **Aquinas, Thomas**; **Augustine of Hippo**; **Boethius, Anicius Manlius Severinus**; **Bonaventure**; **Duns Scotus, John**; **fides quaerens intellectum**; **Ockham, William of**; **scholasticism**

Further reading: Armstrong 1967; Copleston 1952; Kenny 2005; Kenny, Kretzmann, Pinborg and Stump 1982; Marenbon 1987, 1988 and 1998

philosophy, moral see **ethics**

philosophy, process: A philosophy developed by **Alfred North Whitehead** and **Charles Hartshorne**, process philosophy replaces the traditional Western **metaphysics** of being and **substance** with one of becoming and event. For this reason, Whitehead chose as the fundamental metaphysical primitive of his system a basic unit of becoming that he termed an 'actual occasion'. As each actual occasion moves toward being, it undergoes concrescence (a move from subjectivity to objectivity), through which it is 'prehended' by the actual occasions to follow. Each apparent substance (a tree, a **person** and so on) is a society of actual occasions in a flowing process of concrescence and prehension that creates an ongoing, fully relational oscillation between subjectivity and objectivity. Process philosophy holds to panentheism (see **pantheism**) in that the world is viewed as God's body, a collection of actual occasions in a constant dynamic of becoming. In this on-going process, God works through persuasion as he suffers with **creation** through the prehension of the totality of actual occasions. While initially bewildering, process metaphysics is an impressive intellectual achievement and many see it as offering promising resources for an alternative conception of the God/world relation to the 'static substance' of **classical theism**. Philosophically, critics find the system to be deeply counterintuitive, and see inadequate argument to warrant overturning the intuition that there are enduring substances. Theologically, process philosophy stands in tension with the traditional Christian view of God's otherness and sovereignty over creation.

See **pantheism; theology, process; Whitehead, Alfred North**

Further reading: Rescher 2000; Sibley and Gunter 1978; Whittemore 1974

philosophy, reformational see **Dooyeweerd, Herman**

philosophy of religion see **religion, philosophy of**

Philosophy of Religion, British Society for the see **British Society for the Philosophy of Religion**

Plantinga, Alvin (1932–): One of the leading Christian philosophers of the present day, Plantinga has made a major contribution to the current renaissance of Christian philosophy. He was educated at, and later taught at, Calvin College, a university of the Christian Reformed Church, of which church he is also a member, before moving to take up the John A. O'Brien Chair in Philosophy at the University of Notre Dame. His philosophical work is marked by his insistence on the permissibility of his doing philosophy in the light of his Christian faith and by his refusal to follow philosophical fashion for its own sake. His first work (*God and Other Minds*) was in **religious epistemology**, arguing that **belief** in God was just as rational as belief in other minds. He then used insights in modal **logic** to construct a valid **ontological argument** and a rigorous version of the **free-will defence**. This led him into the **problem of foreknowledge and freedom**, in which he rediscovered **Molinism**. More recently Plantinga has returned to **epistemology**, publishing a trilogy of volumes on warrant, that is, that quality enough of which distinguishes knowledge from mere true belief. He argues in the first two volumes (*Warrant: The Current Debate* and *Warrant and Proper Function*) that a belief is warranted only if it is produced by a properly functioning mental faculty aimed at the production of true beliefs. He concludes in the last volume of the trilogy, *Warranted Christian Belief*, that Christian faith is, if true, warranted, and so, if true, counts as knowledge, since, according to Christianity, central Christian beliefs are produced by the 'internal instigation of the Holy Spirit', by which God reveals to people the **truth** of these beliefs. Plantinga cheerfully admits that this account will not appeal to atheists but equally cheerfully disavows any duty to do philosophy to please the atheistic academic community. He has also recently developed a (pre-existing) argument that evolutionary naturalism (see **materialism**) is self-defeating in that if it is true then we have reason to doubt that our minds have evolved to aim at truth and, hence, reason to doubt that it is true. In his landmark lecture, 'Advice to Christian Philosophers', Plantinga insisted that part of the Christian philosopher's duty was to serve the Christian community. This challenge has been enthusiastically taken up by a whole generation of Christian philosophers that looks to Plantinga as its inspiration.

See **argument, ontological; defence, free-will; divinitatis, sensus; epistemology; epistemology, Reformed; epistemology, religious; evil, problem of; foreknowledge and freedom, problem of; freedom, counterfactuals of creaturely; hard-fact/soft-fact debate; Molina, Luis de; necessity, accidental; Ockham, William of; theology, natural; Wolterstorff, Nicholas**

Further reading: Plantinga 1967, 1984 and 2000; Sennett 1998; Tomberlin and van Inwagen 1985

Plato (c. 427–347 BCE): Often described as the greatest of all ancient philosophers, and sometimes as the greatest philosopher ever, Plato was born into an aristocratic Athenian family but fell under the spell of Socrates and so never pursued a proper political career (though he did abortively attempt to influence Sicilian politics), devoting himself instead to philosophy. Plato was also a great stylist and his works, mostly written in the form of a dialogue, are very pleasant to read. His output is usually divided into three periods: early, middle and late. To the category of early dialogues are usually attributed: *Charmides*, *Crito*, *Euthydemus*, *Euthyphro*, *Gorgias*, *Hippias Major*, *Hippias Minor*, *Ion*, *Laches*, *Lysis* and *Protagoras*. These are often called 'Socratic' dialogues because, scholars think, in these dialogues Plato was not so much attempting to construct a pervasive philosophical system, but merely trying to give a reasonably faithful portrayal of the historical Socrates and his habit of asking questions (particularly ones concerning **ethics**) rather than giving answers. Of these, perhaps *Euthyphro* has exercised the greatest influence on Christian philosophers, since it poses the classic question now known as the **Euthyphro dilemma**. The works of Plato's 'middle' period are usually said to include *Phaedo*, *Cratylus*, *Symposium*, *Republic* and *Phaedrus*. In these dialogues it is thought that Plato elaborates his own views on a variety of philosophical topics using Socrates as a mere mouthpiece. *Republic* in particular has exercised a great influence on philosophers of all sorts, including Christian philosophers, particularly with its picture of humans as prisoners in a cave seeing mere shadows and mistaking them for reality until they are liberated and brought into the real world outside. Plato uses this **metaphor** to illustrate the process of philosophical awakening and the turning from transient particulars to the eternal Forms. Many Christian philosophers have, however, taken this as a picture of the intellectual process accompanying salvation, as one's eyes are opened to see spiritual things. The traditional division of Plato's work is completed by considering six dialogues as Plato's late works: *Sophist*, *Statesman*, *Timaeus*, *Critias*, *Philebus* and *Laws*. Out of these perhaps *Timaeus* has been the most important for Christian philosophy, particularly during the period of **medieval philosophy**, because *Timaeus* was the only work of Plato's widely known then. In this dialogue Plato describes the making of the world by a demiurge or divine craftsman, who takes pre-existent matter and fashions it in accordance with the heavenly blueprints of the Forms. Plato's influence on subsequent philosophy has been so great that **Whitehead** said that all philosophy since had been mere 'footnotes to Plato'; his influence survives explicitly as **Neoplatonism**.

See **dilemma, Euthyphro; Neoplatonism**

Further reading: Fine 1999a and 1999b; Kraut 1992; Melling 1987; Plato 1899–1906 and 1997

plenitude, principle of: The principle of plenitude is the principle that God's boundless goodness expresses itself in creating every possible sort of being or, at least, that

God has created as many beings as could possibly coexist (other beings couldn't coexist with actually existing ones). The reason why this principle is held is that it would seem mean of God to restrict **creation** or to deny actuality to possible beings. But since the possible beings would never have existed if God had not created them it is hard to see that God would have wronged anything in not creating them. The principle, much discussed by American historian of ideas Arthur Lovejoy, is found in various expressions in **Neoplatonism, Augustine** and **Aquinas**.

See **Aquinas, Thomas; Augustine of Hippo; Neoplatonism**

Further reading: Lovejoy 1936

Plotinus (c. 205–70 CE): The traditional founder of **Neoplatonism,** Plotinus wrote many wide-ranging essays, which were posthumously collected and published in groups of nine as the *Enneads* by his disciple Porphyry. According to Plotinus, the One (God) transcends every human category, even number and being, preventing any cognition or speech about him. All reality proceeds from the One as a series of timeless emanations of descending order of being beginning with the highest emanation of Mind (*Nous*), the realm of **Plato**'s Forms. Next is the level of **soul,** and then bodies, and finally primary matter, which is so low that it verges on the edge of non-being. Plotinus' **ethics** is focused on the Platonic desire for the human soul to escape embodiment and multiplicity and return to the unity of the One. Plotinus' system presents a number of deep conceptual difficulties including the challenge of explaining how derivative levels of being originate from the higher levels (for example, how matter derives from mind). Moreover, the **transcendence** of the One over all properties/concepts is not only difficult to grasp, but by definition it *cannot* be grasped, a fact that places the system out of the area of rational discourse and into the realm of mysticism. Plotinus' theory contradicts numerous Christian doctrines including the personal and triune **nature of God**. Nevertheless, Plotinus has exercised an enormous influence over much Christian philosophy.

See **Neoplatonism; Plato**

Further reading: Dufour 2002; Gerson 1994; O'Meara 1993; Plotinus 1956; Rist 1967

Polanyi, Michael (1891–1976): A Christian scientist and philosopher of **science** whose book *Personal Knowledge* developed a post-critical **epistemology** that has been influential within modern theology, Polanyi attacked **Enlightenment** conceptions of **reason** in **science** by emphasising factors such as community, personal commitment and aesthetic sense. He also stressed **fallibilism** in his influential definition of 'personal knowledge': 'I may hold firmly to what I believe to be true, even though I know that it might conceivably be false' (1974: 214). Moreover, Polanyi has carefully defended critical **realism**, thereby avoiding the antirealist concerns associated with the work of Thomas Kuhn. In *The Tacit Dimension* Polanyi explored the range of conceptual and sensory information that shape our cognitive life, identifying the extent to which *tacit* knowledge transcends our ability to articulate and conceptualise it. In *Meaning*, his final work, Polanyi counters scientism by arguing that science gains meaning from the wider cultural sphere of the creative imagination, including theology. In all his work Polanyi challenged the hegemonic rule of science by identifying the full range of human experience. He has had a significant impact on theologians seeking a 'post-critical' epistemology. Polanyi has also attracted attention from conservative Protestant theologians and philosophers, although he himself was most attracted to **Tillich**'s articulation of Christian **belief**.

See **epistemology, Reformed; epistemology, religious; fallibilism; science; science and religion; Tillich, Paul**

Further reading: Gelwick 1977; Polanyi 1974 and 1983; Polanyi and Prosch 1975

positivism, logical: A movement that arose out of the group of early twentieth-century philosophers known as the 'Vienna Circle', whose members included Rudolf Carnap and Otto Neurath, logical positivism sought to reduce philosophy to **science** with the **verification principle,** which stated that all meaningful statements are either analytic or have identifiable verification conditions. Statements that fail to fit into one of these categories are, strictly speaking, meaningless. The most notable casualties of this austere principle were **metaphysics, ethics** and theology. Thus, on this view, 'Jesus loves me, this I know' is no more cognitively meaningful than 'Twas brillig, and the slithy toves did gyre and gimble in the wabe'. Logical positivism flourished in the 1920s–30s while being popularised in English philosophy through **A. J. Ayer**'s influential book *Language, Truth and Logic* (1936). The movement maintained supremacy in English-speaking philosophy into the 1940s until internal difficulties, including successive failures to defend the verification principle from the problem of self-referential defeat, led to its abandonment. Despite this traces of it still linger on, for example, in the work of W. V. Quine.

See **Ayer, Alfred Jules; falsification principle; verification/verifiability principle**

Further reading: Ayer 2001; Ayer 2004; Biletzki and Matar 1998

post-mortem existence: Christians believe that (at least some) humans survive the death of the body. All Christians believe that some go to Heaven after death; some (universalists) believe that all go to Heaven. Among those that deny universalism, some hold that those that do not go to Heaven simply go out of existence at death or at the Last Judgment (annihilationists); others hold that those that do not go to Heaven go to **Hell**. The Roman-Catholic tradition also postulates a third post-mortem abode, Purgatory, but Protestants tend to reject this as based on apocryphal Scripture excluded by them from the canon.

See **Hell**

Further reading: Flew 1964, 1984 and 1987; Helm 1989; Penelhum 1970

postmodernism: A term used to identify a broad movement across a number of fields including architecture, art and literature, that is united by its criticism of **Enlightenment** values and goals, 'postmodernism' entered philosophical use in the 1970s and is generally identifiable as involving a rejection of some or all of the following theories or entities: (1) the correspondence theory of **truth**; (2) metaphysical **realism**; (3) 'metanarratives' and universal principles of **reason**; (4) **foundationalism**; (5) essentialism; (6) the possibility of thought without language; and (7) the referential use of language. Postmodernism is closely associated with **continental philosophy** and, in particular, the work of leading deconstructionists such as **Derrida**. Many Christian critics contend that postmodernism is inimical to Christianity at a number of points including its denial of the existence of **natures** (essentialism) and the real reference of language (including the revelatory propositions of Scripture). Even so, a number of Christian philosophers including **Merold Westphal** have found postmodernism to be an ally in certain respects, including its critique of **ontotheology** and rejection of the search for a 'God's eye point-of-view'.

See **Derrida, Jacques; philosophy, continental; Ricoeur, Paul; Westphal, Merold**
Further reading: Caputo and Scanlon 1999; Crowther 2003; Silverman and Welton 1988; Taylor and Winquist 1998

power, counterfactual: To possess counterfactual power over a state of affairs is to possess the power to do something such that, were one to do it, the state of affairs in question would obtain, and the power to do something such that, were one to do it, the state of affairs in question would not obtain. Counterfactual power is thus weaker than causal power. Many Christian philosophers claim that we have counterfactual **power over the past.**
See **past, power over the**
Further reading: Dekker 2000; Flint 1998; Hasker, Basinger and Dekker 2000; Plantinga 1974b

pragmatism: A distinctly American philosophy, pragmatism emerged in Charles Peirce's development and defence of pragmatic efficacy as a criterion for discerning the meaning of words. According to Peirce, meaning can be found in the conceivable effects that a particular assertion might have on life. As a result, statements that have no conceivable effect are dismissed as nonsense. While Peirce did not apply pragmatism beyond these relatively narrow confines, **William James** retooled pragmatism as a theory of **truth**. Hence, in *Pragmatism* James makes the claim that truth is whatever is good or useful in **belief**. Christian philosophers have generally been critical of pragmatism given that it fails to recognise **nature** and truth as the objective ground of pragmatic efficacy.
See **James, William; realism; truth**
Further reading: Goodman 1995; James 1981; Rorty 1982

prayer: A verbal or mental address directed to God, prayer may assume many forms including praise, thanksgiving and confession, but philosophically the most interesting form is petitionary prayer, where a particular request is addressed to God. Such prayers present a puzzle, for if God is **omniscient** he will already know our needs and desires, and if he is **perfectly good** he will desire the best for us. From this it seems to follow that any petition that is good for us, God would already intend to provide, while any petition that is not good for us, God would not fulfil anyway. But if this is the case, then petitionary prayer seems to make no difference. One response is to say that God uses petitionary prayer to develop character within human beings insofar as the simple provision of requests prior to their being made would stunt moral and spiritual growth. Another response is to say that God has ordained to use the prayers of his creatures as a condition of his own action in certain circumstances, and that, thus, what is best for God to do may depend on whether or not we pray.

See **miracle; omnipotence; omniscience**

Further reading: Baelz 1968; Phillips 1965; Stump 1979

predestination: Predestination is God's determining (either timelessly or in ages past) to send some people to Heaven (election) and (in double predestination) some people to **Hell** (reprobation). The principal philosophical question concerning predestination is whether it is compatible with human **freedom**. Compatibilists claim that it is so compatible; incompatibilists deny this. The question acquires added seriousness from the thought that human **moral responsibility** goes hand in hand with freedom: can one be justly punished in Hell if one is predestined to go there? Can God justly receive all the praise for one's salvation if one accepts it without being predestined to do so? Another question is that of the basis for God's predestination: is it conditional on a free human response, as Arminianism claims, or does it depend on nothing other than God's good pleasure, as **Calvinism** maintains?

See **compatibilism; freedom; Hell; incompatibilism; punishment; responsibility, moral**

Further reading: Basinger and Basinger 1986; Garrigou-Lagrange 1939; Helm 1993; Pinnock 1975 and 1989; Pinnock, Rice, Sanders, Hasker and Basinger 1994

principle, falsification see falsification principle

principle, verifiability see verification/verifiability principle

principle, verification see verification/verifiability principle

principle of sufficient reason see sufficient reason, principle of

process philosophy see philosophy, process

process theology see theology, process

property, great-making: A great-making property is one that endows its possessor with some measure of greatness. In other words, its possession makes its possessor greater than he or she would have been without it.

See **greatness, maximal**

Further reading: Hill, Daniel J. 2005; Morris 1991

prophecy see revelation, special

punishment: Punishment is the infliction of something bad (frequently, but not necessarily, pain or a loss of freedom) on a wrongdoer because of a wrong committed. Philosophical debate centres on the question of how, if at all, punishment can be justified. There are two principal schools of thought here: the retribution view, that crimes intrinsically deserve punishment, whatever effects the punishment may have, and the rehabilitation view, that the purpose of punishment is to teach the offender the error of his or her ways and to ensure that he or she does not reoffend. There is also the deterrence view: that punishment exists to deter not just the offender but everyone. One issue that brings out the disagreement among the views is that of capital punishment: supporters of the retribution view tend to allow for capital punishment (at least in theory), whereas supporters of the rehabilitation view regard capital punishment as impermissible, and supporters of the deterrence view are divided. Most Christian philosophers have tended to the retribution view for two reasons: (1) the law of the Old Testament, especially the *lex talionis* ('an eye for an eye, a tooth for a tooth'), seems to be based on the retribution view, and (2) the existence of **Hell** is difficult to reconcile with the deterrence view or the rehabilitation view.

See **Hell**

Further reading: Duff 1986; Hoekema 1986; Honderich 1984; Walker 1991

R

Rahner, Karl (1904–84): Perhaps the leading Roman-Catholic theologian of the twentieth century, Rahner published a series of influential works including *Spirit in the World* (1939), *Hearer of the Word* (1941), *Foundations of Christian Faith* (1976), and his monumental twenty-three-volume collection of essays in *Theological Investigations*. Rahner has had a deep impact on the theology of the Second Vatican Council and contemporary Roman-Catholic theology. In contrast to traditional **Thomism**, which sharply differentiated nature as the foundation of **creation** from **grace** as a supplement to it, Rahner inverts the order in his 'transcendental Thomism', thereby seeing grace as the primary reality from which nature is an abstraction. Rahner believes that this inversion provides a basis to explain both human understanding generally as well as the capacity to receive **revelation**, for both involve the becoming immanent in our understanding of the grace of the **transcendent** God. Indeed, in all experience and cognition we are in fact experiencing God: even the mundane perception of a chair involves God's grace. Rahner uses this picture to explain the mystery of ongoing human cognition as well as the ground and reception of revelation. This picture also provides the framework for Rahner's theory of the **incarnation** not as an unnatural Barthian incursion into the natural order, but instead as a fulfilment of the intrinsic nature of being. While Rahner is relatively conservative doctrinally, his dogmatic affirmations do not always stand easily with his method.

See **Heidegger, Martin; Lonergan, Bernard; Thomism**
Further reading: Rahner 1961–81, 1978 and 1994

rationalism: The traditional philosophical definition of 'rationalism' is 'the doctrine that all of our knowledge comes from or is dependent on **reason,** as opposed to experience'. In this sense, **Descartes, Spinoza** and **Leibniz** are rationalists, and **Plato** was an extreme rationalist (extreme because of his view that we could not know anything about the physical world). In popular usage, however, 'rationalism' is often used for the view that there is no supernatural dimension to life: no God or **soul**. This usage has come about because it is supposed that reason teaches us that there is no supernatural dimension. Finally, there is a theological usage of the term 'rationalism' according to which knowledge of God is claimed to come from reason rather than from Scripture or **religious experience**.

See **Descartes, René; empiricism; Leibniz, Gottfried Wilhelm; Plato; Spinoza, Baruch**

Further reading: Aune 1970; BonJour 1998; Cottingham 1984; Descartes 1979; Leibniz 1973; Plato 1981; Spinoza 1985–

realism: Realism is the view that things exist independently of the mind. There are three main types of realism that are based on that premise: (1) the view that affirms, in opposition to **nominalism**, that **universals** (and perhaps other abstract objects) exist; (2) the view that affirms, in opposition to **idealism**, that things exist apart from the perception or conscious experience of them; (3) the view that affirms, in opposition to **antirealism**, that (most or all) things exist independently of conceptual schemes, that is, our particular ways of thinking about the world. To be a realist in the sense of (1) is to affirm that such a thing as beauty exists in addition to the beautiful particulars that exemplify it. To be a realist in the sense of (2) is to affirm that the tree exists even if there is no one in the quad to perceive it. To be a realist in the sense of (3) is to reject **Kant's** thesis that reality is constituted by our mental concepts, and to deny that existence is only relative to a conceptual scheme. As defined, (3) allows the possibility that some things exist in the realist sense (for example, trees, people) while other things exist only relative to a conceptual scheme (for example, money, chairs). Considered thus far, realism is a metaphysical position, but (3) can also be applied to **truth**. Alethic realism is the conviction that truth obtains independently of thought, language or conceptual schemes. Antirealist theories view truth as something that exists only relative to human thought (coherentism) or the achievement of human ends (**pragmatism**). Many Christian philosophers believe that a Christian **worldview** entails realism, and certainly it would be curious for a Christian to claim that God exists only relative to our conception of God.

See **idealism; philosophy, continental; truth; universals; worldview**

Further reading: Alston 2001; Alston 2002; French, Uehling and Wettstein 1988; Kulp 1997; Wright 1987

reason: Within philosophy 'reason' refers to (1) a faculty or ability in virtue of which one makes appropriate doxastic judgements that have a high likelihood of approximating to **truth**; (2) a rational ground for a **belief** (that is, 'I believe p for the following reason'). While reasonable doxastic judgements ideally find the golden mean between excessive credulity and **scepticism**, the **Enlightenment** conception of reason tended to place an inordinate emphasis upon scepticism as the preeminent reasonable virtue. Enlightenment reason also was conceived as monolithic, with the assumption that all rational individuals would share the same first principles of reason, rules of inference and weighing of evidence leading to doxastic judgements. If this were true, however, one would expect to find much more agreement among the experts in various fields of enquiry than is actually the case. Even so, this does not necessarily warrant the conclusion that there are no universal principles of reason, Aristotle's or Frege's laws of thought being excellent candidates. Indeed, Christians can point out that Jesus is identified as the *logos* (reason, **logic,** word) of God (John 1: 1), a fact that points to reason as an important, indeed essential, aspect of existence. It should not be surprising then that a dominant tradition in Christian anthropology has viewed the ability to reason as of the essence of the image of God.

See a posteriori/a priori; epistemology; faith; fideism; illumination, divine; postmodernism; reason, practical

Further reading: Audi 2003; Bennett 1967; Helm 1999 and 2000; Plantinga and Wolterstorff 1983; Swinburne 2005

reason, practical: Practical reason is the human ability to decide through reflection on the appropriate course of action. Since Socrates (Plato, *Protagoras* 345e) many philosophers have assumed that if one knows the right course of action, one will necessarily act upon it. It appears, however, that original sin has created an affective disorder, such that we may *know* the right course of action, but still opt for the wrong; this is known to philosophers as 'weakness of will' or (from the Greek of Plato and others) *akrasia*. This breakdown of practical reason is poignantly captured in Paul's struggle (Romans 7: 18–24). There is also debate about precisely how one should reason about action: Aristotle introduced the 'practical syllogism' to cover cases in which one reasons from a premise holding out a particular end and a premise holding out a particular means to that end to the conclusion of intending to perform that means to that end.

See ethics; reason

Further reading: Anscombe 1957; Hare 1996; Nozick 1993

reason, principle of sufficient see sufficient reason, principle of

Reformed epistemology see epistemology, Reformed

Reformed theology see **Calvinism**

regenerate: Someone is regenerate ('born again') if he or she is indwelt by the Holy Spirit and has had the image of God in him or her restored to its intended integrity.
Further reading: Helm 1986; Van Mastricht 2002

Reid, Thomas (1710–96): The progenitor of Scottish 'Common-Sense philosophy', a form of **realism,** Reid launched a blistering attack on the 'Way of Ideas'. This is a notion developed in **Descartes** and **Locke** that views mental contents as internal representations of the external world. Reid saw this as placing a 'veil of ideas' between the mind and world that led naturally to **Berkeley**'s **idealism** and **Hume**'s **scepticism.** He developed a trenchant critique of the Way of Ideas in *Inquiry into the Human Mind* (1764). Later, in *Essays on the Intellectual Powers of Man* (1785), Reid develops a form of realism in which perceptions are the direct means by which we experience the world. Reid attacked Hume's scepticism as unliveable, and advocated instead the rationality of basic trust in our sense faculties. Through this Reid became a champion of common-sense intuitions, granting them legitimate philosophical status. His work had a great impact in nineteenth-century America, particularly among conservative theologians of the Princeton school, and has also been an important philosophical source for externalist **epistemology** and the **Reformed epistemology** of **Plantinga** and **Wolterstorff.**
See **epistemology; epistemology, Reformed; Hume, David; Plantinga, Alvin; Wolterstorff, Nicholas**
Further reading: Lehrer 1989; Reid 2000 and 2002; Wolterstorff 2001

relativism see **objectivism**

religion: There is much philosophical discussion about what religion is. It would seem that a religion must have some kind of supernatural commitment: a materialistic creed that claimed that there was nothing but molecules in motion would not, strictly speaking, qualify as a religion, even though in some ways it might function as such (in 1967, the Albanian government made **atheism** the 'state religion', with this designation remaining in effect until 1991). In contrast, a religion need not postulate belief in God or even a god. Most religions have, in addition to an ontological commitment, an ethical commitment too, that is, that certain actions are mandated and others forbidden. The three religions that have exercised the greatest influence over Western philosophy have been Judaism, Christianity and Islam.

See **God, existence of; God, nature of**

Further reading: Basinger 2002; Clouser 2005; Evans 1984; Hick 1989; Meeker and Quinn 2000; Runzo 1993; Ward 1994

Religion, British Society for the Philosophy of see **British Society for the Philosophy of Religion**

religion, philosophy of: Philosophy of religion is the philosophical analysis of the claims of **religion,** particularly the claim that there is a God. Philosophy of religion includes both philosophical defences of religion and philosophical attacks on it.

See **British Society for the Philosophy of Religion; Society of Christian Philosophers**

Further reading: Davies 1998; Quinn and Taliaferro 1997; Taliaferro and Griffiths 2003; Wainwright 1999

religious experience see **experience, religious**

responsibility, moral: One has the moral responsibility to perform certain actions (such as worshipping God) and to avoid others (such as idolatry and murder). Furthermore, one is worthy of moral blame if one does not do what one should or does what one should not. Christian philosophers debate over the origin of this moral responsibility: is it solely from God, or does God also have a responsibility to a morality outside himself? Another area of debate is over whether moral responsibility is compatible with **determinism,** that is, over whether one needs to have **freedom** (understood as per libertarianism) in order to be morally responsible. A special case is the **sin** of Adam and Eve; many Christians believe that our moral responsibility is in some way related to this (for example, by their sin's being imputed to our moral accounts), and there is vigorous debate over how this fits in with our best theories of morality. Another special case is the debate over whether Jesus took moral responsibility for our sins in the **atonement.**

See **atonement; determinism; dilemma, Euthyphro; sin**
Further reading: Beld 2000; Fischer 1986; Lucas 1993; Swinburne 1989a

resurrection: Christians believe that human bodies will return from the dead in a reconstituted form at the advent of the new heaven and earth, and that this general resurrection is prefigured in the resurrection of Jesus Christ. While it would be relatively straightforward for God to create a new body for a disembodied **soul,** Christians complicate things by insisting that the *same* body that dies is resurrected. **Aquinas** interprets this by saying 'by the union of numerically the same soul with numerically the same matter, numerically the same man will be restored' (1905: 4.81). There are, however, many instances where it appears difficult to conceive of even an omnipotent God's effecting a resurrection of this type (for example, that of a body vaporised in a nuclear blast). One troubling scenario debated among the scholastics concerns a cannibal raised on human flesh whose body is entirely constituted by matter from other human bodies. As such, it would seem that once all those other bodies are resurrected, there would be nothing left for the poor cannibal's body.

See **atonement; incarnation**

Further reading: Davis, Stephen 1993; Edwards, Paul 1992; Helm 1989; Swinburne 1993b

revelation: A revelation is a divinely given cognitive disclosure of information and/or non-cognitive experience. For the cognitive conception, revelation principally involves the transfer of new propositional knowledge. For the non-cognitive conception, revelation is something like an ineffable encounter with divine otherness. One classic question concerns how revelation relates to **reason**, and thus whether it can be rational to form **beliefs** from revelation. **John Locke** argued that a putative revelation must always be judged by reason, but this seems to place an unacceptable limit on what God could successfully reveal. A more moderate approach to the problem is to draw parallels between revelation as a doxastic process and non-revelatory doxastic processes. For instance, one could argue that the reception of revelation is sufficiently analogous to sense perception that if beliefs from the latter are rational to accept, so are beliefs from the former. A third option is to regard revelation as irrational but to embrace it as a more fundamental (epistemic) virtue than rationality. This is one construal of **Kierkegaard**'s 'knight of faith'.

See **Enlightenment; fideism; Kierkegaard, Søren Aabye; Locke, John; postmodernism; reason**

Further reading: Alston 1993; Plantinga, Alvin 2000; Plantinga and Wolterstorff 1983; Swinburne 1991

revelation, general: General revelation is the **revelation** of God that comes to all people at all times, for example, through the created order or the voice of conscience.
See **revelation; revelation, special**
Further reading: Berkouwer 1955; Helm 1982

revelation, special: Special revelation is the **revelation** of God that comes to specific people at specific times. Christians believe that Christ is God's supreme self-revelation, but also that God has spoken to his people at various times in the past (and perhaps also in the present) through a mixture of prophets, Church tradition and the inspired Scriptures (there are different opinions over the weight to be accorded each of these). There are philosophical problems over what it means for God to reveal himself, whether a linguistic revelation can do any justice to him, and over whether prophetic predictions of human actions are compatible with the freedom of those actions.
See **revelation; revelation, general**
Further reading: Helm 1982; Wolterstorff 1995

Ricoeur, Paul (1913–2005): A French Christian philosopher, Ricoeur was principally concerned with **hermeneutics**. Before serving in the Second World War (during which he was captured by the Germans), he studied under **Gabriel Marcel** at the Sorbonne; after the war he returned to the Sorbonne, but moved in 1965 to become a professor of philosophy at the newly established university in Nanterre. He also succeeded **Paul Tillich** as Professor of Philosophical Theology at the University of Chicago. Ricoeur was a prolific writer, producing some 20 books and 600 essays in all. In his work Ricoeur stressed both the 'willingness to expose and to abolish idols' and the 'willingness to listen with openness to symbolic and indirect language'. He also emphasised the difference between **persons** and objects (while insisting that this did not provide any commitment to substance **dualism**), and wrote much on the nature of **metaphor** and narrative. Although he gave the Edinburgh Gifford lectures in 1986, Ricoeur did not apply his hermeneutical approach to many explicitly Christian themes; his 1967 work *The Symbolism of Evil* is his most famous foray into this area, though he also co-wrote *Thinking Biblically* (1998) with André Lacocque.

See **hermeneutics; Marcel, Gabriel; Tillich, Paul**

Further reading: Kearney 2004; Lacocque and Ricoeur 1998; Ricoeur 1967, 1977, 1981, 1991, 1996 and 2004; Thompson 1980

Russell, Bertrand Arthur William (1872–1970): A British mathematician, logician and philosopher, Bertrand Russell began philosophical life by going through Kantian and Hegelian phases in which he sought a synthesis of all reality, but then eventually moved (in his words) from viewing the world as a bowl of jelly to as a bucket of shot. Key to his logical atomism was the attempt finally to confirm his childhood fascination with the **certainty** of geometry by reducing arithmetic to **logic**. He sought to do this first via classes and then propositional functions, the latter of which led to his influential essay, 'On Denoting' (1905). This early work culminated in the monumental three-volume *Principia Mathematica* (1910–13), a collaborative effort with **Alfred North Whitehead**. Through these years Russell's **metaphysics** grew increasingly austere as he sought to eradicate **Neoplatonism** from his philosophy. Along with his logical atomism Russell defended an uncompromising **atheism** that challenges one to find dignity by living in the face of 'unyielding despair'. While Russell found some religious satisfaction in mathematics and philosophy (he was fascinated by Pythagoras in particular), he remained a vocal critic of organised **religion**, and of Christianity in particular. His anti-Christian writings are collected in *Why I am Not a Christian* (1957), a fairly conventional set of objections to the morality and rationality of Christian belief. Russell engaged in a famous debate on the **existence of God** with F. C. Copleston, which was aired on the BBC and has frequently been anthologised since. Ever the sceptical empiricist, when asked how he would defend his disbelief in a post-mortem encounter with God, Russell replied: 'Not enough evidence!' Russell's atheism also shows itself in his influential history of philosophy, in which he expresses bafflement at the idea that there could be such a thing as a Christian philosopher such as **Aquinas**. He coped with other philosophers that he respected more, such as **Leibniz**, by simply disregarding their Christian commitments.

See **philosophy, analytical; Whitehead, Alfred North; Wittgenstein, Ludwig Josef Johann**

Further reading: Blackwell and Ruja 1994; Monk 1996 and 2000; Pears 1972; Roberts 1979; Russell 1946, 1957, 1959, 1961 and 1983–; Schilpp 1989; Tait 1975

S

Sartre, Jean-Paul (1905–80): The leading philosopher of **existentialism** and in some ways the leading atheist of the twentieth century, Sartre did at least recognise that his **atheism** was just as much of a philosophical position as another's **theism**. In his earlier writings Sartre interacted with Husserl and **Heidegger,** and wrote on consciousness (which he thought demanded a tacit self-consciousness) and **freedom** (which he thought meant freedom not just from God but from independent moral values). These themes come together in his insistence that human consciousness, or being for itself (*être-pour-soi*), must not become an object, or being in itself (*être-en-soi*), as this would entail a loss of freedom. In his later writings Sartre tried to marry his existentialist insights with **Marxism,** with the result that he lost his earlier emphasis on freedom. Sartre developed these ideas in philosophical monographs such as his magnum opus, *L'être et le néant* (*Being and Nothingness*), in plays such as *Huis Clos* (*No Exit*), biographies such as those of Flaubert and Genet, his autobiography, and novels such as *La Nausée* (*Nausea*). Sartre was offered the Nobel Prize for Literature in 1964, but declined. He, together with his companion Simone de Beauvoir, exercised a great influence over intellectual culture in France and Europe more generally.

See **atheism; existentialism; Heidegger, Martin**

Further reading: Cohen-Solal 1988; Howells 1992; Sartre 1948, 1957, 1958 and 1963

scepticism: Scepticism is the denial of knowledge. It can be held globally, as a denial that anyone (or anyone apart from God) knows anything at all, or locally, concerning a particular subject matter, such as the **existence of God**. Scepticism does not imply non-realism; the sceptic concerning God does not have to affirm that God does not exist. A strong version of scepticism is Pyrrhonian scepticism, which not only denies knowledge but also recommends suspension of belief wherever possible. It is said that Cratylus (fl. c. 400 BCE) took this so far that he even refused to use words at all, communicating by wagging his finger. While some Christian philosophers (for example, Pierre Bayle) have been led by sceptical concerns to embrace **fideism**, most have resisted scepticism not only concerning God but also in other areas, holding that one of the aspects in which humans are made in the image of God is that they have knowledge.

See fideism

Further reading: Hester 1992; Penelhum 1983; Popkin 2003

Schleiermacher, Friedrich Daniel Ernst (1768–1834): Known as the 'Father of Liberal Theology' for his method of accommodating theology to the culture of the late **Enlightenment**, Schleiermacher taught at the University of Berlin alongside **Hegel**, with whom he had a bitter rivalry. His early work *On Religion: Speeches to its Cultured Despisers* (1799) is a forceful interpretation of Christianity within romantic categories that, critics claimed, veers close to **pantheism**. Schleiermacher's radical method and conclusions were based both on his desire to accommodate theology as well as on his belief that **Kant** had undermined the notion that theology could be based on cognitive **revelation**. Within his magnum opus, *Christian Theology*, Schleiermacher sought to reestablish theology based on a non-cognitive aesthetic 'sense of absolute dependence'. On this view, Scripture is not the revealed word of God but human reflection on **religious experience**, a basic assumption that underlies liberal theology today. Schleiermacher raised trenchant criticisms against the coherence of Chalcedonian Christology, opting instead to explain the **incarnation** in virtue of the human **person** of Christ's having been uniquely open to the sense of absolute dependence. This reinterpretation set the standard for many subsequent liberal Christologies. Schleiermacher was also a **Plato** scholar and made important contributions to the foundations of modern **hermeneutics**.

See **Enlightenment; hermeneutics; incarnation; Kant, Immanuel**

Further reading: Schleiermacher 1922, 1958 and 1984–; Williams, Robert R. 1978

scholasticism: The theology 'of the schools', scholasticism developed with the rise of medieval universities (c. twelfth century) and is typified by its rigorous argumentation centred in the *disputation*, a form of argument that would set out the alternative viewpoint and then systematically argue against it. Materially, scholasticism is characterised by the synthesis of Greek (especially Aristotelian) philosophy with Christian theology, paradigmatically modelled in the work of **Thomas Aquinas**. Later scholastics, including **John Duns Scotus** and **William of Ockham**, raised trenchant criticisms against Aquinas and Aristotle. While the scholastic method was heavily critiqued by Protestant reformers such as Martin Luther, the intellectual maturation of Protestant theology brought its own scholasticism by the 1600s, which was eventually to fall under the same criticisms as its medieval counterpart.

See **Abelard, Peter; Anselm of Canterbury; Aquinas, Thomas; Duns Scotus, John; Lombard, Peter; Ockham, William of; philosophy, medieval**

Further reading: Aquinas 1963–80, 1993a and 1993b; Kenny, Kretzmann, Pinborg and Stump 1982; Pieper 2001

science: The modern meaning of 'science' is something like 'a discipline that seeks a programmatic, ordered investigation into the operations of the natural world leading to the discovery of laws of nature and the consequent ability to predict the development of natural systems'; the traditional meaning, coming from the Latin *scientia*, is something like 'any systematic, principled investigation into a given subject matter'. **Descartes**'s rejection of medieval forms and potencies for a mechanical understanding of the universe was crucial for science in the modern sense to advance. Equally important was Francis Bacon's (rather naïve) description of science as consisting in the enumeration of inductive instances leading to the formation of a hypothesis and eventually the identification of physical laws. Today there is a much greater appreciation among philosophers of science for the communal and non-rational aspects of scientific discovery, for instance, in the work of **Michael Polanyi**. The absolutisation of scientific knowledge as the only form is known as 'scientism', a view that is closely aligned with naturalism. The broad definition of 'science' in the traditional sense raises the questions of identifying which other disciplines are appropriately scientific (for example, theology, **hermeneutics**), and which are the appropriate criteria for making such an identification.

See **falsification principle; materialism; science and religion; verification/verifiability principle**

Further reading: Polanyi 1974; Ratzsch 1986; Rosenberg 2000

science and religion: While theology was once termed the 'queen of the sciences' (using 'sciences' in the traditional sense outlined under the entry **science**), in the modern world this title has been claimed by the natural sciences, especially physics. Given that both science and **religion** (or theology) purport to provide knowledge of the world, the question of how they interrelate is inevitable. Many popularly think of a science/religion conflict, as classically captured in Andrew Dixon White's *A History of the Warfare of Science with Theology in Christendom* (1896). But, according to Ian Barbour, this is only one of four models (the conflict model) as to how science and religion might relate. At the opposite extreme, the independence model views science and religion as dealing with wholly different spheres (for example, fact and value). The third and fourth models – dialogue and integration – offer a more nuanced picture of an ongoing conversation between science and religion. On these latter two models the question arises of how particular scientific theories and religious doctrines relate, for instance, the question of how biological **evolution** and divine **creation** relate. Another issue concerns the nature of scientifics law with regard to other issues such as **miracles** and **divine action**.

See **creation; evolution; miracle; religion; science**

Further reading: Barbour 1998; Russell, Stoeger and Coyne 1988; Murphy, Nancy C. 1990; Peacocke 1993; White, Andrew Dickson 1896

scientia media see **knowledge, middle**

Scotus, John Duns see **Duns Scotus, John**

Scripture, Holy see **revelation, special**

sensus divinitas see **divinitas, sensus**

simplicity, divine: The doctrine of divine simplicity is the doctrine that God is absolutely simple. The intuition behind this idea is that any kind of complexity in God is either unseemly in itself, or would mean that God had to depend on his parts in some way. This doctrine comes in a variety of strengths: (1) the most basic form is that God has no spatial parts, or, at least, that his **nature** is not to have such parts; (2) like (1), but with the claim that he has no temporal parts, usually because he is thought to be timeless; (3) like (2), but with the denial that there is logical composition within God's nature; each of God's attributes is identical with each of his attributes, so God's **omnipotence** is the same as his **omniscience** and his **omnipresence** and his **perfect goodness** and his **eternity**; (4) like

(3), but with the addition of the contention that God himself is the same as his nature, that is, his property; (5) like (4), but with the claim that God's existence is identical with his nature, that is, with God himself. Although in **medieval philosophy** it was common to hold the doctrine of divine simplicity in its strongest possible form, in contemporary Christian philosophy this is a good deal rarer, though there are some present-day examples, such as William Mann. Particular problems for Christian philosophers include the reconciliation of divine simplicity with the **doctrine of the Trinity** and with the doctrine of the **incarnation**.

See **eternity; God, nature of; goodness, perfect; omniscience; omnipotence; omnipresence; philosophy, medieval**

Further reading: Hughes 1989; Morris 1991; Plantinga 1980

sin: 'Sin' is used in two senses 'original sin' and 'actual sin'. 'Actual sin' describes those moral wrongs that are actually committed by humans (and other agents). 'Original sin' describes the universal sinfulness shared by all people, which is traceable to the moral fall of the first humans, Adam and Eve. While discussion of original sin is found in patristic theologians, **Augustine** was the theologian that determined the form of the doctrine in the West. One controversial aspect of the Augustinian tradition is the claim that human beings also possess the original *guilt* of the sin of Adam as if we had committed it. This doctrine is controversial given the powerful intuitions that I cannot be guilty of an action if I have not myself committed that action. Another contested issue is the mode of transference of original sin from Adam to his descendents. Realistic theories see original sin as rooted in an actual ontological inheritance, while federal theories see original sin as rooted in God's declaration of imputation. Finally, one might ask whether the theory of **evolution** renders the claim of a historical fall incredible, and, if so, what implications this has for both original sin and salvation. **F. R. Tennant** denied a historical fall, and instead grounded human sinfulness in the vestiges of what were once amoral animal instincts in our ancestors, but which now corrupt our moral being.

See **atonement; Augustine of Hippo; evolution; Tennant, Frederick Robert**

Further reading: Blocher 2001; Plantinga 1995

Society of Christian Philosophers: Organised in 1978 by a group of Christian philosophers led by **William Alston**, this academic society remains open to all Christians that maintain an interest in philosophy. The society meets annually and publishes a leading journal of Christian philosophy, *Faith and Philosophy*. Past presidents include **William Alston, Alvin Plantinga, Marilyn McCord Adams, Robert Merrihew Adams** and **Nicholas Wolterstorff**.

See **Adams, Marilyn McCord; Adams, Robert Merrihew; Alston, William Payne; Plantinga, Alvin; Wolterstorff, Nicholas**

Further reading: *Faith and Philosophy* 1984–; Web site for the Society of Christian Philosophers

soft fact see **hard-fact/soft-fact debate**

soul: While the word 'soul' has multiple meanings and connotations within philosophy, one might identify the core term as referring to the immaterial essence of a living thing, most often of a human **person**. The two predominant views on the soul in Christian thought date back to **Plato** and Aristotle. Plato's conception of the person as a soul attached to a body was taken up by **Augustine**, albeit with a greater emphasis on the goodness of embodiment. In contrast, Aristotle, whose **metaphysics** viewed all things as a combination of matter and form, viewed the person as the body/soul unity, with the soul being the form of the body. This view was adopted by **Aquinas**, though he rejected Aristotle's claim that the soul could not exist apart from the body. While Aristotle thought that plants had a vegetative soul, beasts a soul that was sensate as well as vegetative, and humans a soul that was rational as well as sensate and vegetative, **Descartes**'s radical **dualism** denied souls of all animals but humans. In recent decades the concept of a soul has come under increasing criticism by philosophers such as **Ludwig Wittgenstein** and Gilbert Ryle, with the latter dismissing it as the 'ghost in the machine'. While many philosophers (even Christians such as **Peter van Inwagen**) today reject the soul, owing to commitments to **materialism,** some theologians reject the soul and substance dualism as unbiblical Greek accretions on holistic Hebrew anthropology. Defenders of dualist anthropology (such as **Richard Swinburne**) claim that the concept of the soul can be reconciled with Scripture, and that it has explanatory scope in various areas including the nature of consciousness, personal identity and **freedom.**

See **dualism; metaphysics; nature; Swinburne, Richard; van Inwagen, Peter**

Further reading: Cooper 1989; Corcoran 2001; Swinburne 1997; van Inwagen 1990

Spinoza, Baruch/Benedict (1632–77): Together with **Descartes** and **Leibniz**, Spinoza was one of the great rationalists of the early-modern period. A grinder of lenses by profession, he was ethnically Jewish, but was expelled from his synagogue in Amsterdam for heresy (he was a pantheist: he believed that there was only one **substance**, which he said could equally be called 'God' or 'nature'; all other things were only modifications of this). One of his main works was the *Tractatus de Intellectus Emendatione*, the stated aim of which was to discover 'the life of blessedness for man', which necessitated a search for that 'by whose discovery and acquisition I might be put in possession of a joy continuous and supreme to all eternity'. Spinoza called this 'the intellectual love of God', saying that it consisted in a clear understanding of human **nature**, the universe and the joy essential to humans, which came through realising that we were all just cogs in a deterministic machine. Spinoza's magnum opus, *Ethics demonstrated in a geometrical manner*, was published immediately after his premature death aged forty-five, and is a system of definitions, axioms and theorems proved in the manner of Euclid. Spinoza agreed with Descartes that there were only two attributes of which we had any knowledge: extension and thought. Whereas Descartes thought that these two attributes were incompatible, Spinoza thought that both of these were possessed by the one substance (God/nature); in other words, God/nature was both an infinite thinking thing and an infinite extended thing (and an infinite number of other things beyond our ken). This implies not only that things we normally think of as unextended, such as God, are actually physical, but also that things we usually think of as unthinking, such as rocks, are actually conscious, since they are but modes of the one substance. Spinoza also translated the Old Testament into Dutch, and his writings on the Old Testament in his *Tractatus Theologico-politicus* contributed to the rise of the critical-historical approach. Spinoza also thought that **religions** such as Judaism and Christianity were not primarily repositories of theological

truths, but rather disguised commands about how one should live.

See **Descartes, René; Leibniz, Gottfried Wilhelm; pantheism; rationalism**

Further reading: Hampshire 1988 and 2005; Spinoza 1925–87, 1985– and 1994

spontaneity, liberty of see **freedom**

Stoicism: The Stoics took their name from the *Stoa* or porch in Athens where they taught. The founder of the Stoical school in c. 300 BCE was Zeno of Citium; it was developed by Cleanthes (after whom a character in Hume's *Dialogues* was named) and Chrysippus; and the last of the ancient Stoics were Seneca, Epictetus and Marcus Aurelius, who was emperor of Rome in the second century CE. The Stoics gave a very high place to **reason**, insisting that the world was deterministically ordered in a reasonable fashion by God to give the best possible arrangement of the matter that wholly composed it. The Stoics concluded from this that there was no place for grief or regret, since everything that happened was for the best. The Stoic theory here goes further than Christian theistic **determinism,** since Stoicism affirms that the only bad thing is wickedness, so natural disasters were not viewed by the Stoics as bad things, and the wise man should be indifferent to them. For this reason, the Stoics also shunned 'the passions', notably distress, pity and fear. The Stoics were pantheists or panentheists; they thought that God, being a very fine physical body, was in everything. They also believed in the doctrine of eternal recurrence, that events repeat themselves at various intervals, in which doctrine they influenced **Nietzsche.**

See **determinism; Nietzsche, Friedrich Wilhelm; pantheism**

Further reading: Algra, Barnes, Mansfeld and Schofield 1999; Armstrong 1967; Armstrong and Markus 1960; Arnim 1903–24; Bobzien 1998; Inwood, Michael 2003; Long and Sedley 1987; Rist 1969

subjectivism: Subjectivism about an area holds that reality in that area is subjective, that is, it is determined by the subject. Global subjectivism is the view that each **person** determines the whole of reality for him or herself. This view, though widely accepted outside the philosophical community today, has not found favour within it. More limited kinds of subjectivism have found philosophical adherents: ethical subjectivists hold that each person determines what is right and what is wrong for him or her, and aesthetic subjectivists hold that each person determines what is beautiful and what is ugly for him or her. Christian philosophers have tended to reject ethical subjectivism as incompatible with the Bible's emphasis on the objectivity of sin in God's eyes; there seems also to be a case that what is beautiful and what is ugly are similarly objective in God's eyes.

See **objectivism; postmodernism**

Further reading: Farber 1959; Murphy, Richard T. 1979; Williams, Bernard A. O. 1993

substance: Aristotle defined 'a substance' in his *Categories* as 'what is neither in a subject nor said of a subject', but in his *Metaphysics* as 'a determinate individual that is capable of existing on its own', that is, independently. Aristotle distinguishes two sorts of substance: primary substances (particular individuals, such as Socrates) and secondary substances (species and genera, such as the species of humanity). Many Christian philosophers have insisted that God is, strictly speaking, the only substance, since he is the only thing capable of existing on his own; everything else depends on him for its existence. But when the Nicene Creed describes the Son as being of one substance with the Father, it is not clear whether the framers of the creed had primary or secondary substances in mind, although they do seem to have had one of Aristotle's definitions in mind. That is, it is not clear whether they are saying that the members of the **Trinity** somehow compose a single particular individual (God) or whether they all share in a single genus (deity). Even if God is the only substance in a strict sense of 'substance', there may well be other substances in a looser sense; **Descartes** regarded matter as a single substance; **Locke** regarded individual material things as separate substances 'standing under' their properties. Locke could say nothing, however, about the substance or 'I-know-not-what' itself underlying all the properties, which problem has led some philosophers, such as **Hume**, to reject the concept of substance altogether, in favour of a theory that all that exists are just bundles of properties not inhering in anything. Those that believe in both mental and physical substances are faced with the additional problem of explaining how they interact. **Whitehead** thought that concentration on the concept of substance had led philosophy astray and instead proposed that philosophers should concentrate on the concept of a process; Whitehead's system of thought was termed **process philosophy**.

See **Descartes, René; Hume, David; Locke, John; metaphysics; ontology; philosophy, process; Whitehead, Alfred North**

Further reading: Hoffman and Rosenkrantz 1994 and 1997; van Inwagen 1990; Wiggins 2001; Woolhouse 1993

sufficient reason, principle of: The principle of sufficient reason states that for every fact, event or state of affairs, there is a sufficient reason why that fact, event or state of affairs obtains. **Leibniz** viewed the principle as a first principle of **reason**, and it occupied a particularly important place both in his thought and in that of his student Christian Wolff. Leibniz used the principle in a version of the **cosmological argument**, as well as to explain why God created this particular world. Certainly the principle has a high intuitive appeal: for instance, if money goes missing from your wallet, you proceed on the assumption that there is a reason, while to deny that there is a sufficient reason would simply appear baffling. Despite its initial plausibility, however, the principle remains controversial. For one thing, it has been argued to imply universal **determinism**: that is, if everything that happens does so for a sufficient reason, then everything must happen. On a more contained level, some claim that the principle is false at least at the quantum level where there is an alleged indeterminacy to the position and velocity of fundamental particles.

See **argument, cosmological; determinism; Leibniz, Gottfried Wilhelm; necessity**

Further reading: Gurr 1959; Urban, Wilbur Marshal 1898; Woolhouse 1994

Swinburne, Richard Granville (1934–): The Nolloth Professor of the Philosophy of the Christian Religion at the University of Oxford from 1985 to 2002, Swinburne exercised a strong influence over **analytical philosophy** of **religion**, not only in his native Britain but also in the United States and, lately, in Russia, with which country he has developed strong ties. Swinburne began his philosophical career working on probability theory; this was to play an important part in his subsequent attempt to bring **theism** in general, and Christianity in particular, on an epistemic par with **science**. Swinburne's early work in the philosophy of religion was a trilogy on theism: *The Coherence of Theism* (1977; revised 1993), explicating and defending the logical consistency of the claim that God exists; *The Existence of God* (1979; 2nd edn 2004), his most famous work, arguing that God actually exists using a rigorous Bayesian formulation of the **argument to design**; and *Faith and Reason* (1981; 2nd edn 2005), elucidating the place of rationality in religious **belief**. More recently Swinburne has turned his attention to specifically Christian themes. This has led to a tetralogy in Christian philosophy: *Responsibility and Atonement* (1989), an analysis of the problem of **sin** and God's solution to it; *Revelation* (1992), looking at how God might communicate with humans; *The Christian God* (1994), a rigorous philosophical analysis of the doctrines of the **Trinity** and the **incarnation**; and *Providence and the Problem of Evil* (1998), his attempt at a **theodicy**. Swinburne has also written in defence of the **resurrection** of Jesus and the existence of the **soul**. Swinburne's writings are marked by clarity, thoroughness and a defence in the traditional, reasonable, manner of an orthodox Christian outlook.

See **argument from/to design; theodicy; theology, natural**

Further reading: Swinburne 1989a, 1991, 1993a, 1993b, 1994, 1998, 2004 and 2005

symbol: A symbol is something that stands for something else in some artificial, conventional way (as opposed to the natural way in which black clouds mean that there is rain on the way). Names stand for their bearers, but also the crown can be a symbol of the monarchy. Christian philosophers are interested here in, among other questions, the question of how much of **religious language** is symbolic. Some claim that all of it is symbolic, but this seems to fall foul of the fact that if we do not know what the symbols mean literally, then we do not know what our religious beliefs are, but if we do know what they mean literally then there must be in principle a non-symbolic story to tell.

See **metaphor**

Further reading: Dillistone 1966; Soskice 1985; Todorov 1982a and 1982b

---

T

teleological argument see **argument from/to design**

Tennant, Frederick Robert (1866–1957): A theologian and philosopher of **religion** at Cambridge University, Tennant worked in dogmatic theology primarily on the topic of original **sin**, and in **philosophy of religion** primarily on the application of the **argument to design**. Tennant rejected a state of original righteousness and instead saw sin emerging through gradual **evolution** as the acts of self-preservation in our evolutionary ancestors have been carried into the moral sphere of human existence, leading to the possibility of sin. Tennant's two-volume *Philosophical Theology* develops a 'cosmic teleology' in order to defend the theistic **worldview** as the most reasonable. Hence, for Tennant, **theism** is a rational induction based on evidence for design. Tennant's argument does not depend upon particular instances of design (as in Paley's appeal to the eye) but rather upon the cumulative force of multiple apparent instances of design, from basic order in the world to the aesthetic and ethical human sense.

See **argument from/to design; creation; evolution; God, arguments for the existence of; sin; theology, natural**

Further reading: Bertocci 1938; Tennant 1912, 1928 and 1930

Tertullian, Quintus Septimius Florens (c. 160–c. 220 CE): A brilliant North-African lawyer and theologian, Tertullian was the first to write theology in Latin. Thanks to his original formulations of doctrine and ruthless argument he became one of the most influential theologians of the early Church. Among his many distinctions, Tertullian coined the term **Trinity** (*trinitas*) and developed influential definitions of God as 'one **substance** in three persons' and Christ as 'one **person** in two **natures**'. Interestingly, Tertullian was influenced by the **materialism** of **Stoicism**, and seems to have held that even God exists as a rarefied form of matter, a nuance that was not carried forward by later theologians. Despite his rational and articulate defence of Christian faith, Tertullian is more often remembered among philosophers for his rhetorical extremes that appear to lead to an irrational **fideism**. Among them is his famous question 'What has Athens to do with Jerusalem?' and his description of the **incarnation** in *De carne Christi*: 'the Son of God died; it is by all means to be believed, because it is absurd. And He was buried and rose again; the fact is certain, because it is impossible' (Tertullian 1956: §5). Contrary to popular opinion, however, this is not an irrational statement, but rather a rhetorically appreciable argument that the crucifixion and **resurrection** are plausible precisely because they are so absurd a human being would never have concocted them.

See **fideism; incarnation; materialism; reason; Stoicism; Trinity, doctrine of the**

Further reading: Barnes 1985; Claesson 1974; Dunn 2004; Tertullian 1868–70, 1890–1957; 1954, 1956 and 2003; the Tertullian Project (web site)

theism: Theism is the doctrine that God exists or that a divine being exists.

See **theism, classical; theism, open**

Further reading: Aquinas 1963–80; Hill, Daniel J. 2005; Swinburne 1993a

theism, classical: Classical theism is an approach to the doctrine of God that emphasises unchanging being, divine **transcendence** and sovereignty as captured in a set of divine attributes that typically includes atemporal **eternity, immutability, impassibility** and **divine simplicity.** Classical theism was developed over centuries by theologians critically interacting with important pagan philosophical theology including that of **Plato** (God as Form of the Good), Aristotle (God as Pure Act and Unmoved Mover) and **Plotinus** (God as transcendent One). Exponents of classical theism come from all the major monotheistic traditions including Judaism (Philo, Maimonides), Christianity (**Augustine, Anselm** and **Aquinas**), and Islam (Averroës, Avicenna). Within Christian classical theism, Anselm's conception of God as the greatest conceivable or most perfect being, and Aquinas' identification of God's existence and essence have also been influential concepts. Many Christians today reject classical theism, claiming that concepts of Greek origination like impassibility produce a 'God of the philosophers' that has little relation to the God of biblical **revelation.** While admitting that there may *appear* to be tension between scriptural revelation and classical theism, advocates of the latter argue that there is a deeper concord, and indeed that this is the best way to ensure a theology that is both biblically sound and philosophically coherent.

See **Anselm of Canterbury; Aquinas, Thomas; Aristotelianism; Augustine of Hippo; Boethius, Anicius**

Manilius Severinus; Bonaventure; eternity; Hartshorne, Charles; immutability; impassibility; ontotheology; philosophy, process; simplicity, divine; theism, open; theology, perfect-being; theology, process; transcendence

Further reading: Aquinas 1963–80; Parrish 1997; Swinburne 1993a

theism, open: Open theism is the view of recent popularity that the affirmation that **determinism** is false and that humans have **freedom** as per libertarianism commits one to believing that God does not know future free actions. Open theism is thus a radical solution to the **problem of foreknowledge and freedom**. Its recent proponents have been from the evangelical wing of the Church, and include theologians such as Gregory Boyd and Clark Pinnock, and philosophers such as William Hasker and David Basinger. **Richard Swinburne** and **Peter Geach** have similar views though from different sections of the Church. Most Christian philosophers have not been convinced that open theism is the best solution to the dilemma of freedom and foreknowledge.

See **foreknowledge and freedom, problem of**

Further reading: Hasker 1989; Pinnock, Rice, Sanders, Hasker and Basinger 1994

theodicy: A theodicy is a defence of divine **omnipotence** and **perfect goodness** in the light of the **problem of evil**. In the words of Milton's famous preface to *Paradise Lost*, it is to 'justify the ways of God to men'. According to **Alvin Plantinga**, theodicy should be distinguished from the more modest pursuit of a defence. The former purports to provide an actual explanation for why God allows evil, while the latter simply attempts to demonstrate that the existence of evil and the **existence of God** are not logically incompatible.

See **defence, free-will; defence, greater-good; evil, problem of; Hell**

Further reading: Adams, Marilyn McCord 1999; Farrer 1966; Leibniz 1985; Lewis, C. S. 1940; Swinburne 1998

theology, creation: Creation theology is an attempt to think about God from the evidence of the physical universe around us. A very popular argument from **creation** is the **argument to design**, which claims to find evidence for the existence of an omnipotent, omniscient and perfectly good creator in the physical universe's order, beauty and serviceableness to us. Creation theology was at its highest in the middle of the medieval period, reaching its apogee in **Aquinas'** 'five ways', and it has long been popular in the Roman-Catholic tradition, but it has also received many defenders outside that tradition, from **William Paley** to **Richard Swinburne**.

See **Aquinas, Thomas; argument from/to design; God, nature of; Paley, William; Swinburne, Richard**

Further reading: Aquinas 1963–80; Kretzmann 2001; Swinburne 1993a

theology, natural: Natural theology is not necessarily theologising about nature, but rather reflection about God himself (and associated religious claims) undertaken from the data of general, rather than special, **revelation**. Typically, natural theology is concerned with assertions about the **existence of God** and the **nature of God** that are shared by major forms of monotheism. For much of Christian history natural theology has provided a common framework of concepts that could be shared between Christians and non-Christians, thereby allowing a point of contact in understanding prior to the gospel. Hence, **Aquinas** believed that **reason** could demonstrate the existence of God (natural theology), but that the **doctrine of the Trinity** was a deliverance of **special revelation**. With the **Enlightenment** natural theology gained increasing prominence as a means to meet the demands of sceptical reason. This movement finally terminated in **deism**, which completely limited its theological reflection to truths that are naturally available. The strong emphasis within **Calvinism** upon the cognitive effects of the fall has meant that many theologians within this tradition have been sceptical of the prospects of natural theology. Most notable is **Karl Barth,** who denied that there could be *any* theology apart from special revelation.

See **Barth, Karl; foundationalism; God, arguments for the existence of; reason; revelation; theism, classical**

Further reading: Crombie 2001; Paley 1819; Swinburne 2005

theology, perfect-being: Perfect-being theology is an attempt to analyse the **nature of God** in terms of absolute perfection or **maximal greatness**. The idea is that this is the single defining attribute of God's, and that the other attributes that God is traditionally thought to possess (**omnipotence, omniscience, omnipresence, perfect goodness, eternity**) are derived from it. **Anselm** is the fountainhead for this approach (though there are signs of it in **Augustine**), and it has been recently revived by **Alvin Plantinga** and many others.

See **Anselm of Canterbury; Augustine of Hippo; greatness, maximal; God, nature of; Plantinga, Alvin; property, great-making; theism, classical**

Further reading: Hill, Daniel J. 2005; Morris 1987; Morris 1991; Rogers, Katherin A. 2000

theology, process: A theology that builds upon the **metaphysics** of process philosophy, process theology has numbered among its leading exponents **Charles Hartshorne** and, more recently, John Cobb. Its general characteristics include a rejection of the **metaphysics** of being and **substance**, instead viewing change and event as fundamental both to God and **creation**. Hence, God is in the process of becoming along with all else, as he is present to, and affected by, the development of everything. Process theology has proved attractive to theologians seeking an alternative vision to **classical theism**. It shares certain characteristics with **open theism**, though proponents of the latter affirm *creatio ex nihilo* and generally do not subscribe to process metaphysics. Process theists translate Christian doctrine in accordance with their metaphysics. For instance, the **doctrine of the Trinity** is interpreted through dipolar **theism**, where, according to John Cobb, God the Father is the concrete being, the Son is the 'primordial nature' and the Spirit is the 'consequent nature'.

See **Hartshorne, Charles; Whitehead, Alfred North**

Further reading: Cobb and Griffin 1976; Griffin 2001; Kane and Phillips 1989; Suchocki 1989

theology, Reformed see **Calvinism**

Thomism: Broadly, Thomism is the school of thought that grants special authority to the systematic thought of **Thomas Aquinas** in theological and philosophical issues. More narrowly, Thomism involves the views of those within the Order of Preachers (Dominicans). Early Thomism developed in the fourteenth century as the *Summa Theologiae* replaced **Peter Lombard**'s *Sentences* as a standard textbook among Dominicans. By the eighteenth century Thomism had stagnated owing to a failure to engage with the philosophical shift to a modern **worldview** that dispensed with forms, potencies and final causes. In the early nineteenth century some scholars began advocating a neo-Thomism, a move that came to fruition with Pope Leo XIII's encyclical *Aeterni Patris* (1879), which commended the programmatic use of Aquinas among Roman-Catholic scholars as a response to the challenge of modernity. Initially much of the resulting work was weak in historical sensitivity, but this has been addressed through the work of scholars like Etienne Gilson and **Jacques Maritain**. Neo-Thomism underwent a further permutation with the work of theologians like **Karl Rahner** and **Bernard Lonergan**, who developed a transcendental Thomism that sought greater dialogue with both the **Enlightenment** and the work of philosophers like **Heidegger**. The Second Vatican Council ended the monopoly of Thomism so that Roman-Catholic theologians and philosophers are now free to explore various schools of thought including **process theology**.

See **Aquinas, Thomas; Lonergan, Bernard; Rahner, Karl**

Further reading: Brezik 1981; Grenet 1967; McInerny 1966

Tillich, Paul (1886–1965): A German philosophical theologian, Tillich, under Nazi pressure for his socialistic views, emigrated to the USA in 1934, and then taught at Union Theological Seminary, Harvard, and the University of Chicago, eventually achieving wide public recognition, even appearing on the cover of *Time* magazine. His popular works include collected sermons in *The Courage to Be* (1952) and *The Eternal Now* (1963). Tillich defended a 'method of correlation', in which theological formulation is determined by the present existential questions/concerns of society. In this way theology is ensured apologetic relevance. Among these points of correlation is Tillich's identification of an existential fear of not being and the universality of an 'ultimate concern', which Tillich interprets as God. Since everyone has an ultimate concern, **atheism** is, strictly speaking, impossible. Tillich was critical of **ontotheology**, as he stressed that God is not a being, but the ground of being. Since God transcends existence it is wrong to say that God exists. The answer to our existential struggle is in the 'New Being' (Christ), who offers us the means to the 'essentialisation' that makes us whole. Tillich's *Systematic Theology* (1951, 1957, 1963) is the fullest presentation of his work. Critics contend that the method of correlation produces a theology only as good as the questions being asked, and it is often at this point that a prophetic voice is necessary. Moreover, his theology is overly abstract, and shows little interaction with Scripture.

See **God, existence of; Heidegger, Martin; Neoplatonism; ontotheology**

Further reading: Tillich 1951–63 and 1952

time: **Augustine** famously remarked in his *Confessions*: 'What, then, is time? If no one asks me about it, I know; if someone asks me to explain it, I don't know' (Augustine 1991: XI.xiv). Many Christian philosophers since have followed his example. Aristotle defined time in his *Physics* as the measure of change, but some philosophers have accused him of getting things the wrong way round, claiming that change is the way by which we keep track of time. Christian philosophers have debated whether God is in time or not: in **classical theism**, God is viewed as being outside time, but contemporary Christian philosophers are divided on this question. Those that have said that God is in time have often had a motivation for rejecting

Aristotle's definition, claiming that in the past there was a time when only an unchanging God existed. But perhaps if God is in time he must change, if only to have new memories. Many Christians think that on the 'last day' God will bring time to a halt, but the biblical writings seem to envisage a continuation of actions in the next life (for example, praise of God), and how can one continue to perform actions without time in which to perform them?

See **eternity**

Further reading: Augustine 1991; Ganssle 2001; Le Poidevin 1998; Le Poidevin and McBeath 1993; Prior 2003; Swinburne 1968; Tooley 1997; Zwart 1976

timelessness see **eternity**

transcendence: Transcendence is the relational property of possessing a higher level of existence. For instance, human beings transcend the natural world owing to our capacities in the realm of self-consciousness, **reason** and moral action. The preeminent transcendent being is, of course, God, who, in Christian theology, utterly transcends all else that exists as the creator of it. **Kierkegaard** referred to the gulf between God and **creation** as an 'infinite qualitative difference'. For that reason, **Karl Barth** stressed that God must initiate contact in **revelation**. At the same time, Christian theology also asserts that God is fully immanent within creation, most concretely in the **incarnation**. The relationship between divine transcendence and immanence constitutes one of the most fundamental theological tensions.

See **creation; God, existence of; language, religious; via negativa**

Further reading: Archer, Collier and Porpora 2004; Farley 1962; Westphal, Merold 2004

Trinity, doctrine of the: The doctrine of the Trinity can be stated in two simple propositions:

1. There exists exactly one divine **substance**: God.
2. There exist exactly three divine **persons**: Father, Son and Holy Spirit.

The problems arise in reconciling these two propositions: what is the relation between the persons and the substance? Some Christian philosophers believe that in the Trinity there is one thinker (that is, God) – the challenge for them is to understand how there can be three divine persons. Other Christian philosophers believe that in the Trinity there are three thinkers (that is, the Father, the Son and the Holy Spirit) – the challenge for them is to understand how there can be one God. One suggestion, put forward by **Peter Geach** and **Peter van Inwagen,** is that of relative identity: this allows that the Father can be the same God as, but a different person from, the Son. Another suggestion is that 'the Father is God' is not an identity statement at all, but a mere predication of divinity of the Father. This is often coupled with the claim that the divine substance is merely the divine **nature** – an abstract set of properties instantiated in the divine persons. The charge of tritheism is deflected by the claim that there are not three *independent* gods or Gods, but three divine persons that always cooperate. These theories are *social* theories of the Trinity that stress the plurality; other theories stress the unity of the Trinity, claiming that the three persons are different modes of being of the one divine substance or different aspects of his character.

See **God, nature of; nature; person; philosophy, medieval; substance**

Further reading: Davis, Kendall and O'Collins 1999; Geach 1980; Swinburne 1994; van Inwagen 1995

truth: The property of truth is typically understood to apply to assertions that state what is actually the case. In Aristotle's classic definition, 'to say of what is, that it is and of what is not, that it is not, is true' (1928: IV.7). Among the standard candidates for being truth-*bearers* are propositions, sentences and thoughts. The truth-*maker* is that (if anything) in virtue of which the putative truth-bearer is true. While one common description of the relationship between the truth-bearer and truth-maker is *correspondence*, some query how something like the sentence 'the sun is setting' can correspond to something as different as the event of the sun's setting. One response is to introduce a new metaphysical entity, a 'fact', as the truth-maker, but one can then ask what facts are and how they relate to the world. Some also object that the correspondence theory reifies truth into an opaque relation (we cannot confirm correspondence) that terminates in **scepticism** (we cannot *know* that any of our beliefs is true). The coherence theory of truth focuses on human thought by viewing truth as the property of coherence of one's beliefs. But while coherence is a partial guide to identify truth (for example, an incoherent belief cannot be true), it does not seem that truth can be *reduced* to coherence. For one thing, insofar as there can be two fully coherent belief systems – one in which p is true and the other in which not-p is true – relativism about truth follows. **Pragmatism** about truth looks to human action and sees truth as whatever produces results, but this appears to confuse the *implications* of truth with the actual property of truth. Some Christian theologians argue that truth-bearers must transcend propositions since Jesus claims to be 'the truth' (John 14: 6). It is not clear, however, whether the admittedly broader use of the word 'truth' in the Bible (*emeth, aletheia*) is pre-theoretical, or whether it actually has metaphysical implications.

See James, William; metaphysics; pragmatism; realism
Further reading: Alston 1996; Aristotle 1928; Horwich 1998; Kirkham 1992; Marshall 2000; Wright 1987

universalism see **Hell**

universals: Universals are supposed to be objects that are capable of wholly existing in different places at the same time. This feature distinguishes them from particulars. In **medieval philosophy** the problem of universals was widely discussed; the problem was how universals existed, whether in mind-independent reality as the realists (such as **Thomas Aquinas**) claimed, in concepts in the mind as the conceptualists (such as **William of Ockham**) claimed, or merely in language as the nominalists (such as Roscelin and **Abelard**) claimed. The realists were challenged to explain the relationship between God and universals (did he create them? were they independent of him?), whereas the conceptualists and nominalists were charged with making God's nature fit paltry human minds and language.

See **conceptualism; nominalism; philosophy, medieval**
Further reading: Moreland 2001; Spade 1994; Wolterstorff 1970

univocal: A word is used univocally in two contexts when it has exactly the same meaning in each context. Christian philosophers debate whether words used of God and humans are used univocally.

See **analogy; equivocal; language, religious**
Further reading: Alston 1989a

unregenerate see **regenerate**

van Inwagen, Peter (1942–): The John Cardinal O'Hara Professor of Philosophy at the University of Notre Dame, Peter van Inwagen has written widely in defence of **theism** in general and Christianity in particular. He has also written extensively on **metaphysics,** particularly in defence of libertarianism concerning **freedom.** His writings are distinguished by their clarity, wit and trenchant style.

See **freedom**

Further reading: van Inwagen 1983, 1995 and 1997

van Til, Cornelius (1895–1987): Although in some ways more of a theologian than a philosopher, van Til has exercised a profound influence on many Christian philosophers, especially those committed to **Calvinism.** Although a graduate of the Dutch-Reformed Calvin College, van Til taught all of his life (apart from a brief sojourn at Princeton Theological Seminary) at Westminster Theological Seminary. He is best known for his views on **apologetics:** van Til thought that **sin** had had such a pervasive influence on the human mind that there was no common point of meeting for the **regenerate** mind and the unregenerate mind. He therefore rejected **natural theology** in favour of a concentration on the supreme authority of **special revelation** (that is, the Bible). Van Til did, however, allow that one could engage in a certain form of negative apologetics, by showing how the presuppositions of the non-Christian did not ultimately make sense of life. There is much similarity between van Til's thought and **Reformed epistemology.** Van Til was an ordained minister of the Orthodox Presbyterian Church, and was involved in a famous dispute within that denomination with **Gordon Clark** over whether God's knowledge and human knowledge had a point of contact (as Clark thought) or were totally incomparable (as van Til argued).

See **apologetics; Calvinism; Clark, Gordon Haddon; epistemology, Reformed**

Further reading: Bahnsen 1998; Frame 1995; Geehan 1971; North 1979; Sigward 1997; van Til 1969a and 1969b; www.vantil.info (web site); White, William 1979

verification/verifiability principle: The central principle of **logical positivism,** the verification principle states that the meaning of non-analytic statements is found in their conditions of verification. On this view, all non-analytical statements that do not have verification conditions are deemed meaningless, including all statements of **metaphysics, ethics,** aesthetics and theology. The principle was eventually abandoned for a number of reasons including the problem of self-reference: that is, it could not itself be verified, and thus failed on its own terms to be meaningful. Further, philosophers of **science** now recognise that many scientific postulates cannot be directly verified (or falsified) and are instead abandoned when they become explanatorily degenerative.

See **Ayer, Alfred Jules; falsification principle; positivism, logical**

Further reading: Ayer 2001; Ayer 2004; Hanfling 1981; Popper 1996

via negativa: The via negativa or 'way of negation' is one of the classic four ways to knowledge of God (along with **analogy,** eminence and causality). It is predicated upon the premise that God utterly transcends our categories of thought such that we are limited to an indirect route to knowledge of him since, it is claimed, none of our affirmative statements applies to him. Jewish theologian Maimonides believed that the *via negativa* was the only way to gain knowledge of God, but **Thomas Aquinas** supplemented this method with analogy.

See **analogy; language, religious**

Further reading: Alston 1989a; Jacobs 1997

virtue ethics see **ethics, virtue**

virtues: Ancient philosophers agreed that there were four 'cardinal' virtues: justice, wisdom, courage and moderation. There was disagreement, however, on quite how they were related: was it possible to have one without having the others or were they all really identical? There was also disagreement on whether the virtues could be taught, with **Plato** arguing in *Meno* that they could not. In **medieval philosophy** the three 'theological virtues' of faith, hope and charity (1 Corinthians 13: 13) were added to the four cardinal virtues. All the philosophers of this period assumed that the virtues were objective, accessible to **reason,** and not determined by anything (except perhaps God). Some modern philosophers, notably **Hume**, have rejected this tradition, holding that virtues are determined by human society. There is much philosophical discussion over the place of the virtues in the best theory of **ethics; virtue ethics** is the theory that the virtues are fundamental to our moral thinking. There is also theological discussion over the relationship between virtue and salvation: those from the Protestant tradition have tended to the view that salvation is gratuitous, that is, irrespective of the virtue or vice of the saved, whereas the Roman-Catholic tradition has typically wanted to allow for virtue's accruing some merit to make one less unworthy of salvation in the eyes of God, while always acknowledging that the source of this human virtue is God's **grace**.

See **ethics, virtue**

Further reading: Dent 1984; Foot 1978; Geach 1977a

voluntarism, theological see **ethics, divine command theory of**

warrant see **justification, epistemic**

ways, five see **five ways**

Westphal, Merold (1940–): A Christian philosopher at Fordham University, Merold Westphal has been primarily interested in **continental philosophy** since **Immanuel Kant**, and has become an interpreter of this tradition to practitioners of **analytical philosophy**. While Christian philosophers are often critical of **postmodernism**, Westphal has argued that it has helpfully illuminated human finitude and the effects of original **sin**, which were inadequately appreciated by the **Enlightenment** in its quest to identify transcultural, ahistorical norms of human **nature** and **reason**. Westphal develops a critique of the remaining vestiges of this project by drawing upon many of religion's greatest critics, including **Freud** and Marx. In his dialogue with postmodernists, Westphal sees in **Derrida**'s 'death of the author' a commendable challenge to the Enlightenment conception of the omnipotent and autonomous author. Westphal's critics contend, however, that he has failed to distinguish adequately between those aspects of postmodernism that can be affirmed and those that should be rejected.

See **ontotheology; philosophy, continental; postmodernism**

Further reading: Westphal 1993, 1996, 2001 and 2004

Whitehead, Alfred North (1861–1947): An English mathematician and philosopher, Whitehead began his career in mathematics and, with **Bertrand Russell**, published the monumental *Principia Mathematica* (1910–13), an attempt to reduce all of mathematics to a logical basis. In the final stage of his career at Harvard (1924–47) Whitehead developed his distinctive influential metaphysical system known as **process philosophy** which brought together his religious upbringing (he was the son of an Anglican priest) with a **metaphysics** that he believed fitted the emerging Einsteinian conception of the universe. For Whitehead, the basic metaphysical unit was not **substance**, but rather an 'actual occasion', that is, a basic unit of *process*. Whitehead's God exists in eternal dynamism with the universe. These views were most fully developed in his Gifford Lectures, *Process and Reality* (1929). Whitehead's metaphysics has had relatively little influence among philosophers, but this is perhaps not surprising since it is difficult to borrow a concept from such a complete system. It has, however, been quite influential among Christian theologians.

See **Hartshorne, Charles; metaphysics; philosophy, process; theology, process**

Further reading: Johnson 1983; Schilpp 1951; Whitehead 1929; Wilmot 1979

will, freedom of see **freedom**

William of Ockham see **Ockham/Occam, William of**

Wittgenstein, Ludwig Josef Johann (1889–1951): Among the most influential and revered of twentieth-century philosophers, Wittgenstein was deeply sceptical of traditional philosophy. Wittgenstein came from Austria in 1911 to study with **Bertrand Russell**, and later completed a draft of his first great work, *Tractatus Logico-philosophicus* (1921), while on the battlefield in the First World War. This bold work, written in a terse and enigmatic style, develops a logical analysis of language that seeks to reduce every meaningful utterance to an atomic sentence, which is formally isomorphic with a possible state of affairs. Those sentences that fail this test (including those of **ethics**, theology, philosophy and indeed the *Tractatus* itself) are in fact meaningless. Hence Wittgenstein concluded: 'Whereof one cannot speak thereof one must be silent.' After the publication of this book, Wittgenstein stayed away from formal philosophy for a number of years until in 1928 he returned to Cambridge, where he remained for the rest of his career. Wittgenstein's second great work, the posthumously published *Philosophical Investigations* (1953), differs markedly from the *Tractatus*. Wittgenstein came to eschew **metaphysics** and view philosophy as a therapeutic analysis of forms of life. To this end he concluded that meaning is found in the *use* of language, and through the analysis of use he sought to dissolve many classical philosophical dilemmas, including the mind/body problem and the problem of other minds. Wittgenstein's influence has been substantial. While the *Tractatus* became a seminal text for **logical positivism** Wittgenstein retained a mystical openness to what transcends language. His greater impact, however, has been through *Philosophical Investigations*, a work whose enigmatic comments on **language games**, private language and forms of life have left little of contemporary philosophy and theology untouched.

See **language game**; **Malcolm, Norman**; **philosophy, analytical**; **positivism, logical**; **Russell, Bertrand**

Further reading: Baker and Hacker 1980–96; Fogelin 1987; Glock 1996; Kenny 1994; Kerr 2002; Kripke 1982; Malcolm 1962; Wittgenstein 1958, 1960–, 1975 and 1979

Wolterstorff, Nicholas Paul (1932–): A versatile Christian philosopher from a Calvinist tradition, Wolterstorff taught at Calvin College for thirty years before moving to Yale Divinity School in 1989. Wolterstorff has published in a number of areas including **metaphysics** (*On Universals*, 1970), aesthetics (*Art in Action*, 1980), political philosophy (*Until Justice and Peace Embrace*, 1983) and **hermeneutics** (*Divine Discourse*, 1995). Arguably his greatest influence has been in **Reformed epistemology** and his important historical work supporting it. Wolterstorff developed his epistemological views in *Reason within the Bounds of Religion* (1976), in which he argued that Christian **beliefs** can rationally serve as control beliefs in the formation and evaluation of theories across disciplines. Wolterstorff's historical work on **John Locke** has highlighted that philosopher's **epistemology** of entitlement, which shaped the development of classical **foundationalism**. Further, part of his Gifford Lectures (1995) was developed into *Thomas Reid and the Story of Epistemology* (2001), an important study of the founder of Scottish 'common-sense' philosophy.

See **epistemology, Reformed**; **foundationalism**; **Plantinga, Alvin**; **Reid, Thomas**

Further reading: Sloane 2003; Wolterstorff 1976, 1995, 1996 and 2001

worldview: Derived from the German term Weltanshauung, the word 'worldview' refers to the set of basic **beliefs**

that shape the way one views the world. Given their fundamental status, these beliefs are typically argued *from* rather than argued *for*, though it would seem that one worldview can be abandoned for another, a process one might call 'conversion'. The concept of worldview shares a family resemblance with other widely used terms current in philosophy including 'conceptual scheme' and 'paradigm'. Like those other terms, it has occasionally raised the concern of relativism. Within a realist context, however, the concept has become influential within Christian thought, particularly through the influence of Dutch Reformed theologian **Abraham Kuyper.**

See **Dooyeweerd, Herman; Kuyper, Abraham**

Further reading: Dewitt 2004; Kuyper 1932; Naugle 2002

Bibliography

Abelard, Peter (1849–59), *Opera*, ed. V. Cousin and C. Jourdain, Paris: Durand.

Abelard, Peter (1855), *Opera Omnia*, ed. J.-P. Migne, Paris: Garnier.

Abelard, Peter (1969–87), *Opera Theologica*, i–iii, ed. E. Buytaert and C. Mews, *Corpus Christianorum Continuatio Mediaevalis* 11–13, Turnholti: Brepols.

Abelard, Peter (1977), *Sic et non*, ed. B. Boyer and R. McKeon, Chicago: University of Chicago Press.

Adams, Marilyn McCord (1987), *William Ockham*, 2 vols, Notre Dame, IN: University of Notre Dame Press.

Adams, Marilyn McCord (1999), *Horrendous Evils and the Goodness of God*, Ithaca, NY: Cornell University Press.

Adams, Robert Merrihew (1987), *The Virtue of Faith and Other Essays in Philosophical Theology*, New York: Oxford University Press.

Adams, Robert Merrihew (1994), *Leibniz: Determinist, Theist, Idealist*, Oxford: Oxford University Press.

Albert the Great (1951–), *Opera Omnia*, ed. Bernhard Geyer, Wilhelm Kübel, Mechthild Dryer and Ludger Honnefelder, Aschendorff: Monasterii Westfalorum.

Algra, Keimpe, J. Barnes, J. Mansfeld and M. Schofield (1999), eds, *The Cambridge History of Hellenistic Philosophy*, Cambridge: Cambridge University Press.

Allard, Jean-Louis, and Pierre Germain (1994), *Répertoire bibliographique sur la vie et l'œuvre de Jacques et Raissa Maritain*, Ottawa: Jean-Louis Allard, Université d'Ottawa.

Alston, William P. (1989a), *Divine Nature and Human Language*, Ithaca, NY: Cornell University Press.

Alston, William P. (1989b), *Epistemic Justification: Essays in the Theory of Knowledge*, Ithaca, NY: Cornell University Press.

Alston, William P. (1993), *Perceiving God: The Epistemology of Religious Experience*, Ithaca, NY: Cornell University Press.

Alston, William P. (1996), *A Realist Conception of Truth*, Ithaca, NY: Cornell University Press.

Alston, William P. (2001), *A Sensible Metaphysical Realism*, Aquinas Lecture 2001, Milwaukee: Marquette University Press.

Alston, William P. (2002), ed., *Realism and Antirealism*, Ithaca, NY: Cornell University Press.

Anscombe, G. E. M. (1957), *Intention*, Ithaca, NY: Cornell University Press.

Anscombe, G. E. M. (1981a), *The Collected Philosophical Papers of GEM Anscombe: Vol. 1: From Parmenides to Wittgenstein*, Oxford: Basil Blackwell.

Anscombe, G. E. M. (1981b), *The Collected Philosophical Papers of GEM Anscombe: Vol. 2: Metaphysics and the Philosophy of Mind*, Oxford: Basil Blackwell.

Anscombe, G. E. M. (1981c), *The Collected Philosophical Papers of GEM Anscombe: Vol. 3: Ethics, Religion and Politics*, Oxford: Basil Blackwell.

Anselm of Canterbury (1938–61), *Opera Omnia*, ed. F. S. Schmitt, Edinburgh: Thomas Nelson.

Anselm of Canterbury (1998), *The Major Works*, ed. B. Davies and G. R. Evans, Oxford: Oxford University Press.

Anselm of Canterbury (2000), *Complete Philosophical and Theological Treatises of Anselm of Canterbury*, tr. Jasper Hopkins and Herbert Richardson, Minneapolis: Banning Press.

Aquinas, Thomas (1882–), *Opera Omnia*, Rome: San Tommaso.

Aquinas, Thomas (1905), *Of God and His Creatures: An Annotated Translation (with Some Abridgement) of the Summa Contra Gentiles of St Thomas Aquinas*, tr. Joseph Rickaby, London: G. Bell.

Aquinas, Thomas (1920–5), *Summa Theologica*, tr. the Fathers of the English Dominican Province, London: Burns Oates and Washbourne.

Aquinas, Thomas (1955–7), *On the Truth of the Catholic Faith*, tr. Anton C. Pegis, James F. Anderson, Vernon J. Bourke and Charles J. O'Neill, Garden City, NY: Doubleday.

Aquinas, Thomas (1963–80), *Summa Theologiae*, ed. Thomas Gilby, London: Eyre and Spottiswoode.

Aquinas, Thomas (1993a), *Light of Faith: Compendium of Theology*, tr. Cyril Vollert, 2nd edn, Manchester, NH: Sophia Institute Press.

Aquinas, Thomas (1993b), *Selected Philosophical Writings*, ed. and tr. Timothy McDermott, Oxford: Oxford University Press.

Archer, Margaret Scotford, Andrew Collier and Douglas V. Porpora (2004), *Transcendence: Critical Realism and God*, London: Routledge.

Aristotle (1928), *Aristotle's Metaphysics*, rev. W. D. Ross, 2nd edn, Oxford: Clarendon Press.

Armstrong, Arthur Hilary (1967), ed., *The Cambridge History of Later Greek and Early Medieval Philosophy*, Cambridge: Cambridge University Press.

Armstrong, Arthur Hilary, and Robert Austin Markus (1960), *Christian Faith and Greek Philosophy*, London: Darton, Longman & Todd.

Arnim, Hans von (1903–24), ed., *Stoicorum Veterum Fragmenta*, Leipzig: Teubner.

Atherton, Margaret (1999), ed., *The Empiricists: Critical Essays on Locke, Berkeley, and Hume*, Oxford: Rowman & Littlefield.

Audi, Robert (2003), *Epistemology: A Contemporary Introduction to the Theory of Knowledge*, Routledge Contemporary Introductions to Philosophy, 2nd edn, London: Routledge.

Augustine, Aurelius (1877–1902), *Opera Omnia*, ed. J.-P. Migne, Paris: Garnier.

Augustine, Aurelius (1965–), *Opera Omnia*, Rome: Città Nuova.

Augustine, Aurelius (1990–), *The Works of St Augustine: A Translation for the 21st Century*, ed. John Rotelle and Boniface Ramsey, Brooklyn: New City.

Augustine, Aurelius (1991), *Confessions*, tr. Henry Chadwick, World's Classics, Oxford: Oxford University Press.

Aune, Bruce (1970), *Rationalism, Empiricism and Pragmatism: An Introduction*, New York: Random House.

Ayer, Alfred J. (1978), *Part of My Life*, Oxford: Oxford University Press.

Ayer, Alfred J. (1984), *More of My Life*, London: Collins.

Ayer, Alfred J. (2001), *Language, Truth and Logic*, rev. edn, Harmondsworth: Penguin.

Ayer, Alfred J. (2004), *Writings in Philosophy*, Basingstoke: Palgrave Macmillan.

Ayers, Michael (1993), *Locke*, Arguments of the Philosophers Series, London: Routledge.

Bacon, John (1995), *Universals and Property Instances: The Alphabet of Being*, Aristotelian Society Series Vol. 15, Oxford: Blackwell.

Baelz, Peter R. (1968), *Prayer and Providence: A Background Study*, London: SCM Press.

Bahnsen, Greg L. (1998), *Van Til's Apologetic: Readings and Analysis*, Phillipsburg, NJ: Presbyterian & Reformed.

Baillie, John (1962), *The Sense of the Presence of God*, Gifford Lectures 1961–2, London: Oxford University Press.

Baker, Gordon P., and Peter Michael Stephan Hacker (1980–96), *An Analytical Commentary on the Philosophical Investigations*, 4 vols, Oxford: Blackwell.

Baker, Gordon P., and Peter Michael Stephan Hacker (1984), *Scepticism, Rules and Language*, Oxford: Blackwell.

Baker, Lynne Rudder (2000), *Persons and Bodies: A Constitution View*, Cambridge: Cambridge University Press.

Barbour, Ian G. (1998), *Religion and Science: Historical and Contemporary Issues*, rev. and expanded edn, London: SCM Press.

Barnard, Leslie W. (1967), *Justin Martyr: His Life and Thought*, London: Cambridge University Press.

Barnes, Jonathan (1972), *The Ontological Argument*, London: Macmillan.

Barnes, Timothy D. (1985), *Tertullian: A Historical and Literary Study*, 2nd edn, Oxford: Clarendon Press.

Baron, Marcia W., Philip Pettit and Michael Slote (1997), *Three Methods of Ethics*, Oxford: Blackwell.

Barth, Karl (1936), *Credo*, tr. J. Strathearn McNab, London: Hodder & Stoughton.

Barth, Karl (1956–77), *Church Dogmatics*, tr. G. W. Bromiley, G. T. Thomson, Harold Knight, T. H. L. Parker, W. B. Johnson, James L. M. Haire, Oscar Bussey, A. Hart Edwards, J. W. Edwards, ed. G. W. Bromiley and T. F. Torrance, Edinburgh: T. & T. Clark.

Barth, Karl (1960), *Anselm: Fides quaerens intellectum. Anselm's Proof of the Existence of God in the Context of His Theological Scheme*, tr. I. W. Robertson, The Library of Philosophy and Theology, London: SCM Press.

Barth, Karl (1961), *Church Dogmatics: A Selection*, tr. and ed. Geoffrey W. Bromiley, Edinburgh: T. & T. Clark.

Barth, Karl (1965), *Evangelical Theology: An introduction*, tr. Grover Foley, London: Collins.

Barth, Karl (1968), *Epistle to the Romans*, tr. E. C. Hoskyns, New York: Oxford University Press.

Barth, Karl (1971–), *Gesamtausgabe*, Zurich: Theologischer Verlag.

Barth, Karl (2001), *Dogmatics in Outline*, London: SCM Press.

Basinger, David (2002), *Religious Diversity: A Philosophical Assessment*, Burlington, VT: Ashgate Publishing Company.

Basinger, David, and Randall Basinger (1986), *Predestination & Free Will: Four Views of Divine Sovereignty & Human Freedom*, Downers Grove, IL: Intervarsity Press.

Battenhouse, Roy W. (1955), ed., *A Companion to the Study of St Augustine*, New York: Oxford University Press.

Beaty, Michael D. (1990), ed., *Christian Theism and the Problems of Philosophy*, Library of Religious Philosophy 5, Notre Dame, IN: University of Notre Dame Press.

Behe, Michael (1996), *Darwin's Black Box: The Biochemical Challenge to Evolution*, London: The Free Press.

Beilby, James (2002), ed., *Naturalism Defeated? Essays on Plantinga's Evolutionary Argument against Naturalism*, Ithaca, NY: Cornell University Press.

Beiser, Frederick (1993), ed., *The Cambridge Companion to Hegel*, Cambridge: Cambridge University Press.

Beiser, Frederick (2005), *Hegel*, Routledge Philosophers, London: Routledge.

Beld, Ton van den (2000), ed., *Moral Responsibility and Ontology*, Library of Ethics and Applied Philosophy 7, London: Kluwer Academic.

Bennett, Jonathan (1967), *Rationality: An Essay towards an Analysis*, Studies in Philosophical Psychology, London: Routledge & Kegan Paul.

Berkeley, George (1948–57), *The Works of George Berkeley*, ed. A. A. Luce and T. E. Jessop, Edinburgh: Thomas Nelson.

Berkeley, George (1975), *Philosophical Works*, ed. M. R. Ayers, London: Dent & Sons.

Berkouwer, Gerrit Cornelis (1955), *General Revelation*, Studies in Dogmatics, Grand Rapids, IN: Eerdmans.

Berman, David (1987), *A History of Atheism in Britain: From Hobbes to Russell*, London: Croom Helm.

Berthold, Fred Jr (2004), *God, Evil, and Human Learning: A Critique and Revision of the Free Will Defense in Theodicy*, Albany, NY: State University of New York Press.

Bertocci, Peter (1938), *The Empirical Argument for God in Late British Thought: On the Theism of James Martineau, A. S. Pringle-Pattison, James Ward, W. R. Sorley, and F. R. Tennant*, Cambridge, MA: Harvard University Press.

Biletzki, Anat, and Anat Matar (1998), eds, *The Story of Analytic Philosophy: Plots and Heroes*, Routledge Studies in Twentieth-Century Philosophy, London: Routledge.

Black, Max (1962), *Models and Metaphors*, Ithaca, NY: Cornell University Press.

Blackham, Harold John (1997), *Six Existentialist Thinkers*, London: Routledge.

Blackwell, Kenneth, and Harry Ruja (1994), *A Bibliography of Bertrand Russell*, 3 vols, London: Routledge.

Blocher, Henri (2001), *Original Sin: Illuminating the Riddle*, Downers Grove, IL: InterVarsity.

Blondel, Maurice (1984), *Action: Essay on a Critique of Life and a Science of Practice*, tr. Oliva Blanchette, Notre Dame, IN: University of Notre Dame Press.

Blondel, Maurice (1995), *The Letter on Apologetics and History of Dogma*, tr. Alexander Dru and Illtyd Trethowan, Edinburgh: T. & T. Clark.

Bobzien, Susanne (1998), *Determinism and Freedom in Stoic Philosophy*, New York: Oxford University Press.

Boethius, Anicius Manlius Severinus (1882–91), *Opera Omnia*, ed. J.-P. Migne, Paris: Garnier.

Boethius, Anicius Manlius Severinus (1973), *Boethius: Theological Tractates, Consolation of Philosophy*, ed. and tr. H. F. Stewart, E. K. Rand and S. J. Tester, Cambridge, MA: Harvard University Press.

Boethius, Anicius Manlius Severinus (1990), *Consolatio Philosophiae*, ed. James J. O'Donnell, 2nd edn, Bryn Mawr, PA: Bryn Mawr College.

Boethius, Anicius Manlius Severinus (2000), *De consolatione philosophiae, Opuscula theologica*, ed. C. Moreschini, Leipzig: K. G. Saur (Bibliotheca Teubneriana).

Bonaventure (1882–1902), *Opera Omnia*, tr. F. a Fanna and I. Jeiler, Quarrachi: Collegium S. Bonaventurae.

Bonaventure (2002), *Itinerarium mentis in Deum*, ed. and tr. Philotheus Boehner and Zachary Hayes, St Bonaventure, NY: The Franciscan Institute.

BonJour, Laurence (1998), *In Defense of Pure Reason*, Cambridge: Cambridge University Press.

BonJour, Laurence (2002), *Epistemology: Classic Problems and Contemporary Responses*, Elements of Philosophy, Oxford: Rowman & Littlefield.

Bonner, Gerald (1986), *St Augustine of Hippo: Life and Controversies*, Norwich: Canterbury Press.

Bouwsma, O. K. (1965), *Philosophical Essays*, Lincoln, NE: University of Nebraska Press.

Bouwsma, O. K. (1984), *Without Proof or Evidence: Essays of O. K. Bouwsma*, ed. J. L. Craft and Ronald E. Hustwit, Lincoln, NE: University of Nebraska Press.

Braine, David (1987), *The Reality of Time and the Existence of God: The Project of Proving God's Existence*, Oxford: Clarendon Press.

Brezik, Victor B. (1981), ed., *One Hundred Years of Thomism: Aeterni Patris and Afterwards: A Symposium,* Houston, TX: Center for Thomistic Studies, University of St Thomas.

Brink, Gijsbert van den (1993), *Almighty God: A Study of the Doctrine of Divine Omnipotence*, Studies in Philosophical Theology 7, Kampen: Kok Pharos.

Brom, Luco J. van den (1993), *Divine Presence in the World: A Critical Analysis of the Notion of Divine Omnipresence*, Studies in Philosophical Theology 5, Kampen: Kok Pharos.

Bromiley, Geoffrey W. (1979), *An Introduction to the Theology of Karl Barth*, Edinburgh: T. & T. Clark.

Brower, Jeff, and Kevin Guilfoy (2004), eds, *The Cambridge Companion to Abelard*, New York: Cambridge University Press.

Brown, Peter (1969), *Augustine of Hippo: A Biography*, 2nd edn, Berkeley: University of California Press.

Brown, Warren S., Nancey Murphy and H. Newton Malony (1998), eds, *Whatever Happened to the Soul?: Scientific and Theological Portraits of Human Nature*, Theology and the Sciences, Minneapolis: Fortress Press.

Brümmer, Vincent (2005), *Atonement, Christology, and the Trinity: Making Sense of Christian Doctrine*, Aldershot: Ashgate.

Buber, Martin (1962–4), *Werke*, Munich: Kösel-Verlag.

Buber, Martin (1970), *I and Thou*, tr. Walter Kaufmann, Edinburgh: T. & T. Clark.

Buber, Martin (2001–), *Martin Buber-Werkausgabe*, ed. Paul Mendes-Flohr and Peter Schäfer, Gütersloher: Gütersloher Verlagshaus.

Bultmann, Rudolf (1984), *New Testament and Mythology and Other Basic Writings*, ed. and tr. Schubert M. Ogden, Philadelphia: Fortress Press.

Butler, Joseph (1736), *Analogy of Religion, Natural and Revealed, to the Constitution and Nature*, London: Knapton.

Butler, Joseph (1900), *Works*, ed. J. H. Bernard, London: Macmillan.

Byrne, Peter (1989), *Natural Religion and the Nature of Religion: The Legacy of Deism*, Routledge Religious Studies Series, London: Routledge.

Calvin, John (1863–1900), *Opera Quae Supersunt Omnia*, ed. Wilhelm Baum, Edward Cunitz and Edward Reuss, Brunswick: Schwetschke and Sons.

Calvin, John (1960), *Institutes of the Christian Religion*, tr. Ford Lewis Battles, ed. John T. McNeill, Philadelphia: Westminster Press.

Calvin, John (1992–), *Ioannis Calvini Opera Omnia*, ed. B. G. Armstrong, Geneva: Droz.

Campbell-Jack, Campbell, Gavin McGrath and C. Stephen Evans (2006), eds, *New Dictionary of Christian Apologetics*, Leicester: Inter-Varsity Press.

Caputo, John D. (1986), *The Mystical Element in Heidegger's Thought*, rev. edn, New York: Fordham University Press.

Caputo, John D. (1997), *The Prayers and Tears of Jacques Derrida: Religion without Religion*, The Indiana Series in the Philosophy of Religion, Bloomington, IN: Indiana University Press.

Caputo, John D., and Michael J. Scanlon (1999), eds, *God, the Gift, and Postmodernism*, Indiana Series in the Philosophy of Religion, Bloomington, IN: Indiana University Press.

Carson, D. A. (2000), *The Difficult Doctrine of the Love of God*, Leicester: Inter-Varsity Press.

Carver, Terrell (1991), ed., *The Cambridge Companion to Marx*, Cambridge: Cambridge University Press.

Cassirer, Ernst (1955), *The Philosophy of the Enlightenment*, tr. Fritz C. A. Koelln and James P. Pettegrove, Humanitas: Toward the Study of Man, Boston: Beacon Press.

Cavell, Stanley (1999), *The Claim of Reason: Wittgenstein, Skepticism, Morality, and Tragedy*, rev. edn, Oxford: Oxford University Press.

Caygill, Howard (1995), *A Kant Dictionary*, Oxford: Blackwell.

Chadwick, Henry (1981), *Boethius*, Oxford: Clarendon Press.

Chadwick, Henry (1986), *Augustine*, Oxford: Oxford University Press.

Chappell, Vere (1994), ed., *The Cambridge Companion to Locke*, Cambridge: Cambridge University Press.

Chisholm, R. (1976), *Person and Object*, La Salle, IL: Open Court.

Christopher, Joe R., and Joan K. Ostling (1975), *C. S. Lewis: An Annotated Checklist of Writings about Him and His Works*, Serif Series 30, Kent, OH: Kent State University Press.

Claesson, G. (1974), *Index Tertullianeus*, 3 vols, Paris: Études Augustiniennes.

Clark, Gordon H. (1957), *Thales to Dewey: A History of Philosophy*, Boston: Houghton Mifflin.

Clark, Gordon H. (1982), *Behaviorism and Christianity*, Hobbs, NM: Trinity Foundation.

Clark, Gordon H. (2004), *Christian Philosophy: The Works of Gordon Haddon Clark, Volume 4*, ed. John W. Robbins, Hobbs, NM: Trinity Foundation.

Clark, Mary T. (1972), ed., *An Aquinas Reader*, London: Hodder and Stoughton.

Clifford, William Kingdon (1901), *Lectures and Essays*, Vol. 2, ed. Leslie Stephen and Frederick Pollock, 2nd edn, London: Macmillan.

Clouser, Roy A. (2005), *The Myth of Religious Neutrality: An Essay on the Hidden Role of Religious Belief in Theories*, 2nd edn, Notre Dame, IN: University of Notre Dame Press.

Cobb, John B., Jr, and David Ray Griffin (1976), *Process Theology*, Philadelphia: Westminster Press.

Cohen-Solal, Annie (1988), *Sartre: A Life*, tr. Anna Cancogn, ed. Norman MacAfee, London: Heinemann.

Cole, Peter, and John Lee (1994), *Religious Language*, Philosophy of Religion 1, Bromsgrove: Abacus Educational Services.

Colish, Marcia L. (1994), *Peter Lombard*, 2 vols, Brill's Studies in Intellectual History 41, Leiden: Brill.

Conway, Michael A. (2000), *The Science of Life: Maurice Blondel's Philosophy of Action and Scientific Method*, Frankfurt am Main: Peter Lang.

Cooper, John W. (1989), *Body, Soul, and Life Everlasting: Biblical Anthropology and the Monism-Dualism Debate*, Grand Rapids, MI: Eerdmans.

Copan, Paul, and William Lane Craig (2004), *Creation out of Nothing: A Biblical, Philosophical and Scientific Exploration*, Grand Rapids, MI: Baker Academic.

Copleston, Frederick C. (1952), *Medieval Philosophy*, Home Study Books 16, London: Methuen.

Corcoran, Kevin (2001), ed., *Soul, Body, and Survival: Essays on the Metaphysics of Human Persons*, Ithaca, NY: Cornell University Press.

Cottingham, John (1984), *Rationalism*, London: Paladin Books.

Cottingham, John (1992), ed., *The Cambridge Companion to Descartes*, Cambridge: Cambridge University Press.

Covell, Charles (1992), *The Defence of Natural Law: A Study of the Ideas of Law and Justice in the Writings of Lon L. Fuller, Michael Oakeshot, F. A. Hayek, Ronald Dworkin and John Finnis*, Basingstoke: Macmillan, now Palgrave Macmillan.

Craig, William Lane (1979), *The Kalam Cosmological Argument*, Library of Philosophy and Religion, London: Macmillan.

Craig, William Lane (1980), *The Cosmological Argument from Plato to Leibniz*, Library of Philosophy and Religion, London: Macmillan.

Craig, William Lane (1987), *The Only Wise God: The Compatibility of Divine Foreknowledge and Human Freedom*, Grand Rapids, MI: Baker Book House.

Craig, William Lane (1991), *Divine Foreknowledge and Human Freedom: The Coherence of Theism: Omniscience*, Brill's Studies in Intellectual History 19, Leiden: Brill.

Craig, William Lane, and J. P. Moreland (2000), eds, *Naturalism: A Critical Analysis*, Routledge Studies in Twentieth-Century Philosophy, London: Routledge.

Craig, William Lane, and Quentin Smith (1995), *Theism, Atheism, and Big Bang Cosmology*, Oxford: Clarendon Press.

Crampton, W. Gary (1999), *The Scripturalism of Gordon H. Clark*, Hobbs, NM: Trinity Foundation.

Creel, Richard (1985), *Divine Impassibility: An Essay in Philosophical Theology*, Cambridge: Cambridge University Press.

Crisp, Roger, and Michael Slote (1997), *Virtue Ethics*, New York: Oxford University Press.

Crombie, Alexander (2001), *Natural Theology, or, Essays on the Existence of Deity and of Providence, on the Immateriality of the Soul and a Future State*, Bristol: Thoemmes.

Cross, Richard (1999), *Duns Scotus*, Great Medieval Thinkers, Oxford: Oxford University Press.

Cross, Richard (2002), *The Metaphysics of the Incarnation: Thomas Aquinas to Duns Scotus*, Oxford: Oxford University Press.

Cross, Richard (2004), *Duns Scotus on God*, Aldershot: Ashgate.

Crowther, Paul (2003), *Philosophy after Postmodernism: Civilized Values and the Scope of Knowledge*, Routledge Studies in Twentieth-Century Philosophy 16, London: Routledge.

Darwall, Stephen L. (2002a), ed., *Consequentialism*, Blackwell Readings in Philosophy 7, Oxford: Blackwell.

Darwall, Stephen L. (2002b), ed., *Deontology*, Blackwell Readings in Philosophy 9, Oxford: Blackwell.

Darwall, Stephen L. (2002c), ed., *Virtue Ethics*, Blackwell Readings in Philosophy 10, Oxford: Blackwell.

Davies, Brian (1992), *The Thought of Thomas Aquinas*, Oxford: Oxford University Press.

Davies, Brian (1998), *Philosophy of Religion: A Guide to the Subject*, London: Cassell.

Davies, Brian, and Brian Leftow (2004), eds, *The Cambridge Companion to Anselm*, Cambridge: Cambridge University Press.

Davis, Richard (2001), *The Metaphysics of Theism and Modality*, American University Studies, Series V, Philosophy Vol. 189, New York: Peter Lang.

Davis, Stephen (1993), *Risen Indeed*, London: SPCK.

Davis, Stephen (2004), ed., *The Incarnation: An Interdisciplinary Symposium on the Incarnation of the Son of God*, Oxford: Oxford University Press.

Davis, Stephen, Daniel Kendall and Gerald O'Collins (1999), eds, *The Trinity: An Interdisciplinary Symposium on the Trinity*, Oxford: Oxford University Press.

Dekker, Eef (2000), *Middle Knowledge*, Studies in Philosophical Theology 20, Leuven: Peeters.

Dembski, William A. (1998), *The Design Inference: Eliminating Chance through Small Probabilities*, Cambridge Studies in Probability, Induction, and Decision Theory, Cambridge: Cambridge University Press.

Dembski, William A. (1999), *Intelligent Design: The Bridge between Science & Theology*, Downers Grove, IL: InterVarsity Press.

Dennett, Daniel C. (1996), *Darwin's Dangerous Idea: Evolution and the Meanings of Life*, Penguin Science, London: Penguin.

Dent, N. J. H. (1984), *The Moral Psychology of the Virtues*, Cambridge: Cambridge University Press.

DePaul, Michael R (2001), ed., *Resurrecting Old-Fashioned Foundationalism*, Studies in Epistemology and Cognitive Theory, Oxford: Rowman & Littlefield.

Derrida, Jacques (1998), *Of Grammatology*, tr. Gayatri Chakravorty Spivak, Baltimore, MD: Johns Hopkins University Press.

Derrida, Jacques (2001), *Acts of Religion*, ed. Gil Anidjar, London: Routledge.

Descartes, René (1969–75), *Œuvres*, ed. Charles Adam and Paul Tannery, 11 vols, Paris: Vrin.

Descartes, René (1979), *Meditations on First Philosophy*, tr. Donald A. Cress, Indianapolis: Hackett.

Descartes, René (1984–91), *The Philosophical Writings of Descartes*, tr. John Cottingham, Robert Stoothoff and Dugald Murdoch, 3 vols, Cambridge: Cambridge University Press.

Desmond, William (2003), *Hegel's God: A Counterfeit Double?*, Aldershot: Ashgate.

Dewitt, Richard (2004), *Worldviews: An Introduction to the History and Philosophy of Science*, Oxford: Blackwell.

Diamond, Malcolm L., and Thomas V. Litzenburg, Jr (1975), *The Logic of God*, Indianapolis, IN: Bobbs-Merrill.

Dillistone, F. W. (1966), ed., *Myth and Symbol*, Theological Collections (SPCK) 7, London: SPCK.

Dooyeweerd, Herman (1975), *A New Critique of Theoretical Thought*, tr. David H. Freeman and William S. Young, Lampeter: Edwin Mellen Press.

Dorner, Isaak August (1994), *Divine Immutability: A Critical Reconsideration*, tr. Robert R. Williams and Claude Welch, Fortress Texts in Modern Theology, Minneapolis: Fortress Press.

Dowey, Edward A. Jr (1994), *The Knowledge of God in Calvin's Theology*, 3rd edn, Grand Rapids, MI: Eerdmans.

Dreyfus, Hubert L. (1990), *Being-in-the-world: A Commentary on Heidegger's Being and Time, Division I*, Cambridge, MA: MIT Press.

Ducasse, Curt John (1924), *Causation and the Types of Necessity*, University of Washington Publications in the Social Sciences Vol. 1, no. 2, Seattle: University of Washington Press.

Duff, R. A. (1986), *Trials and Punishments*, Cambridge: Cambridge University Press.

Dufour, Richard (2002), *Plotinus: A Bibliography, 1950–2000*, Leiden: Brill.

Dummett, Michael A. E. (1993), *Origins of Analytical Philosophy*, London: Duckworth.

Dunn, Geoffrey D. (2004), *Tertullian*, The Early Church Fathers, London: Routledge.

Duns Scotus, John (1950–), *Opera Omnia*, ed. Charles Balic, Luca Modric and Barnabas Hechich, Vatican City: Typis Polyglottis Vaticanis.

Duns Scotus, John (1987), *Philosophical Writings*, tr. Allan B. Wolter, Indianapolis: Hackett Publishing Company.

Duns Scotus, John (1997–), *Opera Philosophica*, ed. Romauld Green and Timothy B. Noone, St Bonaventure, NY: The Franciscan Institute.

Duriez, Colin (2002), *The C. S. Lewis Encyclopedia: A Comprehensive Guide to His Life, Thought and Writings*, London: Azure.

Earman, John (1986), *A Primer on Determinism*, Dordrecht: Reidel.

Easton, Patricia, T. M. Lennon and G. Sebba (1992), *Bibliographia Malebranchiana: A Critical Guide to the Malebranche Literature into 1989*, Edwardsville: Southern Illinois Press.

Edwards, James C. (1990), *The Authority of Language: Heidegger, Wittgenstein, and the Threat of Philosophical Nihilism*, Tampa: University of South Florida Press.

Edwards, Jonathan (1970), *The Great Christian Doctrine of Original Sin Defended*, ed. Clyde A. Holbrook, New Haven, CT: Yale University Press.

Edwards, Jonathan (1971), *Treatise on Grace, and Other Posthumously Published Writings*, ed. Paul Helm, Cambridge: James Clarke.

Edwards, Jonathan (1974), *The Works of Jonathan Edwards*, Edinburgh: Banner of Truth Trust.

Edwards, Paul (1992), ed., *Immortality*, Philosophical Topics, Toronto: Macmillan.

Edwards, Paul (2004), *Heidegger's Confusions*, Amherst, NY: Prometheus Books.

Evans, C. Stephen (1984), *Philosophy of Religion: Thinking About Faith*, Contours of Christian Philosophy, Leicester: Inter-Varsity Press.

Evans, C. Stephen (1998), *Faith beyond Reason: A Kierkegaardian Account*, Grand Rapids, MI: Eerdmans.

Ewing, Alfred Cyril (1961), *Idealism: A Critical Survey*, 3rd edn, London: Methuen.

Fackenheim, Emil Ludwig (1968), *The Religious Dimension in Hegel's Thought*, Bloomington, IN: Indiana University Press.

Faith and Philosophy (1984–), Journal of the Society of Christian Philosophers.

Fakhry, Majid (1958), *Islamic Occasionalism and Its Critique by Averroës and Aquinas*, London: Allen & Unwin.

Farber, Marvin (1959), *Naturalism and Subjectivism*, American Lecture Series No. 367, Springfield, IL: Charles C. Thomas.

Farley, Edward (1962), *The Transcendence of God: A Study in Contemporary Philosophical Theology*, London: Epworth Press.

Farrer, Austin (1966), *Love Almighty and Ills Unlimited: An Essay on Providence and Evil*, Nathaniel Taylor Lectures for 1961, London: Collins.

Feuerbach, Ludwig (1967–), *Gesammelte Werke*, ed. Werner Schuffenhauer, Berlin: Akademie-Verlag.

Feuerbach, Ludwig (1997), *The Essence of Christianity*, ed. Robert M. Baird and Stuart E. Rosenbaum, tr. George Eliot, Amherst, NY: Prometheus.

Fiddes, Paul (1989), *Past Event and Present Salvation: The Christian Idea of Atonement*, Louisville, KY: Westminster John Knox Press.

Fine, Gail (1999a), ed., *Plato 1: Metaphysics and Epistemology*, Oxford: Oxford University Press.

Fine, Gail (1999b), ed., *Plato 2: Ethics, Politics, Religion, and the Soul*, Oxford: Oxford University Press.

Finnis, John M. (1983), *Fundamentals of Ethics*, Washington DC: Georgetown University Press.

Finnis, John M. (1980), *Natural Law and Natural Rights*, Clarendon Law Series, Oxford: Clarendon Press.

Fischer, John Martin (1986), ed., *Moral Responsibility*, London: Cornell University Press.

Fischer, John Martin (1989), ed., *God, Foreknowledge, and Freedom*, Stanford Series in Philosophy, Stanford, CA: Stanford University Press.

Fischer, John Martin (2005), ed., *Free Will*, 4 vols, London: Routledge.

Fitzgerald, Allan D. (1999), ed., *Augustine through the Ages: An Encyclopedia*, Grand Rapids, MI: Eerdmans.

Flew, Antony (1964), ed., *Body, Mind, and Death: Readings Selected, Edited, and Furnished with an Introductory Essay by Antony Flew*, Problems of Philosophy Series, New York: Macmillan.

Flew, Antony (1966), *God and Philosophy*, London: Hutchinson.

Flew, Antony (1984), *God, Freedom, and Immortality: A Critical Analysis*, Buffalo, NY: Prometheus Books.

Flew, Antony (1987), *The Logic of Mortality*, Oxford: Basil Blackwell.

Flew, Antony (1993), *Atheistic Humanism*, The Prometheus Lectures, Buffalo, NY: Prometheus Books.

Flew, Antony (1998), *How to Think Straight: An Introduction to Critical Reasoning*, Amherst, NY: Prometheus Books.

Flew, Antony, and Gary Habermas (2004), 'My Pilgrimage from Atheism to Theism', *Philosophia Christi*, 6: 2, pp. 197–211.

Flew, Antony, and Alasdair MacIntyre (1955), eds, *New Essays in Philosophical Theology*, The Library of Philosophy and Theology, London: SCM Press.

Flint, Thomas P. (1998), *Divine Providence: The Molinist Account*, Ithaca, NY: Cornell University Press.

Fogelin, Robert J. (1987), *Wittgenstein*, London: New York.

Foot, Philippa (1978), *Virtues and Vices*, Oxford: Blackwell.

Forbes, Graeme (1985), *The Metaphysics of Modality*, Clarendon Library of Logic and Philosophy, Oxford: Clarendon Press.

Foster, John (1985), *Ayer*, London: Routledge & Kegan Paul.

Frame, John M. (1995), *Cornelius Van Til: An Analysis of His Thought*, Phillipsburg, NJ: Presbyterian & Reformed.

French, Peter, Theodore E. Uehling, Jr, and Howard K. Wettstein (1988), eds, *Realism and Antirealism*, Midwest Studies in Philosophy 12, Minneapolis: University of Minnesota Press.

Freud, Sigmund (1928), *The Future of an Illusion*, tr. W. D. Robson-Scott, International Psycho-analytical Library 15, London: Hogarth Press.

Freud, Sigmund (1953–74), *The Standard Edition of the Complete Psychological Works of Sigmund Freud*, tr. and ed. J. Strachey et al., 24 vols, London: Hogarth Press.

Fried, Charles (1978), *Right and Wrong*, Cambridge, MA: Harvard University Press.

Gadamer, Hans-Georg (2003), *Truth and Method*, 2nd rev. edn, tr. and rev. Joel Weinsheimer and Donald G. Marshall, New York: Continuum.

Gamble, Richard C. (1992), *Articles on Calvin and Calvinism*, New York: Garland Publishing Co.

Ganssle, Gregory (2001), ed., *God & Time: Four Views*, Nottingham: IVP.

Garrett, Don, and Edward Barbanell (1997), eds, *Encyclopedia of Empiricism*, London: Fitzroy Dearborn.

Garrigou-Lagrange, Réginald (1939), *Predestination*, tr. Bede Rose, London: B. Herder.

Gaukroger, Stephen (1995), *Descartes: An Intellectual Biography*, Oxford: Clarendon Press.

Gauthier, David P. (1970), ed., *Morality and Rational Self-interest*, Englewood Cliffs, NJ: Prentice-Hall.

Gay, Peter (1968), *Deism: An Anthology*, New York: Krieger.

Gay, Peter (1973), *The Enlightenment: A Comprehensive Anthology*, New York: Simon and Schuster.

Geach, Peter (1972), *Logic Matters*, Oxford: Blackwell.

Geach, Peter (1977a), *The Virtues*, Cambridge: Cambridge University Press.

Geach, Peter (1977b), *Providence and Evil*, The Stanton Lectures, Cambridge: Cambridge University Press.

Geach, Peter (1980), *Reference and Generality: An Examination of Some Medieval and Modern Theories*, Contemporary Philosophy, 3rd edn, London: Cornell University Press.

Geach, Peter (2000), *God and the Soul*, Key Texts (South Bend, IN), 2nd edn, South Bend, IN: St. Augustine's Press.

Geehan, E. R. (1971), *Jerusalem & Athens: Critical Discussions on the Philosophy and Apologetics of Cornelius Van Til*, Nutley, NJ: Presbyterian and Reformed.

Geisler, Norman L. (1973), *The Christian Ethic of Love*, Grand Rapids: Zondervan.

Geisler, Norman L. (1976), *Christian Apologetics*, Grand Rapids: Baker Book House.

Geisler, Norman L. (1998), *Baker Encyclopedia of Christian Apologetics*, Grand Rapids: Baker Books.

Geivett, R. Douglas, and Gary R. Habermas (1997), eds, *In Defense of Miracles: A Comprehensive Case for God's Action in History*, Downers Grove, IL: InterVarsity Press.

Geivett, R. Douglas, and Brendan Sweetman (1993), eds, *Contemporary Perspectives on Religious Epistemology*, Oxford: Oxford University Press.

Gelwick, Richard (1977), *The Way of Discovery: An Introduction to the Thought of Michael Polanyi*, New York: Oxford University Press.

Gerson, Lloyd Phillip (1994), *Plotinus*, The Arguments of the Philosophers, London: Routledge.

Gettier, Edmund (1963), 'Is Justified True Belief Knowledge?', *Analysis*, 23, pp. 121–3.

Geyer, Bernhard (1919–33), *Peter Abaelards logische Schriften, Beiträge zur Geschichte der Philosophie und Theologie des Mittelalters* (XXI 1–4), Münster: Aschendorff.

Gilson, Etienne (1960), *The Christian Philosophy of Saint Augustine*, New York: Random House.

Gilson, Etienne (1965), *The Philosophy of St Bonaventure*, tr. I. Trethowan and F. Sheed, Paterson, NJ: St Anthony Guild.

Glock, Hans-Johann (1996), *A Wittgenstein Dictionary*, Oxford: Blackwell.

Goodman, Russell B. (1995), *Pragmatism: A Contemporary Reader*, London: Routledge.

Goodman, Russell B. (2005), ed., *Pragmatism*, 4 vols, Critical Concepts in Philosophy, London: Routledge.

Gormally, Luke (1994), *Moral Truth and Moral Tradition: Essays in Honour of Peter Geach and Elizabeth Anscombe*, Blackrock, Co. Dublin: Four Courts Press.

Grant, Robert M. (1996), *Irenaeus of Lyons*, London: Routledge.

Grenet, Paul (1967), *Thomism: An Introduction*, tr. James F. Ross, New York: Harper & Row.

Griffin, David Ray (2001), *Reenchantment without Supernaturalism: A Process Philosophy of Religion*, Ithaca, NY: Cornell University Press.

Gross, Barry R. (1970), *Analytic Philosophy: An Historical Introduction*, Pegasus Traditions in Philosophy, New York: Pegasus.

Guignon, Charles B. (1993), ed., *The Cambridge Companion to Heidegger*, Cambridge Companions, Cambridge: Cambridge University Press.

Guignon, Charles B., and Derk Pereboom (2001), ed., *Existentialism: Basic Writings*, 2nd edn, Cambridge: Hackett Publishing.

Gunton, Colin (1989), *The Actuality of Atonement: A Study of Metaphor, Rationality and the Christian Tradition*, Edinburgh: T. & T. Clark.

Gurr, John Edwin (1959), *The Principle of Sufficient Reason in Some Scholastic Systems 1750–1900*, Milwaukee: Marquette University Press.

Guyer, Paul (1992), ed., *The Cambridge Companion to Kant*, Cambridge: Cambridge University Press.

Hahn, Lewis E. (1992), *The Philosophy of A. J. Ayer*, The Library of Living Philosophers, Vol. XXI, Chicago: Open Court.

Hales, Steven D. (2002), ed., *Analytic Philosophy: Classic Readings*, Belmont, CA: Wadsworth.

Hall, Roland (1978), *Fifty Years of Hume Scholarship: A Bibliographical Guide*, Edinburgh: Edinburgh University Press.

Hampshire, Stuart (1988), *Spinoza*, Pelican Philosophy Series, Harmondsworth: Penguin.

Hampshire, Stuart (2005), *Spinoza and Spinozism*, Oxford: Clarendon Press.

Hanfling, Oswald (1981), *Logical Positivism*, New York: Columbia University Press.

Hannay, Alastair, and Gordon Daniel (1997), eds, *The Cambridge Companion to Kierkegaard*, Cambridge: Cambridge University Press.

Hare, John (1996), *The Moral Gap: Kantian Ethics, Human Limits and God's Assistance*, Oxford Studies in Theological Ethics, Oxford: Clarendon Press.

Hare, John (2001), *God's Call: Moral Realism, God's Commands, and Human Autonomy*, Grand Rapids, MI: Eerdmans.

Harris, Michael (2003), *Divine Command Ethics: Jewish and Christian Perspectives*, Philosophical Ideas in Debate, London: Routledge.

Hart, Hendrik (1984), *Understanding Our World: An Integral Ontology*, Christian Studies Today, London: University Press of America.

Hartshorne, Charles (1965), *Anselm's Discovery: A Re-examination of the Ontological Proof for God's Existence*, Open Court Library of Philosophy, La Salle: IL: Open Court.

Hartshorne, Charles (1976), *Aquinas to Whitehead: Seven Centuries of Metaphysics of Religion*, Aquinas Lecture 1976, Milwaukee: Marquette University Press.

Hartshorne, Charles (1948), *The Divine Relativity: A Social Conception of God*, New Haven, CT: Yale University Press.

Hasker, William (1983), *Metaphysics: Constructing a World View*, Contours of Christian Philosophy, Leicester: Inter-Varsity Press.

Hasker, William (1989), *God, Time, and Knowledge*, Cornell Studies in the Philosophy of Religion, Ithaca, NY: Cornell University Press.

Hasker, William, David Basinger and Eef Dekker (2000), *Middle Knowledge: Theory and Applications*, Contributions to Philosophical Theology 4, Frankfurt am Main: Peter Lang.

Haught, John F. (2000), *God after Darwin: A Theology of Evolution*, Boulder, CO: Westview Press.

Hebblethwaite, Brian, and Edward Henderson (1990), *Divine Action: Studies Inspired by the Philosophical Theology of Austin Farrer*, Edinburgh: T. & T. Clark.

Hegel, Georg Wilhelm Friedrich (1968–), *Gesammelte Werke*, ed. Rheinisch-Westfälischen Akademie der Wissenschaften, Hamburg: Felix Meiner.

Hegel, Georg Wilhelm Friedrich (1977), *Phenomenology of Spirit*, tr. A. V. Miller, Oxford: Clarendon Press.

Hegel, Georg Wilhelm Friedrich (1984), *Lectures on the Philosophy of Religion*, Vol. 1, *Introduction and the Concept of Religion*, ed. Peter C. Hodgson, tr. R. F. Brown, Berkeley: University of California Press.

Heidegger, Martin (1975–), *Gesamtausgabe*, Frankfurt am Main: Vittorio Klostermann.

Heidegger, Martin (1977), *Basic Writings: From Being and Time (1927) to The Task of Thinking (1964)*, ed. David Farrell Krell, New York: Harper & Row.

Heidegger, Martin (2002), *Being and Time: A Translation of Sein und Zeit*, tr. Joan Stambaugh, Chicago: University of Chicago Press.

Helm, Paul (1973), *The Varieties of Belief*, Muirhead Library of Philosophy, London: George Allen & Unwin.

Helm, Paul (1981), ed., *Divine Commands and Morality*, Oxford: Oxford University Press.

Helm, Paul (1982), *Divine Revelation: The Basic Issues*, Foundations for Faith, London: Marshall Morgan & Scott.

Helm, Paul (1986), *The Beginnings: Word and Spirit in Conversion*, Edinburgh: Banner of Truth Trust.

Helm, Paul (1987), ed., *Objective Knowledge: A Christian Perspective*, Leicester: Inter-Varsity Press.

Helm, Paul (1988), *Eternal God: A Study of God Without Time*, Oxford: Clarendon Press.

Helm, Paul (1989), *The Last Things: Death, Judgment, Heaven, Hell*, Edinburgh: Banner of Truth Trust.

Helm, Paul (1993), *The Providence of God*, Leicester: Inter-Varsity Press.

Helm, Paul (1994), *Belief Policies*, Cambridge Studies in Philosophy, Cambridge: Cambridge University Press.

Helm, Paul (1998), *Calvin and the Calvinists*, Edinburgh: Banner of Truth.

Helm, Paul (1999), *Faith and Reason*, Oxford Readers, Oxford: Oxford University Press.

Helm, Paul (2000), *Faith with Reason*, Oxford: Oxford University Press.

Helm, Paul (2004), *John Calvin's Ideas*, Oxford: Oxford University Press.

Helm, Paul, and Oliver D. Crisp (2003), eds, *Jonathan Edwards: Philosophical Theologian*, Aldershot: Ashgate.

Herrick, Jim (2003), *Humanism: An Introduction*, Great Britain: Rationalist Association Press.

Hester, Marcus (1992), *Faith, Reason, and Skepticism: Essays*, 8th James Montgomery Hester Seminar, Philadelphia: Temple University Press.

Hick, John (1957), *Faith and Knowledge: A Modern Introduction to the Problem of Religious Knowledge*, Ithaca, NY: Cornell University Press.

Hick, John (1976), *Death and Eternal Life*, London: Collins.

Hick, John (1977), *Evil and the God of Love*, 2nd edn, London: Macmillan.

Hick, John (1989), *An Interpretation of Religion: Human Responses to the Transcendent*, New Haven, CT: Yale University Press.

Hick, John, and Arthur C. McGill (1967), eds, *The Many-faced Argument: Recent Studies on the Ontological Argument for the Existence of God*, London: Macmillan.

Hill, Charles (2004), ed., *The Glory of the Atonement*, Downers Grove, IL: InterVarsity.

Hill, Daniel J. (2005), *Divinity and Maximal Greatness*, Routledge Studies in the Philosophy of Religion Vol. 2, London: Routledge.

Hintikka, Jaakko (1973), *Time & Necessity: Studies in Aristotle's Theory of Modality*, Oxford: Clarendon Press.

Hobbes, Thomas (1839–45), *English Works of Thomas Hobbes of Malmesbury*, ed. Sir William Molesworth, London: J. Bohn.

Hodges, Wilfrid (2001), *Logic*, 2nd edn, London: Penguin.

Hoekema, David (1986), *Rights and Wrongs: Coercion, Punishment, and the State*, Selinsgrove, PA: Susquehanna University Press.

Hoffman, Joshua, and Gary S. Rosenkrantz (1994), *Substance among Other Categories*, Cambridge: Cambridge University Press.

Hoffman, Joshua, and Gary S. Rosenkrantz (1997), *Substance: Its Nature and Existence*, London: Routledge.

Holmes, Arthur F. (1984), *Ethics: Approaching Moral Decisions*, Contours of Christian Philosophy, Leicester: Inter-Varsity Press.

Honderich, Ted (1984), *Punishment: The Supposed Justifications*, rev. edn, Harmondsworth: Penguin.

Hong, Nathaniel J., Kathryn Hong and Regine Prenzel-Guthrie (2000), *Cumulative Index to Kierkegaard's Writings: The Works of Søren Kierkegaard*, Kierkegaard's Writings 26, Princeton, NJ: Princeton University Press.

Hooker, Michael (1982), ed., *Leibniz: Critical and Interpretive Essays*, Manchester: Manchester University Press.

Hopkins, Jasper (1972), *A Companion to the Study of St Anselm*, Minneapolis: University of Minnesota Press.

Horton, John, and Susan Mendus (1994), eds, *After MacIntyre: Critical Perspectives on the Work of Alasdair MacIntyre*, Cambridge: Polity.

Horwich, Paul (1998), *Truth*, 2nd edn, Oxford: Clarendon Press.

Houlgate, Stephen (1998), ed., *The Hegel Reader*, Oxford: Blackwell.

Howard-Snyder, Daniel (2004), 'Alston, William Payne (1921–)', in John R. Shook (ed.), *The Dictionary of Modern American Philosophers*, Bristol: Thoemmes Press.

Howells, Christina (1992), ed., *The Cambridge Companion to Sartre*, Cambridge: Cambridge University Press.

Hughes, Christopher (1989), *On a Complex Theory of a Simple God: An Investigation in Aquinas' Philosophical Theology*, Ithaca, NY: Cornell University Press.

Hull, David Lee (2001), *Science and Selection: Essays on Biological Evolution and the Philosophy of Science*, Cambridge Studies in Philosophy and Biology, Cambridge: Cambridge University Press.

Hume, David (1874–5), *The Philosophical Works of David Hume*, ed. T. H. Green and T. H. Grose, 4 vols, London: Longmans, Green.

Hume, David (1974), *Enquiries Concerning Human Understanding and Concerning the Principles of Morals*, ed. P. H. Nidditch, Oxford: Clarendon Press.

Hunt, John (1970), *Pantheism and Christianity*, Port Washington, NY: Kennikat Press.

Hustwit, Ronald E. (1992), *Something about O. K. Bouwsma*, London: University Press of America.

Ingham, Mary Beth (2003), *Scotus for Dunces: An Introduction to the Subtle Doctor*, St Bonaventure, NY: The Franciscan Institute.

Inwood, Brad (2003), ed., *The Cambridge Companion to the Stoics*, Cambridge: Cambridge University Press.

Inwood, Michael (1983), *Hegel*, The Arguments of the Philosophers, London: Routledge.

Inwood, Michael (1992), *A Hegel Dictionary*, Oxford: Blackwell.

Irenaeus, St (1883–4), *The Writings of Irenaeus*, tr. Alexander Roberts and W. H. Rambaut, Ante-Nicene Christian Library 5, 9, 2 vols, Edinburgh: T. & T. Clark.

Irenaeus, St (1992), *Against the Heresies*, tr. Dominic J. Unger, Ancient Christian Writers no. 55, New York: Paulist Press.

Isham, C. J., Nancy Murphy and Robert John Russell, (1993), eds, *Quantum Cosmology and the Laws of Nature: Scientific Perspectives on Divine Action*, Vatican City State: Vatican Observatory.

Israel, Jonathan I. (2001), *Radial Enlightenment: Philosophy and the Making of Modernity 1650–1750*, Oxford: Oxford University Press.

Jackson, Frank (1987), *Conditionals*, Philosophical Theory, Oxford: Blackwell.

Jackson, Frank (1991), ed., *Conditionals*, Oxford Readings in Philosophy, Oxford: Oxford University Press.

Jacobs, Louis (1997), *The Via Negativa in Jewish and Christian Thought: The Zohar and the Cloud of Unknowing Compared*, Essex Papers in Theology and Society 14, Colchester: Centre for the Study of Theology in the University of Essex.

Jaki, Stanley, L. (1995), *Lord Gifford and His Lectures: A Centenary Retrospect*, 2nd edn, Edinburgh: Scottish Academic Press.

James, William (1920), *The Varieties of Religious Experience: A Study in Human Nature*, Gifford Lectures 1901–2, London: Longmans, Green.

James, William (1975–), *The Works of William James*, ed. Frederick Burkhardt, London: Harvard University Press.

James, William (1979), *The Will to Believe and Other Essays in Popular Philosophy*, The Works of William James Vol. 6, Cambridge, MA: Harvard University Press.

James, William (1981), *Pragmatism*, ed. Bruce Kuklick, Cambridge: Hackett.

Jantzen, Grace M. (1984), *God's World, God's Body*, London: Darton, Longman, and Todd.

Jaspers, Karl (1956), *Reason and Existenz: Five Lectures*, tr. William Earle, London: Routledge & Kegan Paul.

Jaspers, Karl (1969–71), *Philosophy*, tr. E. B. Ashton, Chicago: University of Chicago Press.

Jaspers, Karl (1971), *Philosophy of Existence*, tr. Richard F. Grabau, Oxford: Blackwell.

Jaspers, Karl (2000), *Karl Jaspers: Basic Philosophical Writings: Selections*, 2nd edn, ed. and tr. Edith Ehrlich, Leonard H. Ehrlich and George B. Pepper, Amherst, NY: Humanity.

Jay, Eric George (1946), *The Existence of God: A Commentary on St Thomas Aquinas' Five Ways of Demonstrating the Existence of God*, London: SPCK.

Johnson, Allison H. (1983), *Whitehead and His Philosophy*, Lanham, MD: University Press of America.

Jolley, Nicholas (1994), ed., *The Cambridge Companion to Leibniz*, Cambridge: Cambridge University Press.

Jolley, Nicholas (2005), *Leibniz*, Routledge Philosophers, London: Routledge.

Justin Martyr (1861), *The works now extant of S. Justin the martyr*, tr. G. J. Davie, A library of fathers of the Holy Catholic Church, Oxford: Parker.

Justin Martyr (1876–81), *Iustini philosophi et martyris opera quae feruntur omnia*, ed. J. C. Th. Otto, Corpus apologetarum Christianorum saeculi secundi, 3rd edn, 5 vols, Ienae: Prostat in Libraria H. Dufft.

Justin Martyr (2003), *Dialogue with Trypho*, ed. Michael Slusser and Thomas P. Halton, tr. Thomas B. Falls, Selections from the Fathers of the Church Vol. 3, Washington DC: Catholic University of America Press.

Kalsbeek, L. (2002), *Contours of a Christian Philosophy: An Introduction to Herman Dooyeweerd's Thought*, ed. Bernard Zylstra and Josina van Nuis Zylstra, Lampeter: Edwin Mellen Press.

Kane, Robert (2002), ed., *Free Will*, Blackwell Readings in Philosophy 3, Oxford: Blackwell.

Kane, Robert (2005), *A Contemporary Introduction to Free Will*, Fundamentals of Philosophy Series, Oxford: Oxford University Press.

Kane, Robert, and Stephen H. Phillips (1989), *Hartshorne, Process Philosophy, and Theology*, Albany, NY: State University of New York Press.

Kant, Immanuel (1902–44), *Gesammelte Schriften*, ed. Hrsg. von der Königlich-Preussischen Akademie der Wissenschaften zu Berlin, Berlin: Reimer.

Kant, Immanuel (1956), *Critique of Practical Reason*, tr. Lewis White Beck, Library of Liberal Arts, no. 52, Indianapolis: Liberal Arts Press.

Kant, Immanuel (1959), *Foundations of the Metaphysics of Morals and What Is Enlightenment*, tr. Lewis White Beck, Indianapolis: Bobbs-Merrill.

Kant, Immanuel (1960), *Religion within the Limits of Reason Alone*, tr. Theodore M. Greene and Hoyt H. Hudson, New York: Harper.

Kant, Immanuel (1992–), *Cambridge Edition of the Works of Immanuel Kant*, tr. and ed. Paul Guyer and Allen W. Wood, Cambridge: Cambridge University Press.

Kearney, Richard (2003), *Continental Philosophy in the 20th Century*, Routledge History of Philosophy Vol. 8, London: Routledge.

Kearney, Richard (2004), *On Paul Ricoeur: The Owl of Minerva*, Aldershot: Ashgate.

Kenny, Anthony (1969a), ed., *Aquinas: A Collection of Critical Essays*, London: Macmillan.

Kenny, Anthony (1969b), *The Five Ways: St. Thomas Aquinas' Proofs of God's Existence*, Studies in Ethics and the Philosophy of Religion, London: Routledge & Kegan Paul.

Kenny, Anthony (1979), *The God of the Philosophers*, Oxford: Clarendon Press.

Kenny, Anthony (1980), *Aquinas*, Oxford: Oxford University Press.

Kenny, Anthony (1983), *Faith and Reason*, Bampton Lectures in America 22, Guildford: Columbia University Press.

Kenny, Anthony (1985), *A Path from Rome: An Autobiography*, London: Sidgwick & Jackson.

Kenny, Anthony (1986), *Rationalism, Empiricism and Idealism*, Oxford Paperbacks, Oxford: Oxford University Press.

Kenny, Anthony (1992), *What Is Faith?: Essays in the Philosophy of Religion*, Oxford: Oxford University Press.

Kenny, Anthony (1994), ed., *The Wittgenstein Reader*, Oxford: Blackwell.

Kenny, Anthony (1997), *A Life in Oxford*, London: John Murray.

Kenny, Anthony (2004), *The Unknown God: Agnostic Essays*, London: Continuum.

Kenny, Anthony (2005), *Medieval Philosophy*, A New History of Western Philosophy 2, Oxford: Clarendon Press.

Kenny, Anthony, Norman Kretzmann, Jan Pinborg and Eleonore Stump (1982), eds, *The Cambridge History of Later Medieval Philosophy from the Rediscovery of Aristotle to the Disintegration of Scholasticism 1100–1600*, Cambridge: Cambridge University Press.

Kerr, Fergus (2002), *Theology after Wittgenstein*, London: SPCK.

Kierkegaard, Søren (1962–4), *Søren Kerkegaards samlede vaerker*, ed. A. B. Drachmann, J. L. Heiberg and H. O. Lange, Copenhagen: Gyldendal.

Kierkegaard, Søren (1978–), *Kierkegaard's Writings*, ed. Edna H. Hong and Howard V. Hong, Princeton, NJ: Princeton University Press.

Kierkegaard, Søren (1985), *Philosophical Fragments; Johannes Climacus*, ed. and tr. Howard V. Hong and Edna H. Hong, Kierkegaard's Writings 7, Princeton, NJ: Princeton University Press.

Kierkegaard, Søren (1992), *Concluding Unscientific Postscript to Philosophical Fragments*, 2 vols, ed. and tr. Howard V. Hong and Edna H. Hong, Kierkegaard's Writings, 12.1–2, Princeton, NJ: Princeton University Press.

Kierkegaard, Søren (1995), *Works of Love*, ed. and tr. Howard V. Hong and Edna H. Hong, Kierkegaard's Writings 16, new edn, Princeton, NJ: Princeton University Press.

Kierkegaard, Søren (2000), *The Essential Kierkegaard*, ed. Howard V. Hong and Edna H. Hong, Princeton, NJ: Princeton University Press.

Kim, Jaegwon, and Ernest Sosa (2000), eds, *Epistemology: An Anthology*, Blackwell Philosophy Anthologies 11, Malden, MA: Blackwell Publishers.

Kirkham, Richard (1992), *Theories of Truth: A Critical Introduction*, Cambridge, MA; London: MIT Press.

Kirwan, Christopher (1989), *Augustine*, London: Routledge & Kegan Paul.

Klein, Peter D. (1981), *Certainty: A Refutation of Scepticism*, Brighton: Harvester.

Knight, Kelvin (1998), *The MacIntyre Reader*, Oxford: Polity Press.

Kolakowski, Leszek (1981), *Main Currents of Marxism: Its Origins, Growth, and Dissolution*, tr. P. S. Falla, Oxford: Oxford University Press.

Konyndyk, Kenneth (1986), 'Faith and Evidentialism', in *Rationality, Religious Belief, and Moral Commitment: New Essays in the Philosophy of Religion*, ed. Robert Audi and William Wainwright, Ithaca: Cornell University Press, pp. 82–108.

Kraut, Richard (1992), ed., *The Cambridge Companion to Plato*, Cambridge: Cambridge University Press.

Kreeft, Peter J. (1993), *Christianity for Modern Pagans: Pascal's Pensées Edited, Outlined, and Explained*, San Francisco: Ignatius Press.

Kretzmann, Norman (1997), *The Metaphysics of Theism: Aquinas's Natural Theology in Summa contra gentiles I*, Oxford: Clarendon Press.

Kretzmann, Norman (2001), *The Metaphysics of Creation: Aquinas's Natural Theology in Summa contra gentiles II*, Oxford: Clarendon Press.

Kretzmann, Norman, and Eleonore Stump (1993), eds, *The Cambridge Companion to Aquinas*, Cambridge: Cambridge University Press.

Kripke, Saul (1981), *Naming and Necessity*, rev. edn, Oxford: Blackwell.

Kripke, Saul (1982), *Wittgenstein on Rules and Private Language*, Oxford: Blackwell.

Kulp, Christopher B. (1997), ed., *Realism, Antirealism and Epistemology*, Studies in Epistemology and Cognitive Theory, Oxford: Rowman & Littlefield Publishers.

Küng, Hans (1994), *Infallible?: An Unresolved Enquiry*, London: SCM Press.

Kurtz, Paul (1997), *The Courage to Become: The Virtues of Humanism*, Westport, CT: Praeger.

Kuyper, Abraham (1932), *Calvinism: Being the Six 'Stone' Lectures Given at Princeton Theological Seminary, USA*, London: Sovereign Grace Union.

Kuyper, Abraham (1998), *Abraham Kuyper: A Centennial Reader*, ed. James D. Bratt, Grand Rapids, MI: Eerdmans.

Kvanvig, Jonathan L. (1993), *The Problem of Hell*, Oxford: Oxford University Press.

Lacocque, André, and Paul Ricoeur (1998), *Thinking Biblically: Exegetical and Hermeneutical Studies*, tr. David Pellauer, Chicago: University of Chicago Press.

Lapointe, François H., and Claire Lapointe (1977), eds, *Gabriel Marcel and His Critics: An International Bibliography (1928–1976)*, London: Garland Publishing.

Le Poidevin, Robin (1996), *Arguing for Atheism: An Introduction to the Philosophy of Religion*, London: Routledge.

Le Poidevin, Robin (1998), ed., *Questions of Time and Tense*, Oxford: Clarendon Press.

Le Poidevin, Robin, and Murray McBeath (1993), eds, *The Philosophy of Time*, Oxford Readings in Philosophy, Oxford: Oxford University Press.

Lear, Jonathan (2005), *Freud*, Routledge Philosophers, London: Routledge.

Lee, Sang Hyun (2005), ed., *A Companion to the Theology of Jonathan Edwards*, Princeton: Princeton University Press.

Leftow, Brian (1991), *Time and Eternity*, Cornell Studies in the Philosophy of Religion, Ithaca, NY: Cornell University Press.

Lehrer, Keith (1989), *Thomas Reid*, The Arguments of the Philosophers, London: Routledge.

Leibniz, Gottfried Wilhelm (1923–), *Sämtliche Schriften und Briefe*, ed. Deutsche Akademie der Wissenschaften, Berlin: Akademie-Verlag.

Leibniz, Gottfried Wilhelm (1965), *Monadology and Other Essays*, tr. Paul Schrecker and Anne Martin Schrecker, Indianapolis: Bobbs-Merrill.

Leibniz, Gottfried Wilhelm (1969), *Philosophical Papers and Letters: A Selection*, ed. and tr. Leroy E. Loemker, 2nd edn, Synthese Historical Library: Texts and Studies in the History of Logic and Philosophy, Dordrecht: Reidel.

Leibniz, Gottfried Wilhelm (1973), *Philosophical Writings*, ed. G. H. R. Parkinson, tr. Mary Morris and G. H. R. Parkinson, London: J. M. Dent & Sons.

Leibniz, Gottfried Wilhelm (1985), *Theodicy: Essays on the Goodness of God, the Freedom of Man, and the Origin of Evil*, ed. Austin Farrer, tr. E. M. Huggard, La Salle, IL: Open Court.

Leibniz, Gottfried Wilhelm (1998), *Philosophical Texts*, ed. Richard Francks and R. S. Woolhouse, Oxford Philosophical Texts, Oxford: Oxford University Press.

Leslie, John (2001), *Infinite Minds: A Philosophical Cosmology*, Oxford: Oxford University Press.

Lesser, M. X. (1981), *Jonathan Edwards: A Reference Guide*, Boston: G. K. Hall.

Lesser, M. X. (1994), *Jonathan Edwards: An Annotated Bibliography, 1979–1993*, Westport, CT: Greenwood.

Levine, Michael P. (1994), *Pantheism: A Non-Theistic Conception of Deity*, London: Routledge.

Lewis, C. S. (1940), *The Problem of Pain*, The Christian Challenge Series, London: Centenary Press.

Lewis, C. S. (1947), *Miracles*, London: G. Bles.

Lewis, C. S. (1952), *Mere Christianity: A Revised and Amplified Edition, with a New Introduction, of the Three Books, Broadcast Talks, Christian Behaviour, and Beyond Personality*, London: G. Bles.

Lewis, C. S. (1960), *The Four Loves*, London: G. Bles.

Lewis, David K. (1986a), *Counterfactuals*, rev. edn, Oxford: Blackwell.

Lewis, David K. (1986b), *On the Plurality of Worlds*, Oxford: Blackwell.

Lewis, Harry A. (1991), *Peter Geach: Philosophical Encounters*, Synthese Library 213, London: Kluwer.

Lieu, Samuel N. C. (1994), *Manichaeism in Mesopotamia and the Roman East*, Religions in the Graeco-Roman World 118, Leiden: Brill.

Lisska, Anthony (1996), *Aquinas's Theory of Natural Law: An Analytic Reconstruction*, Oxford: Oxford University Press.

Locke, John (1975–), *The Clarendon Edition of the Works of John Locke*, ed. Peter H. Nidditch, Oxford: Clarendon Press.

Locke, John (1999), *The Reasonableness of Christianity: as Delivered in the Scriptures*, ed. John C. Higgins-Biddle, Oxford: Clarendon Press.

Lombard, Peter (1971–81), *Sententiae in IV libris distinctae*, ed. Ignatius Brady, 2 vols, Spicilegium Bonaventurianum 4–5, Grottaferrata: Editiones Collegii S. Bonaventurae Ad Claras Aquas.

Lonergan, Bernard (1957), *Insight: A Study of Human Understanding*, London: Longmans, Green.

Lonergan, Bernard (1972), *Method in Theology*, New York: Herder and Herder.

Long, A. A., and D. N. Sedley (1987), *The Hellenistic Philosophers*, 2 vols, Cambridge: Cambridge University Press.

Loux, Michael (1970), ed., *Universals and Particulars: Readings in Ontology*, Garden City, NY: Anchor Books.

Lovejoy, Arthur O. (1936), *The Great Chain of Being: A Study in the History of an Idea*, Cambridge, MA: Harvard University Press.

Lowe, E. Jonathan (1996), *Subjects of Experience*, Cambridge: Cambridge University Press.

Lowe, E. Jonathan (2005), *Locke*, Routledge Philosophers, London: Routledge.

Löwith, Karl (1995), *Martin Heidegger and European Nihilism*, ed. Richard Wolin, tr. Gary Steiner, European Perspectives, New York: Columbia University Press.

Lucas, J. R. (1970), *The Freedom of the Will*, Oxford: Clarendon Press.

Lucas, J. R. (1993), *Responsibility*, Oxford: Clarendon Press.

McInerny, Ralph M. (1966), *Thomism in an Age of Renewal*, Notre Dame: University of Notre Dame Press.

McInerny, Ralph M. (1988), *Art and Prudence: Studies in the Thought of Jacques Maritain*, Notre Dame, IN: University of Notre Dame Press.

MacIntyre, Alasdair (1953), *Marxism: An Interpretation*, London: SCM Press.

MacIntyre, Alasdair (1959), *Difficulties in Christian belief*, London: SCM Press.

MacIntyre, Alasdair (1972), ed., *Hegel: A Collection of Critical Essays*, Modern Studies in Philosophy, Garden City, NY: Anchor Books.

MacIntyre, Alasdair (1985), *After Virtue*, London: Duckworth.

MacIntyre, Alasdair (1988), *Whose Justice? Which Rationality?*, London: Duckworth.

MacIntyre, Alasdair (1990), *Three Rival Versions of Moral Enquiry: Encyclopaedia, Genealogy, and Tradition; Being Gifford Lectures Delivered in the University of Edinburgh in 1988*, Gifford Lectures, Notre Dame, IN: University of Notre Dame Press.

MacIntyre, Alasdair (1995), *Marxism and Christianity*, 2nd edn, London: Duckworth.

MacIntyre, Alasdair (2002), *A Short History of Ethics: A History of Moral Philosophy from the Homeric Age to the 20th Century*, 2nd edn, London: Routledge.

MacIntyre, Alasdair, and Paul Ricoeur (1969), *The Religious Significance of Atheism*, Bampton Lectures in America 18, New York: Columbia University Press.

Mackinnon, D. M. (1974), *The Problem of Metaphysics*, Cambridge: Cambridge University Press.

McNeill, William, and Karen S. Feldman (1998), eds, *Continental Philosophy: An Anthology*, Blackwell Philosophy Anthologies, Oxford: Blackwell.

Magnus, Bernd, and Kathleen Marie Higgins (1996), eds, *The Cambridge Companion to Nietzsche*, Cambridge: Cambridge University Press.

Malcolm, Norman (1959), *Dreaming*, Studies in Philosophical Psychology, London: Routledge & Kegan Paul.

Malcolm, Norman (1962), *Ludwig Wittgenstein: A Memoir*, London: Oxford University Press.

Malcolm, Norman (1963), *Knowledge and Certainty*, Englewood Cliffs, NJ: Prentice Hall.

Malebranche, Nicolas (1958–84), *Œuvres complètes de Malebranche*, ed. A. Robinet, 20 vols, Paris: J. Vrin.

Malebranche, Nicolas (1980a), *The Search after Truth*, tr. Thomas M. Lennon and Paul J. Olscamp, Columbus: Ohio State University Press.

Malebranche, Nicolas (1980b), *Dialogue between a Christian Philosopher and a Chinese Philosopher on the Existence and Nature of God*, tr. D. A. Iorio, Washington DC: Catholic University Press.

Marcel, Gabriel (1965), *Being and Having*, Fontana Library of Theology and Philosophy, tr. Katharine Farrer, London: Collins.

Marcel, Gabriel (2001), *The Mystery of Being*, tr. G. S. Fraser, South Bend, IN: St Augustine's Press.

Marenbon, John (1987), *Later Medieval Philosophy (1150–1350): An Introduction*, London: Routledge & Kegan Paul.

Marenbon, John (1988), *Early Medieval Philosophy (480–1150): An Introduction*, 2nd edn, New York: Routledge.

Marenbon, John (1997), *The Philosophy of Peter Abelard*, Cambridge: Cambridge University Press.

Marenbon, John (1998), ed., *Medieval Philosophy*, Routledge History of Philosophy 3, London: Routledge.

Marenbon, John (2003), *Boethius*, Great Medieval Thinkers, Oxford: Oxford University Press.

Maritain, Jacques (1944), *An Introduction to Philosophy*, tr. E. I. Watkin, London: Sheed and Ward.

Maritain, Jacques (1948), *Jacques Maritain: Son œuvre philosophique*, Paris: Bibliothèque de la Revue Thomiste.

Maritain, Jacques (1955), *An Essay on Christian Philosophy*, tr. Edward H. Flannery, New York: Philosophical Library.

Maritain, Jacques (1982–), *Œuvres complètes de Jacques et Raïssa Maritain*, 15 vols, Fribourg (Switzerland): Éditions universitaires.

Maritain, Jacques (1995–), *The Collected Works of Jacques Maritain*, ed. Theodore M. Hesburgh, Ralph McLnerny, Frederick Crosson and Bernard Doering. Notre Dame: University of Notre Dame Press.

Marrone, Steven P. (2001), *The Light of Thy Countenance: Science and Knowledge of God in the Thirteenth Century*, Vol. 1: *Doctrine of Divine Illumination*, Studies in the History of Christian Thought Vol. 98, Leiden: Brill.

Marrou, Henri (1957), *St Augustine and His Influence through the Ages*, tr. P. Hepburne-Scott, New York: Harper Torchbooks.

Marsden, George (2003), *Jonathan Edwards: A Life*, New Haven, CT: Yale University Press.

Marshall, Bruce (2000), *Trinity and Truth*, Cambridge Studies in Christian Doctrine, Cambridge: Cambridge University Press.

Martin, Christopher (1988), ed., *Thomas Aquinas: Introductory Readings*, London: Routledge & Kegan Paul.

Martinich, Aloysius P. (1995), *A Hobbes Dictionary*, London: Blackwell.

Martinich, Aloysius P. (2005), *Hobbes*, Routledge Philosophers, London: Routledge.

Martinich, Aloysius P., and David Sosa (2001), eds, *Analytic Philosophy: An Anthology*, Blackwell Philosophy Anthologies, Oxford: Blackwell.

Mavrodes, George (1993), 'The God above the Gods: Can the High Gods Survive?' in Eleonore Stump, ed., *Reasoned Faith: Essays in Philosophical Theology in Honor of Norman Kretzmann*, Ithaca, NY: Cornell University Press, pp. 179–203.

May, Gerhard (1994), *Creatio ex Nihilo: The Doctrine of 'Creation out of Nothing' in Early Christian Thought*, Edinburgh: T. & T. Clark.

Meeker, K., and P. Quinn (2000), eds, *The Philosophical Challenge of Religious Diversity*, New York: Oxford University Press.

Melling, David J. (1987), *Understanding Plato*, Opus, Oxford: Oxford University Press.

Melsen, Andrew G van (1965), *Evolution and Philosophy*, Duquesne Studies, Philosophy Series 19, Pittsburgh, PA: Duquesne University Press.

Merricks, Trenton (2001), *Objects and Persons*, Oxford: Oxford University Press.

Meyer, Gerbert, and Albert Zimmermann (1980), *Albertus Magnus – Doctor Universalis 1280/1980*, Mainz: Matthias-Grunewald.

Meynell, Hugo A. (1991), *An Introduction to the Philosophy of Bernard Lonergan*, 2nd edn, Toronto: University of Toronto Press.

Meynell, Hugo (1991), *An Introduction to the Theology of Bernard Lonergan*, 2nd edn, Library of Philosophy and Religion, London: Macmillan.

Midgley, Mary (2002), *Evolution as a Religion: Strange Hopes and Stranger Fears*, rev. edn, London: Routledge.

Mill, John Stuart (1963–), *Collected Works of John Stuart Mill*, ed. J. M. Robson, Toronto: University of Toronto Press.

Mirecki, Paul, and Jason BeDuhn (2001), eds, *The Light and the Darkness: Studies in Manichaeism and Its World*, Nag Hammadi and Manichaean Studies 50, Leiden: Brill.

Molina, Luis de (1953), *Liberi Arbitrii cum Gratiae Donis, Divina Praescientia, Providentia, Praedestinatione et Reprobatione Concordia*, ed. J. Rabeneck, Oña: Collegium Maximum.

Molina, Luis de (1988), *On Divine Foreknowledge: Part IV of the Concordia*, tr. A. J. Freddoso, Ithaca: Cornell University Press.

Moltmann, Jürgen (1974), *The Crucified God: The Cross of Christ as the Foundation and Criticism of Christian Theology*, tr. R. A. Wilson and John Bowden, London: SCM Press.

Monk, Ray (1996), *Bertrand Russell*, Vol. 1, *The Spirit of Solitude*, London: Jonathan Cape.

Monk, Ray (2000), *Bertrand Russell: 1921–1970*, Vol. 2, *The Ghost of Madness*, London: Jonathan Cape.

Moran, Denis P. (1992), *Gabriel Marcel: Existentialist Philosopher, Dramatist, Educator*, Lanham, MD: University Press of America.

Moreland, J. P. (2001), *Universals*, Central Problems of Philosophy, Chesham: Acumen.

Moreland, J. P., and William Lane Craig (2003), *Philosophical Foundations for a Christian Worldview*, Downers Grove, IL: InterVarsity Press.

Morris, Thomas V. (1986), *The Logic of God Incarnate*, Ithaca, NY: Cornell University Press.

Morris, Thomas V. (1987), *Anselmian Explorations: Essays in Philosophical Theology*, Notre Dame, IN: University of Notre Dame Press.

Morris, Thomas V. (1988), ed., *Divine and Human Action*, Ithaca, NY: Cornell University Press.

Morris, Thomas V. (1991), *Our Idea of God: An Introduction to Philosophical Theology*, Contours of Christian Philosophy, Leicester: Inter-Varsity Press.

Morris, Thomas V. (1992), *Making Sense of It All: Pascal and the Meaning of Life*, Grand Rapids, MI: Eerdmans.

Morris, Thomas V. (1994), ed., *God and the Philosophers: The Reconciliation of Faith and Reason*, Oxford: Oxford University Press.

Moser, Paul K. (1987), ed., *A Priori Knowledge*, Oxford: Oxford University Press.

Muller, Richard (2000), *The Unaccommodated Calvin: Studies in the Foundation of a Theological Tradition*, Oxford: Oxford University Press.

Muller, Richard (2003), *After Calvin: Studies in the Development of a Theological Tradition*, Oxford: Oxford University Press.

Murphy, Mark C. (2003), *Alasdair MacIntyre*, Cambridge: Cambridge University Press.

Murphy, Nancey C. (1990), *Theology in the Age of Scientific Reasoning*, Cornell Studies in the Philosophy of Religion, Ithaca, NY: Cornell University Press.

Murphy, Nancey C., Brad J. Kallenberg and Mark Thiessen Nation (1997), *Virtues & Practices in the Christian Tradition: Christian Ethics after MacIntyre*, Harrisburg, PA: Trinity Press International.

Murphy, Richard T. (1979), *Hume and Husserl: Towards Radical Subjectivism*, Phaenomenologica 79, Boston: M. Nijhoff.

Nadler, Steven (1993), ed., *Causation in Early Modern Philosophy: Cartesianism, Occasionalism, and Preestablished Harmony*, University Park, PA: Pennsylvania State University Press.

Nadler, Steven (2000), ed., *The Cambridge Companion to Malebranche*, Cambridge Companions to Philosophy, Cambridge: Cambridge University Press.

Nagel, Thomas (1970), *The Possibility of Altruism*, Oxford: Clarendon Press.

Nagel, Thomas (1986), *The View from Nowhere*, New York: Oxford University Press.

Nash, Ronald H. (1968), *The Philosophy of Gordon H. Clark: A Festschrift*, Philadelphia: Presbyterian and Reformed.

Naugle, David K. (2002), *Worldview: History of a Concept*, Grand Rapids, MI: Eerdmans.

Nicholi, Armand M. (2003), *The Question of God: C. S. Lewis and Sigmund Freud Debate God, Love, Sex, and the Meaning of Life*, London: Free Press.

Nietzsche, Friedrich Wilhelm (1909–13), *The Complete Works*, ed. Oscar Levy, London: Allen & Unwin.

Nietzsche, Friedrich Wilhelm (1967–), *Werke*, ed. Georgio Colli and Mazzino Montinari, Berlin: Walter de Gruyter.

Nietzsche, Friedrich Wilhelm (1968), *Basic Writings of Nietzsche*, tr. and ed. Walter Kaufmann, New York: Modern Library.

Nietzsche, Friedrich Wilhelm (1977), *A Nietzsche Reader*, tr. and ed. R. J. Hollingdale, Harmondsworth: Penguin.

Nietzsche, Friedrich Wilhelm (1980), *Sämtliche Werke*, ed. Georgio Colli and Mazzino Montinari, Berlin: Walter de Gruyter.

Nietzsche, Friedrich Wilhelm (1995), *Nietzsche: A Critical Reader*, tr. Peter R. Sedgwick, Oxford: Blackwell.

Nietzsche, Friedrich Wilhelm (1995–), *The Complete Works of Friedrich Nietzsche*, ed. Ernst Behler, Stanford, CA: Stanford University Press.

Noonan, Harold (1980), *Objects and Identity*, The Hague: Nijhoff.

North, Gary (1979), *Foundations of Christian Scholarship: Essays in the Van Til Perspective*, A Chalcedon Study, Vallecito, CA: Ross House Books.

Nozick, Robert (1993), *The Nature of Rationality*, Princeton: Princeton University Press.

Nygren, Anders (1982), *Agape and Eros*, tr. Philip S. Watson, rev. edn, London: SPCK.

O'Meara, Dominic J. (1982), ed., *Neoplatonism and Christian Thought*, Studies in Neoplatonism Vol. 3, Norfolk, VA: International Society for Neoplatonic Studies.

O'Meara, Dominic J. (1993), *Plotinus: An Introduction to the Enneads*, rev. edn., Oxford: Clarendon Press.

Oberman, Heiko Augustinus (1983), *The Harvest of Medieval Theology: Gabriel Biel and Late Medieval Nominalism*, 3rd edn, Durham, NC: Labyrinth Press.

Ockham, William of (1967–88), *Opera Philosophica et Theologica*, ed. Philotheus Boehner, Gedeon Gál, and Stephen F. Brown, St Bonaventure, NY: The Franciscan Institute.

Ockham, William of (1974), *Ockham's Theory of Terms: Part I of the Summa Logicae*, tr. Michael J. Loux, London: University of Notre Dame Press.

Ockham, William of (1980), *Ockham's Theory of Propositions: Part II of the Summa Logicae*, tr. Alfred J. Freddoso and Henry Schuurman, London: University of Notre Dame Press.

Ockham, William of (1983), *Predestination, God's Foreknowledge, and Future Contingents*, tr. Marilyn McCord Adams and Norman Kretzmann, 2nd edn, Indianapolis: Hackett.

Ockham, William of (1990), *Philosophical Writings: A Selection*, tr. Philotheus Boehner, rev. Stephen F. Brown, Indianapolis, IN: Hackett.

Oderberg, David (1993), *The Metaphysics of Identity over Time*, London: Macmillan.

Oderberg, David, and Timothy Chappell (2004), *Human Values: New Essays on Ethics and Natural Law*, Basingstoke: Palgrave Macmillan.

Ogden, Schubert M. (1962), *Christ without Myth: A Study Based on the Theology of Rudolf Bultmann*, London: Collins.

Oman, John (1931), *Grace and Personality*, 4th edn. Cambridge: Cambridge University Press.

Oppy, Graham (1995), *Ontological Arguments and Belief in God*, Cambridge: Cambridge University Press.

Origen (1857), *Origenis opera omnia*, ed. J.-P. Migne, Patrologiae cursus completus, series graeca, Turnholti: Brepols.

Origen (1878), *The Writings of Origen*, tr. Frederick Crombie, Ante-Nicene Christian Library vol. 10, Edinburgh: T. & T. Clark.

Origen (1936), *On First Principles*, tr. G. W. Butterworth, London: SPCK.

Origen (1980), *Contra Celsum*, tr. Henry Chadwick, Cambridge: Cambridge University Press.

Owen, Huw Parri (1965), *The Moral Argument for Christian Theism*, London: George Allen & Unwin.

Paley, William (1819), *Natural Theology or, Evidences of the Existence and Attributes of the Deity Collected from the Appearances of Nature*, 16th edn, London: F. C. and J. Rivington.

Paley, William (1825), *The Complete Works of William Paley*, 5 vols, London: J. F. Dove for G. Cowie.

Paley, William (1849), *A View of the Evidences of Christianity*, Cambridge: Cambridge University Press.

Pannenberg, Wolfhart (1968), *Jesus – God and Man*, tr. Lewis L. Wilkins and Duane A. Priebe, London: SCM Press.

Pannenberg, Wolfhart (1976), *Theology and the Philosophy of Science*, tr. Francis McDonagh, London: Darton, Longman, and Todd.

Pannenberg, Wolfhart (1985), *Anthropology in Theological Perspective*, tr. Matthew J. O'Connell, Philadelphia: Westminster Press.

Pannenberg, Wolfhart (1991–8), *Systematic Theology*, 3 vols, tr. Geoffrey W. Bromiley, Grand Rapids, MI: Eerdmans.

Papineau, David (1993), *Philosophical Naturalism*, Oxford: Blackwell.

Parfit, Derek (1984), *Reasons and Persons*, Oxford: Oxford University Press.

Parrish, Stephen E. (1997), *God and Necessity: A Defense of Classical Theism*, Lanham, MD: University Press of America.

Pascal, Blaise (1965), *Pensées*, Paris: Larousse.

Pascal, Blaise (1998–), *Œuvres complètes*, ed. Michel Le Guern, Bibliothèque de la pléiade 34, Paris: Gallimard.

Pasnau, Robert (1997), *Theories of Cognition in the Later Middle Ages*, Cambridge, UK; New York: Cambridge University Press.

Peacocke, Arthur R. (1993), *Theology for a Scientific Age*, enl. edn, London: SCM Press.

Pears, David F. (1972), ed., *Bertrand Russell: A Collection of Critical Essays*, New York: Doubleday.

Penelhum, Terence (1970), *Survival and Disembodied Existence*, Studies in Philosophical Psychology, London: Routledge & Kegan Paul.

Penelhum, Terence (1971), *Problems of Religious Knowledge*, Philosophy of Religion Series, London: Macmillan.

Penelhum, Terence (1973), ed., *Immortality*, Basic Problems in Philosophy Series, Belmont, CA: Wadsworth.

Penelhum, Terence (1983), *God and Skepticism: A Study in Skepticism and Fideism*, Philosophical Studies Series in Philosophy 28, Dordrecht: D. Reidel.

Penelhum, Terence (1985), *Butler*, London: Routledge & Kegan Paul.

Penelhum, Terence (1995), *Reason and Religious Faith*, Focus Series, Oxford: Westview Press.

Pennock, Robert T. (2001), ed., *Intelligent Design Creationism and Its Critics: Philosophical, Theological, and Scientific Perspectives*, Cambridge, MA: MIT Press.

Phillips, D. Z. (1965), *The Concept of Prayer*, London: Routledge and Kegan Paul.

Phillips, D. Z. (1970), *Death and Immortality*, New Studies in the Philosophy of Religion, London: Macmillan.

Phillips, D. Z. (1988), *Faith after Foundationalism*, London: Routledge.

Phillips, D. Z. (1993), *Wittgenstein and Religion*, Swansea Studies in Philosophy, London: Macmillan.

Pieper, Joseph (2001), *Scholasticism: Personalities and Problems of Medieval Philosophy*, tr. Richard and Clara Winston, South Bend, IN: St Augustine's Press.

Pinnock, Clark H. (1975), ed., *Grace Unlimited*, Minneapolis: Bethany Fellowship.

Pinnock, Clark H. (1989), ed., *The Grace of God, the Will of Man: A Case for Arminianism*, Grand Rapids, MI: Academie Books.

Pinnock, Clark H., Richard Rice, John Sanders, William Hasker and David Basinger (1994), *The Openness of God: A Biblical Challenge to the Traditional Understanding of God*, Downers Grove, IN: InterVarsity Press.

Plantinga, Alvin (1965), ed., *The Ontological Argument: From St Anselm to Contemporary Philosophers*, Garden City, NY: Anchor.

Plantinga, Alvin (1967), *God and Other Minds*, Ithaca, NY: Cornell University Press.

Plantinga, Alvin (1974a), *God, Freedom, and Evil*, New York: Harper & Row.

Plantinga, Alvin (1974b), *The Nature of Necessity*, Clarendon Library of Logic and Philosophy, Oxford: Clarendon Press.

Plantinga, Alvin (1980), *Does God Have a Nature?* The Aquinas Lecture 1980, Milwaukee: Marquette University Press.

Plantinga, Alvin (1984), 'Advice to Christian Philosophers', *Faith and Philosophy*, 1: 3, pp. 253–71.

Plantinga, Alvin (2000), *Warranted Christian Belief*, Oxford: Oxford University Press.

Plantinga, Alvin, and Nicholas Wolterstorff (1983), *Faith and Rationality: Reason and Belief in God*, Notre Dame: University of Notre Dame Press.

Plantinga, Cornelius (1995), *Not the Way It's Supposed to Be*, Grand Rapids, MI: Eerdmans.

Plato (1899–1906), *Platonis opera*, ed. John Burnet, Oxford: Clarendon Press.

Plato (1977), *Euthyphro; Apology of Socrates; Crito*, ed. John Burnet, Oxford: Clarendon Press.

Plato (1981), *Five Dialogues, Euthyphro, Apology, Crito, Meno, Phaedo*, tr. G. M. A. Grube, Indianapolis, IN: Hackett.

Plato (1997), *Complete Works*, ed. John M. Cooper, Cambridge: Hackett.

Plotinus (1956), *The Enneads*, tr. Stephen MacKenna, 3rd edn, rev. B. S. Page, London: Faber & Faber.

Pohle, Joseph (1938), *God: His Knowability, Essence, and Attributes: A Dogmatic Treatise*, 8th edn, ed. Arthur Preuss, Pohle-Preuss Series of Dogmatic Text-books 1, St Louis, MO: B. Herder.

Polanyi, Michael (1974), *Personal Knowledge: Towards a Post-Critical Philosophy*, Chicago: University of Chicago Press.

Polanyi, Michael (1983), *The Tacit Dimension*, Gloucester, MA: P. Smith.

Polanyi, Michael, and Harry Prosch (1975), *Meaning*, Chicago: University of Chicago Press.

Popkin, Richard H. (2003), *The History of Scepticism: From Savonarola to Bayle*, rev. edn, Oxford: Oxford University Press.

Popper, Karl R. (1996), *Conjectures and Refutations: The Growth of Scientific Knowledge*, rev. and corr. edn, London: Routledge.

Price, Henry H. (1936), *Truth and Corrigibility*, Oxford: Clarendon Press.

Price, Henry H. (1969), *Belief*, London: George Allen & Unwin.

Prior, Arthur N. (2003), *Papers on Time and Tense*, ed. Per Hasle, 2nd edn, Oxford: Oxford University Press.

Prosch, Harry (1986), *Michael Polanyi: A Critical Exposition*, Albany, NY: State University of New York Press.

Pyle, Andrew (2003), *Malebranche*, London: Routledge.

Quinn, Philip L. (1978), *Divine Commands and Moral Requirements*, Clarendon Library of Logic and Philosophy, Oxford: Clarendon Press.

Quinn, Philip L., and Charles Taliaferro (1997), eds, *A Companion to the Philosophy of Religion*, Oxford: Blackwell.

Rahner, Karl (1961–81), *Theological Investigations*, 20 vols, London: Darton, Longman, and Todd.

Rahner, Karl (1978), *Foundations of Christian Faith: An Introduction to the Idea of Christianity*, tr. William V. Dych, London: Darton, Longman, and Todd.

Rahner, Karl (1994), *Spirit in the World*, tr. William Dychf, New York: Continuum.

Ramsey, Ian T. (1957), *Religious Language: An Empirical Placing of Theological Phrases*, Library of Philosophy and Theology, London: SCM Press.

Ramsey, Ian T. (1971), *Words about God*, London: SCM Press.

Ratzsch, Del (1986), *Philosophy of Science: The Natural Sciences in Christian Perspective*, Contours of Christian Philosophy, Leicester: Inter-Varsity Press.

Rayment-Pickard, Hugh (2003), *Impossible God: Derrida's Theology*, Aldershot: Ashgate.

Rea, Michael C. (2002), *World without Design: The Ontological Consequences of Naturalism*, Oxford: Clarendon Press.

Reid, Thomas (2000), *An Inquiry into the Human Mind on the Principles of Common Sense: A Critical Edition*, ed. Derek R. Brookes, Edinburgh Edition of Thomas Reid, Edinburgh: Edinburgh University Press.

Reid, Thomas (2002), *Essays on the Intellectual Powers of Man: A Critical Edition*, ed. Derek Brookes, Edinburgh Edition of Thomas Reid, Edinburgh: Edinburgh University Press.

Reppert, Victor (2003), *C. S. Lewis's Dangerous Idea: In Defense of the Argument from Reason*, Downers Grove, IL: InterVarsity.

Rescher, Nicholas (2000), *Process Philosophy: A Survey of Basic Issues*, Pittsburgh: University of Pittsburgh Press.

Ricoeur, Paul (1967), *The Symbolism of Evil*, tr. Emerson Buchanan, New York: Harper & Row.

Ricoeur, Paul (1977), *The Rule of Metaphor: Multi-disciplinary Studies of the Creation of Meaning in Language*, tr. Robert Czerny, University of Toronto Romance Series 37, Toronto: University of Toronto Press.

Ricoeur, Paul (1981), *Hermeneutics and the Human Sciences: Essays on Language, Action and Interpretation*, ed. and tr. John B. Thompson, Cambridge: Cambridge University Press.

Ricoeur, Paul (1991), *From Text to Action: Essays in Hermeneutics, II*, tr. Kathleen Blamey and John B. Thompson, Northwestern University Studies in Phenomenology and Existential Philosophy, Evanston, IL: Northwestern University Press.

Ricoeur, Paul (1996), *The Hermeneutics of Action*, ed. Richard Kearney, Philosophy and Social Criticism, London: Sage.

Ricoeur, Paul (2004), *The Conflict of Interpretations: Essays in Hermeneutics*, ed. Don Ihde, new edn, London: Continuum.

Rist, John Michael (1967), *Plotinus: The Road to Reality*, Cambridge: Cambridge University Press.

Rist, John Michael (1969), *Stoic Philosophy*, Cambridge: Cambridge University Press.

Rist, John Michael (1985), *Platonism and Its Christian Heritage*, Collected Studies Series 221, London: Variorum Reprints.

Rist, John Michael (1994), *Augustine: Ancient Thought Baptized*, Cambridge: Cambridge University Press.

Robbins, John W. (1989), *Gordon H. Clark: Personal Recollections*, Hobbs, NM: Trinity Foundation.

Roberts, George W. (1979), ed., *Bertrand Russell Memorial Volume*, London: George Allen & Unwin.

Robinson, Howard (1993), ed., *Objections to Physicalism*, Oxford: Clarendon Press.

Rockmore, Tom (2004), *On Foundationalism: A Strategy for Metaphysical Realism*, Lanham, MD: Rowman & Littlefield.

Rogers, Ben (2000), *A. J. Ayer: A Life*, London: Vintage.

Rogers, Katherin A. (2000), *Perfect Being Theology*, Reason and Religion, Edinburgh: Edinburgh University Press.

Rorty, Richard (1982), *Consequences of Pragmatism: Essays 1972–1980*, Minneapolis: University of Minnesota Press.

Rorty, Richard (1991), *Objectivity, Relativism, and Truth: Philosophical Papers I*, Cambridge: Cambridge University Press.

Rosemann, Philipp W. (2004), *Peter Lombard*, Great Medieval Thinkers, New York: Oxford University Press.

Rosen, Stanley (1969), *Nihilism: A Philosophical Essay*, New Haven: Yale University Press.

Rosenberg, Alex (2000), *Philosophy of Science: A Contemporary Introduction*, Routledge Contemporary Introductions to Philosophy, London: Routledge.

Ross, James (1981), *Portraying Analogy*, Cambridge: Cambridge University Press.

Rowe, William L. (1975), *The Cosmological Argument*, Princeton: Princeton University Press.

Rowe, William L. (2001), ed., *God and the Problem of Evil*, Blackwell Readings in Philosophy 1, Malden, MA: Blackwell.

Rudavsky, Tamar (1985), ed., *Divine Omniscience and Omnipotence in Medieval Philosophy: Islamic, Jewish and Christian Perspectives*, Synthese Historical Library 25, Lancaster: Reidel.

Ruf, Henry (1989), ed., *Religion, Ontotheology, and Deconstruction: Seminar on the Future of Ontotheology*, God and the Contemporary Discussion, New York: Paragon House.

Runzo, Joseph (1993), *World Views and Perceiving God*, New York: St. Martin's Press.

Russell, Bertrand (1946), *History of Western Philosophy and Its Connection with Political and Social Circumstances from the Earliest Times to the Present Day*, London: George Allen & Unwin.

Russell, Bertrand (1957), *Why I Am Not a Christian and Other Essays on Religion and Related Subjects*, ed. Paul Edwards, London: George Allen & Unwin.

Russell, Bertrand (1959), *My Philosophical Development*, London: George Allen & Unwin.

Russell, Bertrand (1961), *The Basic Writings of Bertrand Russell, 1903–1959*, London: George Allen & Unwin.

Russell, Bertrand (1983–), *The Collected Papers of Bertrand Russell*, ed. Kenneth Blackwell, London: George Allen & Unwin.

Russell, Robert John, William R. Stoeger and George V. Coyne (1988), eds, *Physics, Philosophy, and Theology: A Common Quest for Understanding*, Vatican City State: Vatican Observatory.

Ryle, Gilbert (1949), *The Concept of Mind*, London: Hutchinson.

Sartre, Jean-Paul (1948), *Existentialism and Humanism*, tr. Philip Mairet, London: Methuen.

Sartre, Jean-Paul (1957), *Being and Nothingness: An Essay on Phenomenological Ontology*, tr. Hazel E. Barnes, London: Methuen.

Sartre, Jean-Paul (1958), *No Exit*, tr. Paul Bowles, New York: Samuel French.

Sartre, Jean-Paul (1963), *Nausea*, tr. Robert Baldick, Harmondsworth: Penguin.

Schacht, Richard (1983), *Nietzsche*, Arguments of the Philosophers, London: Routledge & Kegan Paul.

Scharfstein, Ben-Ami (1993), *Ineffability: The Failure of Words in Philosophy and Religion*, SUNY Series toward a Comparative Philosophy of Religions, Albany: State University of New York Press.

Scheffler, Samuel (1988), *Consequentialism and Its Critics*, Oxford Readings in Philosophy, Oxford: Oxford University Press.

Schilpp, Paul Arthur (1951), ed., *The Philosophy of Alfred North Whitehead*, The Library of Living Philosophers 3, 2nd edn, New York: Tudor Publishing Co.

Schilpp, Paul Arthur (1981), ed., *The Philosophy of Karl Jaspers*, The Library of Living Philosophers 9, augmented edn, La Salle, IL: Open Court.

Schilpp, Paul Arthur (1989), ed., *The Philosophy of Bertrand Russell*, The Library of Living Philosophers 5, 5th edn, La Salle, IL: Open Court.

Schilpp, Paul Arthur, and Maurice Friedman (1967), eds, *The Philosophy of Martin Buber*, The Library of Living Philosophers 12, La Salle, IL: Open Court.

Schleiermacher, Friedrich (1922), *The Christian Faith in Outline*, tr. D. M. Baillie, Edinburgh: W. F. Henderson.

Schleiermacher, Friedrich (1958), *On Religion: Speeches to Its Cultured Despisers*, tr. John Oman, New York: Harper & Row.

Schleiermacher, Friedrich (1984–), *Kritische Gesamtausgabe*, ed. Hans-Joachim Birkner and Gerhard Ebeling, Berlin: de Gruyter.

Schroeder, William Ralph (2005), *Continental Philosophy: A Critical Approach*, Oxford: Blackwell.

Sebba, G. (1959), *Nicolas Malebranche, 1638–1715: A Preliminary Bibliography*, Athens: University of Georgia Press.

Sennett, James F. (1998), ed., *The Analytic Theist: An Alvin Plantinga Reader*, Grand Rapids, MI: Eerdmans.

Senor, Thomas D. (1995), *The Rationality of Belief and the Plurality of Faith: Essays in Honor of William P. Alston*, Ithaca, NY: Cornell University Press.

Sessions, William Lad (1994), *The Concept of Faith: A Philosophical Investigation*, Cornell Studies in the Philosophy of Religion, Ithaca, NY: Cornell University Press.

Shakespeare, Steven (2001), *Kierkegaard, Language and the Reality of God*, Aldershot: Ashgate.

Shapiro, Gary, and Alan Sica (1984), eds, *Hermeneutics: Questions and Prospects*, Amherst, MA: University of Massachusetts Press.

Sherry, Patrick (1976a), 'Analogy Reviewed', *Philosophy*, 51, pp. 337–45.

Sherry, Patrick (1976b), 'Analogy Today', *Philosophy*, 51, pp. 431–46.

Shults, F. LeRon (1999), *The Postfoundationalist Task of Theology: Wolfhart Pannenberg and the New Theological Rationality*, Grand Rapids, MI: Eerdmans.

Sibley, Jack R., and Pete A. Y. Gunter (1978), *Process Philosophy: Basic Writings*, Washington, DC: University Press of America.

Sider, Theodore (2001), *Four-Dimensionalism: An Ontology of Persistence and Time*, Oxford: Oxford University Press.

Sigward, Eric (1997), *The Works of Cornelius Van Til, 1895–1987*, CD-ROM, New York: Labels Army.

Silverman, Hugh J., and Donn Welton (1988), eds, *Postmodernism and Continental Philosophy*, Selected Studies in Phenomenology and Existential Philosophy 13, Albany: State University of New York.

Singer, Irving (1984–7), *The Nature of Love*, 3 vols, Chicago: University of Chicago Press.

Sloane, Andrew (2003), *On Being a Christian in the Academy: Nicholas Wolterstorff and the Practice of Christian Scholarship*, Paternoster Biblical and Theological Monographs, Carlisle: Paternoster Press.

Smith, John E., Harry S. Stout and Kenneth P. Minkema (1995), eds, *A Jonathan Edwards Reader*, New Haven, CT: Yale.

Solomon, Robert C., and David Sherman (2003), *The Blackwell Guide to Continental Philosophy*, Blackwell Philosophy Guides 12, Oxford: Blackwell.

Sorrell, Tom (1996), ed., *The Cambridge Companion to Hobbes*, Cambridge: Cambridge University Press.

Sosa, Ernest, and Tooley, Michael (1993), eds, *Causation*, Oxford: Oxford University Press.

Soskice, Janet Martin (1985), *Metaphor and Religious Language*, Oxford: Clarendon Press.

Spade, Paul Vincent (1994), *Five Texts on the Mediaeval Problem of Universals: Porphyry, Boethius, Abelard, Duns Scotus, Ockham*, Cambridge: Hackett.

Spinoza, Baruch (1925–87), *Opera*, ed. Carl Gebhardt, 5 vols, Heidelberg: Carl Winters.

Spinoza, Baruch (1985–), *The Collected Writings of Spinoza*, ed. and tr. Edwin Curley, Princeton: Princeton University Press.

Spinoza, Baruch (1994), *A Spinoza Reader: The Ethics and Other Works*, ed. and tr. Edwin Curley, Princeton: Princeton University Press.

Stalnaker, Robert (1999), *Context and Content*, Oxford: Oxford University Press.

Statman, Daniel (1997), *Virtue Ethics*, Cambridge: Edinburgh University Press.

Steenberghen, Fernand van (1970), *Aristotle in the West: The Origins of Latin Aristotelianism*, tr. Leonard Johnson, 2nd edn, Louvain: Nauwelaerts Publishing House.

Steenberghen, Fernand van (1980), *Thomas Aquinas and Radical Aristotelianism*, Washington, DC: Catholic University of America Press.

Stein, Stephen J. (1996), ed., *Jonathan Edwards's Writings: Text, Context, Interpretation*, Bloomington: Indiana University Press.

Stonehouse, N. B., and Paul Woolley (1967), *The Infallible Word: A Symposium by the Members of the Faculty of Westminster Theological Seminary*, rev. edn, Philadelphia, PA: Presbyterian and Reformed.

Stroud, Barry (1981), *Hume*, London: Routledge.

Stump, Eleonore (1979), 'Petitionary Prayer', *American Philosophical Quarterly*, 16: 2, pp. 81–91.

Stump, Eleonore (2003), *Aquinas*, London: Routledge.

Stump, Eleonore, and Norman Kretzmann (2001), eds, *The Cambridge Companion to Augustine*, Cambridge: Cambridge University Press.

Sturch, Richard (1990), *The New Deism: Divine Intervention and the Human Condition*, Bristol: Bristol Press.

Sturch, Richard (1991), *The Word and the Christ: An Essay in Analytical Christology*, Oxford: Clarendon Press.

Suchocki, Marjorie Hewitt (1989), *God, Christ, Church: A Practical Guide to Process Theology*, New York: Crossroad.

Swinburne, Richard (1968), *Space and Time*, London: Macmillan.

Swinburne, Richard (1989a), *Responsibility and Atonement*, Oxford: Clarendon Press.

Swinburne, Richard (1989b), ed., *Miracles*, Philosophical Topics, London: Collier Macmillan.

Swinburne, Richard (1991), *Revelation*, Oxford: Clarendon Press.

Swinburne, Richard (1993a), *The Coherence of Theism*, rev. edn, Oxford: Clarendon Press.

Swinburne, Richard (1993b), *The Resurrection of God Incarnate*, Oxford: Clarendon Press.

Swinburne, Richard (1994), *The Christian God*, Oxford: Clarendon Press.

Swinburne, Richard (1997), *The Evolution of the Soul*, rev. edn, Oxford: Clarendon Press.

Swinburne, Richard (1998), *Providence and the Problem of Evil*, Oxford: Clarendon Press.

Swinburne, Richard (2001), *Epistemic Justification*, Oxford: Clarendon Press.

Swinburne, Richard (2004), *The Existence of God*, 2nd edn, Oxford: Clarendon Press.

Swinburne, Richard (2005), *Faith and Reason*, 2nd edn, Oxford: Clarendon Press.

Tait, Katharine (1975), *My Father Bertrand Russell*, New York: Harcourt Brace Jovanovich.

Taliaferro, Charles, and Paul J. Griffiths (2003), *Philosophy of Religion: An Anthology*, Blackwell Philosophy Anthologies 20, Oxford: Blackwell.

Taylor, Victor E., and Charles E. Winquist (1998), eds, *Postmodernism: Critical Concepts*, Routledge Critical Concepts, London: Routledge.

Teichmann, Roger (2000), ed., *Logic, Cause & Action: Essays in Honour of Elizabeth Anscombe*, Royal Institute of Philosophy Supplement 46, Cambridge: Cambridge University Press.

Tennant, Frederick R. (1912), *The Concept of Sin*, Cambridge: Cambridge University Press.

Tennant, Frederick R. (1928), *Philosophical Theology*, Vol. 1, *The Soul and Its Faculties*, Cambridge: Cambridge University Press.

Tennant, Frederick R. (1930), *Philosophical Theology*, Vol. 2, *The World, the Soul, and God*, Cambridge: Cambridge University Press.

Tertullian, Quintus Septimius Florens (1868–70), *The writings of Quintus Sept. Flor. Tertullianus*, tr. P. Holmes and A. S. Thelwall, Ante-Nicene Christian Library 11, 15, 18, 3 vols, Edinburgh: T. & T. Clark.

Tertullian, Quintus Septimius Florens (1890–1957), *Quinti Septimi Florentis Tertulliani Opera*, ed. J. W. P. Borleffs, V. Bulhart, W. A. Hartel, H. Hoppe, E. Kroymann, A. Reifferscheid and Georg Wissowa, Corpus scriptorum ecclesiasticorum Latinorum Vol. 20, 47, 69–70, 76, 5 vols, Vindobonae: Hoelder-Pichler-Tempsky.

Tertullian, Quintus Septimius Florens (1954), *Opera*, ed. E. Dekkers, Corpus Christianorum Series Latina 1–2, 2 vols, Turnhout: Brepols.

Tertullian, Quintus Septimius Florens (1956), *De Carne Christi Liber: Treatise on the Incarnation*, tr. Ernest Evans, London: SPCK.

Tertullian, Quintus Septimius Florens (2003), *Apology: De Spectaculis*, tr. T. R. Glover, Loeb Classical Library 250, Cambridge, MA: Harvard University Press.

Thiselton, Anthony C. (1992), *New Horizons in Hermeneutics*, Grand Rapids, MI: Zondervan.

Thompson, John Brookshire (1981), *Critical Hermeneutics: A Study in the Thought of Paul Ricoeur and Jürgen Habermas*, Cambridge: Cambridge University Press.

Thompson, Silvanus Phillips (1907), *Intuitional Religion: A Study of Divine Illumination*, London: West, Newman & Co.

Thrower, J. (1971), *A Short History of Western Atheism*, London: Pemberton Publishing Co.

Tillich, Paul (1951–63), *Systematic Theology*, 3 vols, Chicago: University of Chicago Press.

Tillich, Paul (1952), *The Courage to Be*, London: J. Nisbet.

Todorov, Tzvetan (1982a), *Symbolism and Interpretation*, tr. Catherine Porter, London: Routledge & Kegan Paul.

Todorov, Tzvetan (1982b), *Theories of the symbol*, tr. Catherine Porter, Oxford: Blackwell.

Toland, John (1999), *Christianity not Mysterious*, Works in the History of British Deism, London: Thoemmes Press.

Tomberlin, James E. (2000), ed., *Action and Freedom*, Philosophical Perspectives 14, Oxford: Blackwell.

Tomberlin, James E., and Peter van Inwagen (1985), eds, *Alvin Plantinga*, Philosophical Profiles, Dordrecht: D. Reidel.

Tooley, Michael (1997), ed., *Time, Tense, and Causation*, Oxford: Clarendon Press.

Tooley, Michael (1999), ed., *The Nature of Properties: Nominalism, Realism, and Trope Theory*, Analytical Metaphysics 3, London: Garland.

Torrance, Thomas F. (1962), *Karl Barth: An Introduction to His Early Theology*, London: SCM Press.

Torrance, Thomas F. (1978), *Space, Time, and Incarnation*, Oxford: Oxford University Press.

Torrance, Thomas F. (1990), *Karl Barth, Biblical and Evangelical Theologian*, Edinburgh: T. & T. Clark.

Tracy, Thomas F. (1994), ed., *The God Who Acts: Philosophical and Theological Explorations*, University Park, PA: Pennsylvania State University Press.

Trigg, Joseph (1998), *Origen*, London: Routledge.

Urban, Linwood, and Douglas N. Walton (1978), eds, *Power of God: Readings on Omnipotence and Evil*, New York, NY: Oxford University Press.

Urban, Wilbur Marshall (1898), *The History of the Principle of Sufficient Reason: Its Metaphysical and Logical Foundations*, Princeton Contributions to Philosophy, Princeton, NJ: Princeton University Press.

Van Inwagen, Peter (1983), *An Essay on Free Will*, Oxford: Clarendon Press.

Van Inwagen, Peter (1990), *Material Beings*, Ithaca, NY: Cornell University Press.

Van Inwagen, Peter (1995), *God, Knowledge, and Mystery: Essays in Philosophical Theology*, Ithaca, NY: Cornell University Press.

Van Inwagen, Peter (1997), *The Possibility of Resurrection and Other Essays in Christian Apologetics*, Boulder, CO: Westview Press.

Van Inwagen, Peter (2002), *Metaphysics*, Dimensions of Philosophy, Cambridge, MA: Westview.

Van Mastricht, Peter (2002), *Treatise on Regeneration*, ed. Brandon G. Withrow, Morgan, PA: Soli Deo Gloria.

Van Til, Cornelius (1969a), *A Survey of Christian Epistemology*, In Defense of the Faith Vol. II, 2nd edn, Ripon, CA: den Dulk Christian Foundation.

Van Til, Cornelius (1969b), *A Christian Theory of Knowledge*, Philadelphia, PA: Presbyterian and Reformed.

Vanhoozer, Kevin J. (2001), ed., *Nothing Greater, Nothing Better: Theological Essays on the Love of God*, 6th Edinburgh Conference in Christian Dogmatics, Rutherford House, Grand Rapids, MI: Wm. B. Eerdmans Pub. Co.

Velde, Rudi te (2005), *Aquinas on God*, Aldershot: Ashgate.

Vesey, Godfrey (1982), ed., *Idealism Past and Present*, Royal Institute of Philosophy Lecture Series 13, Cambridge: Cambridge University Press.

Virgoulay, René (1992), *L'Action de Maurice Blondel, 1993: relecture pour un centenaire*, Bibliothèque des Archives de philosophie, Paris: Beauchesne.

Wainwright, William J. (1999), *Philosophy of Religion*, 2nd edn, London: Wadsworth.

Walker, Nigel (1991), *Why Punish?*, OPUS, Oxford: Oxford University Press.

Wallis, Richard T. (1995), *Neoplatonism*, 2nd edn, London: Duckworth.

Walls, Jerry L. (1992), *Hell: The Logic of Damnation*, Library of Religious Philosophy 9, Notre Dame, IN: University of Notre Dame Press.

Ward, Keith (1994), *Religion and Revelation: A Theology of Revelation in the World's Religions*, Oxford: Clarendon Press.

Warnock, Geoffrey (1953), *Berkeley*, Harmondsworth: Penguin.

Wartofsky, Marx W. (1977), *Feuerbach*, Cambridge: Cambridge University Press.

Webster, John H. (2000), ed., *The Cambridge Companion to Karl Barth*, Cambridge: Cambridge University Press.

Weinandy, Thomas (1985), *Does God Change? The Word's Becoming in the Incarnation*, Studies in Historical Theology Vol. 4, Still River, MA: St Bede's Publications.

Weinandy, Thomas (2000), *Does God Suffer?* Edinburgh: T. & T. Clark.

Weisheipl, James A. (1974), *Friar Thomas D'Aquino*, Garden City, NY: Doubleday.

Weisheipl, James A. (1980), ed., *Albertus Magnus and the Sciences: Commemorative Essays*, Toronto: Pontifical Institute of Medieval Studies.

Wendel, François (1987), *Calvin: Origins and Development of His Religious Thought*, tr. Philip Mairet, Durham, NC: Labyrinth Press.

Westphal, Jonathan (1995), ed., *Certainty*, Hackett Readings in Philosophy, Indianapolis: Hackett.

Westphal, Merold (1993), *Suspicion and Faith: The Religious Uses of Modern Atheism*, Grand Rapids, MA: Eerdmans.

Westphal, Merold (1996), *Becoming a Self: A Reading of Kierkegaard's Concluding Unscientific Postscript*, Purdue University Press Series in the History of Philosophy, West Lafayette, IN: Purdue University Press.

Westphal, Merold (2001), *Overcoming Onto-Theology: Toward a Postmodern Christian Faith*, Perspectives in Continental Philosophy no. 21, New York: Fordham University Press.

Westphal, Merold (2004), *Transcendence and Self-Transcendence: On God and the Soul*, Indiana Series in the Philosophy of Religion, Bloomington, IN: Indiana University Press.

White, Andrew Dickson (1896), *A History of the Warfare of Science with Theology in Christendom*, 2 vols, London: Macmillan.

White, William (1979), *Van Til: Defender of the Faith: An Authorized Biography*, Nashville: Thomas Nelson.

Whitehead, Alfred North (1929), *Process and Reality: An Essay in Cosmology*, Gifford Lectures 1927–8, Cambridge: Cambridge University Press.

Whitney, Barry L. (1998), ed., *Theodicy: An Annotated Bibliography on the Problem of Evil, 1960–1991*, 2nd edn, Bowling Green, OH: Philosophy Documentation Center, Bowling Green State University.

Whittemore, Robert C. (1974), ed., *Studies in Process Philosophy*, Tulane Studies in Philosophy Vol. 23, New Orleans: Tulane University.

Wierenga, Edward (1989), *The Nature of God*, Ithaca: Cornell University Press.

Wiggins, David (2001), *Sameness and Substance Renewed*, Cambridge: Cambridge University Press.

Wiles, Maurice (1993), *God's Action in the World: The Bampton Lectures for 1986*, London: SCM Press.

Williams, Bernard A. O. (1973), *Problems of the Self*, Cambridge: Cambridge University Press.

Williams, Bernard A. O. (1985), *Ethics and the Limits of Philosophy*, London: Fontana.

Williams, Bernard A. O. (1993), *Subjectivism: First Thoughts*, Cambridge: Cambridge University Press.

Williams, Robert R. (1978), *Schleiermacher the Theologian: The Construction of the Doctrine of God*, Philadelphia: Fortress Press.

Williams, Thomas (2003), ed., *The Cambridge Companion to Duns Scotus*, New York: Cambridge University Press.

Wills, Garry (1999), *Saint Augustine*, London: Weidenfeld and Nicolson.

Wilmot, Laurence F. (1979), *Whitehead and God: Prolegomena to Theological Construction*, Waterloo, ON: Wilfrid Laurier University Press.

Wilson, Margaret Dauler (1982), *Descartes*, London: Routledge.

Wippel, John F. (1993), *Thomas Aquinas on the Divine Ideas*, Etienne Gilson Series 16, Toronto: Pontifical Institute of Mediaeval Studies.

Wippel, John F., and Allan B. Wolter (1969), eds, *Medieval Philosophy: From St. Augustine to Nicholas of Cusa*, Readings in the History of Philosophy, London: Collier-Macmillan.

Witham, Larry (2005), *The Measure of God: Our Century-Long Struggle to Reconcile Science & Religion*, San Francisco: HarperCollins.

Wittgenstein, Ludwig (1958), *Philosophical Investigations*, tr. G. E. M. Anscombe, 2nd edn, Oxford: Blackwell.

Wittgenstein, Ludwig (1960–), *Schriften*, ed. Friedrich Waismann, Frankfurt: Suhrkamp.

Wittgenstein, Ludwig (1975), *Tractatus Logico-philosophicus*, tr. D. F. Pears and B. F. McGuinness, Routledge Classics, rev. edn, London: Routledge.

Wittgenstein, Ludwig (1979), *On Certainty*, ed. G. E. M. Anscombe and G. H. von Wright, tr. G. E. M. Anscombe and Denis Paul, corrected edn, Oxford: Blackwell.

Wolfe, David L. (1982), *Epistemology: The Justification of Belief*, Contours of Christian Philosophy, Leicester: Inter-Varsity Press.

Wolter, Allan B. (1990), *The Philosophical Theology of John Duns Scotus*, ed. Marilyn McCord Adams, Ithaca, NY: Cornell University Press.

Wolter, Allan B. (2003), *Scotus and Ockham: Selected Essays*, St Bonaventure, NY: The Franciscan Institute.

Wolterstorff, Nicholas (1970), *On Universals: An Essay in Ontology*, London: University of Chicago Press.

Wolterstorff, Nicholas (1976), *Reason within the Bounds of Religion*, Grand Rapids, MI: Eerdmans.

Wolterstorff, Nicholas (1995), *Divine Discourse: Philosophical Reflections on the Claim That God Speaks*, Cambridge: Cambridge University Press.

Wolterstorff, Nicholas (1996), *John Locke and the Ethics of Belief*, Cambridge Studies in Religion and Critical Thought, Cambridge: Cambridge University Press.

Wolterstorff, Nicholas (2001), *Thomas Reid and the Story of Epistemology*, Modern European Philosophy, Cambridge: Cambridge University Press.

Wood, W. Jay (1998), *Epistemology: Becoming Intellectually Virtuous*, Contours of Christian Philosophy, Leicester: Inter-Varsity Press.

Woolhouse, R. S. (1993), *Descartes, Spinoza, Leibniz: Concept of Substance in Seventeenth-Century Metaphysics*, New York: Routledge.

Woolhouse, R. S. (1994), ed., *Gottfried Wilhelm Leibniz: Critical Assessments*, Vol. 1, *Metaphysics and Its Foundations 1: Sufficient Reason, Truth, and Necessity*, Routledge Critical Assessments of Leading Philosophers, London: Routledge.

Wright, Crispin (1987), *Realism, Meaning, and Truth*, Oxford: Blackwell.

Wykstra, Stephen (1989), 'Toward a Sensible Evidentialism: On the Notion "Needing Evidence"', in William Rowe and William Wainwright (eds), *Philosophy of Religion*, New York: Harcourt Brace Jovanovich, pp. 426–37.

Yandell, Keith (1994), *The Epistemology of Religious Experience*, Oxford: Oxford University Press.

Yolton, John W. (1993), *A Locke Dictionary*, Oxford: Blackwell.

Zagzebski, Linda Trinkaus (1991), *The Dilemma of Freedom and Foreknowledge*, Oxford: Clarendon Press.

Zagzebski, Linda Trinkaus (2004), *Divine Motivation Theory*, Cambridge: Cambridge University Press.

Zwart, P. J. (1976), *About Time: A Philosophical Inquiry into the Origin and Nature of Time*, Oxford: North-Holland Publishing Co.

Web sites

British Society for the Philosophy of Religion. http://www.socialsciences.manchester.ac.uk/philosophy/BSPR/BSPR.htm

The Dooyeweerd Centre for Christian Philosophy. http://www.redeemer.on.ca/Dooyeweerd-Centre/

The Gifford Lectures. http://www.giffordlectures.org

Hopkins, Jasper, Page on Anselm. http://www.jasper-hopkins.info

Institute for Christian Studies. http://www.icscanada.edu/

Society of Christian Philosophers Home Page. http://www.siu.edu/~scp/

Sudduth, Michael, Analytic Philosophy of Religion Page. http://www.homestead.com/philofreligion/

The Tertullian Project. http://www.tertullian.org/

Van Til, Cornelius. http://www.vantil.info/